1968

SATHER CLASSICAL LECTURES

Volume Twenty-nine

Poetic, Scientific, and other
FORMS OF DISCOURSE

POETIC, SCIENTIFIC
and other
FORMS of DISCOURSE

A New Approach to Greek and Latin Literature

BY
JOSHUA WHATMOUGH

UNIVERSITY OF CALIFORNIA PRESS
Berkeley and Los Angeles : MCMLVI

University of California Press
Berkeley and Los Angeles
California

Cambridge University Press
London, England

Copyright, 1956, by
The Regents of the University of California

Library of Congress Catalogue Card No. 56-11900

Printed in the United States of America
By the University of California Printing Department

TO

G.V.T.WH.

T. E.WH.G., J. J.T.WH., AND

A. D. G.

C.WH.G.

It's words that make the world go round.

Louis A. MacKay

PREFACE

THE University of California was but one-and-thirty years old when, in 1899, Benjamin Ide Wheeler, the centenary of whose birth fell on 15 July of last year (1954), was called from Cornell, where he had taught Comparative Philology, to be its president. For a brief time he had been an instructor in German at Harvard. California's gain was Cornell's loss. It was the loss also of Comparative Philology, that now somewhat outmoded title, the title by which my Harvard chair is called, and which dimly recalls the emergence of comparative and historical Indo-European grammar out of the critical study of Greek and Latin literature. Since then still other disciplines have branched off the ancient trunk, the latest of all being what can only be called Mathematical Linguistics. Thus the old union of Mathematics and Classics seems about to be renewed in those Comparative Philologists who continue to cultivate their Greek and Latin.

It must be supposed that I owe the invitation to serve as Sather Professor, the oldest of the University's visiting professorships, to what vestiges of competence in the Classics still cling to my reputation. These lectures are intended to plead for two things: first, the understanding of Greek or Latin literature, or of both, through a firm knowledge of the original language; and second, enjoyment of the literature as such, stripped of all unnecessary externals, and especially of those forms of criticism which amount to nothing more than the mere exchange of opinion.

In the first lecture we shall see, with the comic trimeter as the hindrance, how understanding is subordinated to rule. One of the more important shapes that rule takes in language is analogy, a matter which Wheeler did much to illuminate as long ago as 1887, though his treatise on *Analogy in Language* hardly brought him as much renown as his doctoral dissertation (Heidelberg) on Greek nominal accent (1885), the formulation of the law that still goes by his name, that in Attic Greek nouns and adjectives that ended in the metrical and accentual pattern $-\cup\acute{\cup}$ became paroxytone, thus ποικίλος but χθαμαλός, βουκόλος but συφορβός. Yet there are some exceptions to the rule; for analogy played its part—and also anomaly.

It might be supposed that students of the history of Greek and Latin have worshiped most the fetish of analogy. We shall see that the textual critics are idolaters too. What imposes more insurmountable barriers to understanding than a modern critical annotated text? Take an edition of a single play of Aeschylus that fills three volumes; or of a single book of Vergil that fills one large and closely printed octavo. Twentieth-century humanity is not to have its imagination seized or fertilized in this way. All my study of the ways of words leads me to the conclusion that at many points the principles of textual criticism have done violence to the text, and not least in the insistence upon rule (upon analogy, that is) of meter or rule of grammar; conclusions drawn from arguments by analogy have a certain likelihood, depending on the evidence—they are not themselves certain.

It is the thesis of these lectures that literature is a highly specialized variety of a system of communication, namely, language. The first requirement for any scientific theory is that it shall make possible deductions that agree with laws actually derived from observation. This, I believe, is the case: that the deductions drawn from my theory do in fact agree with laws of language based upon observation. That I may not be misunderstood at the outset, let me add that these are not mechanical laws. Literature is purposive action of a kind too prevalent among mankind to support the behaviorist thesis that man is entirely controlled by physical laws, and not at all by intelligence and reason. It will be observed, in the second place, that the relation of cause and effect, so much admired in the last century, finds no mention in these pages; stress is placed on functional relations. Those who wish to appreciate the argument are invited to read the works of Shannon, Mandelbrot, and Guiraud mentioned in the notes to several chapters, where they will find clearly stated the premises upon which its contentions rest; it is no longer dependent merely on Zipf's pioneer work.

I have found it necessary to consider evidence from a great variety of fields of research in not all of which can I claim equal competence; I begin, therefore, by craving the indulgence of experts, who may feel inclined to criticize—there cannot but be some errors in a book that ranges so widely. But I make no apologies for an attempt to effect a synthesis of supporting evidence that converges from so many different directions upon a single conclusion. Since the conclusion, however, has a bearing upon some questions of educational practice, and since my own experience has formed my thoughts on these questions, I have found it unavoidable here and there to indulge in recollections of an autobiographical sort. Instead of trying to disguise their source, I have stated them frankly in the first person, and to those who think this practice needs apology I am content to offer it.

A fuller account of some of the argument may be had from my book *Language* (Secker and Warburg, London 1955).[1] In particular I must warn the reader that some established technical terms are, unfortunately, misleading. "Information" (pp. 103, 196, 223 below, etc.) would have been better called "conformation" by those who introduced the concept of a measure, not of what each unit of "information" teaches or tells, of what is learned, but of the element of surprise, fruitful or not, which the unit concerned brings on the average; again, a word or epilegma is what results from the association of a given meaning with an ensemble of phonemes or graphemes susceptible of a given grammatical function (Meillet); "bound" means incapable of standing alone, "bounded" means delimited at beginning and end; and so forth.

I thank most warmly all those who welcomed me to Berkeley in the spring of 1955, and those who did so much for my ma-

---

[1] And St Martin's Press, New York 1956.

terial comfort there; and especially Professor Arthur E. Gordon, Chairman of the Department of Classics at the University of California. To Professors H. R. W. Smith, Louis A. MacKay, and Joseph E. Fontenrose I am indebted for a careful scrutiny of my manuscript, for much helpful advice, and for the correction of real blunders. Mr Harold A. Small, Professor W. H. Alexander, and their colleagues at the University of California Press, have given unstintingly of their time and interest at every stage of the production of this book, and deserve my hearty thanks.

J. Wh.

30 June 1955

CONTENTS

GRAPHS

I

Scholar's Progress

Methods and Results

IT IS A precarious deed to borrow a title, even if you modify it, and justified only if you make it your own. A *Passionate Pilgrim* had been written by William Shakespeare long before Francis Turner Palgrave, the compiler of the *Golden Treasury*, invited one of those comparisons that are said to be odious, when in 1858 he published his, under the pseudonym Henry J. Thurstan;[1] not the only Palgrave mystification of nomenclature: for F. T. Palgrave's own father, Sir Francis Palgrave, the son of Meyer Cohen, a stockbroker and a Jew, had abandoned his faith and family name in 1823[2] in favor of the maiden name of his wife's mother, adopting Christianity at the same time. Henry James published a story called *A Passionate Pilgrim* in 1875; but that was a horse of a very different color.

The subject of this first lecture, "Scholar's Progress," recalls, I suppose, *Pilgrim's Progress*; but it also recalls *Rake's Progress*; the present century has produced a *Jade's Progress* (by J. Storer Clouston, 1928) and *Patriot's Progress* (by Henry Williamson, 1930), and doubtless others. The juncture *confessio fidei* (lecture VIII) seems to be at least as old as Gregory the Great, and as recent as the late Dean Inge, who used it as the heading of one of his "outspoken essays." For my *religio grammatici* (lecture VI) I make my apologies to Sir Thomas Browne, whose *religio medici*,

---

[1] Reissued, with an Introduction by R. Brimley Johnson, in 1926 (London: Peter Davies). For the pseudonym, see p. v of this reissue. Cf. *The Times Literary Supplement*, 6 January 1927, p. 9.

[2] See *The Palgrave Family* (Norwich 1878, for private distribution only), a copy of which I have consulted in the Harvard College Library; p. 185 gives a copy of the Grant of Arms to Sir Francis Palgrave, 1823, and recites his change of name. So far as I can find there is no mention of these facts (nn. 1, 2) by Gwenllian F. Palgrave, *Francis Turner Palgrave* (London 1899).

you will recall, was "a private exercise, directed to himself"; not to Gilbert Murray, who also once wrote a *religio grammatici*,[3] for he strikes me as *criticus* more than *grammaticus*, and "literary criticism" as incongruous a juncture as "literary scholarship" (the title of a work published in 1941) or as "coöperative scholarship," an evident contradiction in terms, since coöperation implies at least a modicum of work.

In a note on "Triballic" in Aristophanes, published in *CP* 47, 1952, 26, I read at *Birds* 1615 νὴ Βελσοῦρδον, i.e. "per Campestrem." Perhaps it is time to disclose my reasons for resorting to an unpopular "license" in emendation, the violation of a metrical canon. Any proposal to correct a verse alarms a scholar because it makes a laborious demand upon a man who is by definition a person of leisure, by entailing the work of reading and considering the context. But a proposal which involves consideration of meter may also call for consideration of half a hundred or more lines and contexts. Dislike of unusual toil of this degree makes one or more familiar apologies. We hear at once of respect due to the authority of metrical canons, or of manuscripts, or of scholia, whichever disguise seems best to fit the case, since rarely can all of them be worn at once. If we respect the scholia, or what the scholia are said to say, then we must repudiate the authority of the manuscripts which flout the metrical canon.

"I do not know whether" (*nescio an*) it is in the favor of the reading that it produces a scazon. But I do know that it is in its favor that it makes good sense, as those who respect manuscript authority should admit from Cicero *in Pisonem* 85, where (*Iouis*) *Velsuri* was corrupted into *Vrii* by Turnebus. And it is also in its favor that in an oath it makes good meter:

ἀνόσια πάσχω ταῦτα ναὶ μὰ τὰς Νύμφας
πολλοῦ μὲν οὖν δίκαια ναὶ μὰ τὰς κράμβας.

<hr />

[3] This was the title of his Presidential Address to the Classical Association of England and Wales in 1918 (published in London the same year), to which he made reference in his later Presidential Address to the same Association in 1954 (cf. *Proceedings of the Classical Association* 51, 1954, p. 9). It was also the title of my Presidential Address to the Linguistic Society of America on 29 December 1951 (see *Language* 28, no. 2, pt. 2, April 1952, p. 6).

The analogists have not fudged these two verses, perhaps because they do not read Eupolis, or Athenaeus. In an oath we have the fourth or the second foot of a senarius divided ∪ ∪ₓ – (νὴ | Δία, μὴ seven times in the *Frogs* alone), and many tribrachs have been eliminated[4] by "emendation." Even in the sixth foot ∪ ∪ ∪ is not infrequent, χοιρίδιον (*Ach.* 777), θυλάκιον (*Frogs* 1203), where "emendation" is unwarrantable. If it is argued that in these and in φειδίτια, δελφάκια, σαρκίδια, ληκύθιον the *i* is consonantal (after δ, κ, τ, θ), then the verse is choliambic. Theoretically, at *Ach.* 100, σάτρα (Old Persian *xšaθra-*) may be argued ∪ ⌣, but Greek has ἐξαιθραπεύω and ἐξαιτραπεύω, not to mention σαδράπας and σαδράπῃσιν. However, Rav. has αστρα and there is an Old Persian *aštrā*; if the line actually contains *Xšayāršan* (Ξέρξης) concealed in ἐξάρξαν, then *xšaθra* is less probably to be found in σάτρα, and the references to gold in 102–108 would prompt a search for some word meaning "gold" (Avestic *zaray-* "yellow," *zaranya-* "gold," Thracian ζηλτα "gold"). But the line is not Greek, permissible phonematic sequences may readily be invoked to suggest a number of Persian words, and nothing positive is to be asserted about the final foot.

[4] J. W. White, *Verse of Greek Comedy* (1912), parr. 106, 120–121. Cf. Tucker's *Frogs*, p. xxxix. White cites the divided νὴ Δία from *Frogs* 41, 164, 285, 288, 738, 863, 1433. At 1203 θυλάκιον codd. : θύλακον edd., so 1216 ληκύθιον R : λήκυθον edd. (cf. 1214), notwithstanding ἐν τοῖς ἰαμβείοισι of Aristophanes himself (1204). Frag. 547 (Triphales) ends with ἀργυρίδιον, but this, if a senarius ending, leaves ∪ ∪ (not ∪ ∪ ∪) in the sixth foot; *Lys.* 906 Μυρρίνιον. See now the second edition of W. J. W. Koster's *Traité de métrique grecque*, Leiden 1953, pp. 100–101 (on ἀνὴρ γίγνεται at the end of *Wasps* 207, θυλάκιον *Frogs* 1203 with its triple – – ∪ ∪ –) and 105–106 on Porson's canon (not a "law"). Observe also the comments of Rogers (Appendix) on *Frogs* 1203 (θυλάκιον): "A tribrach is so seldom found at the end of an iambic line . . . that Porson (at *Med.* 139, p. 35, 1824) considers this passage to be *insigniter corruptum*, while Reisig would substitute κυάθιον, and Bothe and Fritzsche read θύλακον. But 'nice customs curtsey to great' necessity; and subsequent editors have seen that a first paeon – ∪ ∪ ∪ is necessary here"; and of Tucker (*Frogs* 979) τίς τοῦτ' ἔλαβε : τίς τόδ' Bentley: ". . . but the metrical objection is not certain. In *Nub.* 1386–89 there are three lines of the scansion ⌣ = | ∪ – | against one of the scansion ⌣ = | ∪ – | ⌣ = | ∪ ⌣, and even in the trimeter dialogue a tribrach [∪ ∪ ∪] sometimes stands in the last foot (Introd. p. xxxviii)"—xxxix: "φειδίτια (Antiph. *Arch.* 3), δελφάκια (Eubul. *Amalth.* 9), σαρκίδια (Diph. *Apl.* 2), ληκύθιον (Anon. 40); Aristoph. χοιρίδιον (*Ach.* 777), θυλάκιον (*Ran.* 1203); . . . to 'correct' all such cases is quite unwarrantable." Add: *Ran.* 1231 ληκύθιον.

Or take *Equites* 635 "καὶ Μόθων Dobr. Zacher from schol. (Neil)" : μόθωνες mss. In the same line βερέσχεθοι (-τοι *gloss. Oxy.* 1801) ἁπ. λεγ. with β (for φ) is not Attic (Macedonian, Thracian?); nor κόβαλοι, which is Thracian or Phrygian; nor (634) σκίταλοι (cf. Att. σχίσις sens. obsc.), which is Western Greek (Elean or Aetolian). The ancients knew that μόθων was Laconian; it occurs also in *Equ.* 697, a line which in R ends περιεκκόκκαυσα (– ⌣), -κόκκυσα other mss., Su[i]das, -κόκκασα Photius, vulg. Why the difficulty? Because κόκκῡ (cf. Latin *cūculus*), κόκκυξ (-ῡγος) have long *ū*, and therefore we expect ῡ in the aorist. The assertion that the scholiast read the singular Μόθων appears to have been perpetuated from Brunck (1810), who took it from Kuster (1710), an assertion borne out neither by the scholium, nor by Su[i]das M. 1188, nor by Harpocration 206.3 (Schol. *Plut.* 279, Dübner 1842, p. 556): fudge! These, together with Su[i]das Σ 630 (s.v. σκίταλοι), define μόθων, but quote Μόθωνες παρὰ 'Αριστοφάνει. Only schol. *Equ.* 634, which is a curtailed form of the rest, by omitting the quotation, hints falsely of μόθων in the text. But scholars are sheep and follow one another through the same hole in the wall that Kuster breached, without once stopping to examine his right. And it is easier to remove all "offending" verses than to discover which do not offend, and why. By the year 5955, or whatever system of reckoning years is then in use, all the lines of Shakespeare and Milton that show inverted stresses will have been removed by hacks calling themselves professors of English, lines, that is, such as the following from Macbeth:

Ónly | for them, and mine eternal jewel   (3.1.68–69)
Gív'n to | the common enemy of man.
Whóle as | the marble, founded as the rock.   (3.4.22)
Whát, sir, | not yet at rest?   (2.1.12)

Vaúlting | ambition, which o'erleaps itself   (1.7.27)
If good,| whý do | I yield to that suggestion?   (1.3.134)
And yet, dark night | strángles | the trav'lling lamp.   (2.4.7)
Súch I | account thy love. | Árt thou | afeard?   (1.7.39)

Cúrses, | not loud but deep, | móuth-hon|our, breath. (5.3.27)
How now, my lord; | why do | you keep alone?   (3.2.8)
I have begun to plant | thee, ànd | will labour
To make thee full of growing. | Nóble | Banquo.   (1.4.28–29)

Or Milton's verses (which I take from Robert Bridges, *Milton's Prosody*, Oxford 1921, pp. 41–43), from *Paradise Lost:*

Régions | of sorrow, doleful shades, where peace.   (1.65)
A mind | nót to | be chang'd by Place or Time.   (1.253)
For one restraint, | Lórds of | the world besides.   (1.32)
Illumine, what is low | ráise and | support.   (1.23)
Of Thrones and mighty Seraphim | próstrate.   (6.841)
Úni|vérsal | reproach, far worse to bear.   (6.34)
In their | tríple | Degrees; | Régions | to which.   (5.750)
As a despite | dón a|gaínst the | most High.   (6.906)

Bridges himself overstepped the necessary limit to inversion, which Milton had observed. Modern editors of Aristophanes have corrupted the text by refusing to allow even a limited inversion (of quantity). In itself the matter is of small moment compared with the understanding and enjoyment of the play, and I do not press my reading in *Birds* 1615 if a better is offered. What the character of Triballic was, will be set forth in lecture III.

Βελσοῦρδος[5] came to my attention in collecting divine names for *The Dialects of Ancient Gaul* (*DAG*); ὀλβεττήρ (cf. *CP* 37, 1942, 97) was a by-product of collecting Messapic texts. But ὀλβεττέρ᾽ ἆρον is Greek. Another text that proceeds from the mouth of the speaker is the ƵOᐯAⴾ pictured in *RA* 4ᵉ sér. 15, 1910, 225. Reverse writing is common enough in curses; but any attempt to interpret the text as Messapic is beside the mark. The latest seems to be *Rend. Lincei* (Cl. Filol.) 8, 1953, 348: unfortunately *blo[ssius]* is Latin; the Messapic is *blatθes*. The question of rhythm (*HSCP* 39, 1928, 4) has no certain answer, for the amount of text is too short to show clearly with what kind and length of verse we have to do; but certainly -ω may

---

[5] Other forms of this divine name (see *REG* 26, 1913, 247) will be discussed in lecture III, below.

be shortened before a vowel (Kühner-Blass 1 i 198). No reading, however, that makes no sense whatever can be right.

The mss. of Aristophanes show a number of trimeters that have – ⏝ in the sixth foot, some of which, but not all, must be corrected since the verse is otherwise faulty (e.g. a syllable short); see *Thesm.* 480, 1002, 1133, 1171; *Ran.* 1448; frag. 622; *Pl.* 361, 461; *Nub.* 638 (since no Greek word begins θμ-)—a short syllable before -θμ- is the anomaly,[6] wherever it occurs (cf. the statistics given by Naylor, *CQ* 1, 1907, 7; and by Tucker, *CR* 11, 1897, 342; Kühner-Blass ed. 3 1 i, 1890, p. 305); τοὔνομ (!) OCT *Lys.* 853 is of course a misprint; 1220 (in 1219 ποιήσαιμι); *Equ.* 1346, 1373, 1401. I have not made a complete survey, but the following instances of violation of the law of the final cretic are well known.

Ἄτλας, ὁ χαλκέοισι νώτοις οὐρανὸν	(*Ion* 1)
κἀμοί. τὸ δ᾽ εὖ μάλιστα γ᾽ οὕτω γίγνεται	(*IT* 580)
νωμῶν, ὅ τ᾽ ἐσθλὸς Ἀριόμαρδος Σάρδεσι	(*Persae* 321)
ἅ μοι προσελθὼν σῖγα σήμαιν᾽ εἴτ ἔχει	(*Phil.* 22)
καὶ στεμματοῦτε καὶ κατάρχεσθ᾽, εἰ δοκεῖ	(*Heracl.* 529)

Such statistics as are available, however, show that as touching both tribrachs in the sixth foot, and scazons, if all are to be reduced to |⏝ ⏝|, then the uniformity involves us in a self-perpetuating circular argument. As for *Birds* 1615, Süvern (see Rogers ad loc.) proposed ἀναβαίνει τρεῖς.

---

[6] But let me make myself clear. I know that Attic tragedians scan ἀνάρϊθμος, ἀρϊθμός (Kühner-Blass 306, who cite, besides Sapph. *S.* 20.10, Aesch. *Pers.* 40, Eur. *Ba.* 1335, Soph. *OT* 167, 179, *El.* 232, *Aj.* 604, Eur. *El.* 1132). But this was at first anomalous; it is not Homeric. It was anomalous in the sense that, since θμ- does not begin a word, it may begin a syllable (leaving the preceding syllable open) only by violating a habit of the language. The difficulty is usually overcome on the assumption that medially a syllabic division was made between θ and μ (as between τ and ρ), whereby a syllable before -θμ- might be regarded as "common" (and therefore might be counted short if it contained a short vowel). But the question is, how did the Greeks of the Classical period pronounce it? Cultivated people do seem to have adopted this trick of pronunciation (-θ–μ-); but the man in the street? Or the cultivated pronunciation of prose? And in comedy (*Nub.* 638, cf. 1203)? Here too the old pronunciation was abandoned, as the evidence of modern Greek shows. What had begun as an anomaly came in the end to be accepted as normal.

There are two fallacies. The first is to argue on the principle that verses are made up of feet. Schoolboys and undergraduates with no sense of rhythm, compose, or used to compose, verses on this principle, trying to keep their wits, and doing so, if at all, only with considerable difficulty, on sense, idiom, grammar, prosody, and meter, all at once: the place of the caesura, of the spondee, of dividing the tribrach, the law of the final cretic, anapaestic license with proper names, and suchlike elementary matters. They confused composition and scansion, as if Aeschylus or Sophocles wrote after the manner of a modern schoolboy. But not even the Greek and Latin languages are made up of feet, but of words, phrases, and sentences. The problem is not to inspect "feet" and fit them into a line, but, given words, word groups, and phrases, to know their rhythm and to match this rhythm with a highly determined pattern that permits certain rhythmical variants and no others; and to achieve at the same time a flow (rhythm) of speech, Greek speech, in natural groups which shall both be metrical and have meaning.

There are twelve chief types of iambic verse, e.g. iamb or spondee + bacchius or amphibrachys [caesura] + cretic + double iamb; with syllaba anceps and, sparingly, certain resolutions of – into ∪ ∪, as *O.T.* 386

$$λάθρα μ' \mid ὑπελθὼν \parallel ἐκβαλεῖν \mid ἱμείρεται$$
$$\smile \; - \;\; \mid \cup - \mid - \;\; \parallel - \mid \cup - \;\; \mid \cup - \mid \cup -$$

or 826

$$μητρὸς \mid ζυγῆναι \parallel καὶ πατέρα \mid κατακτάνειν.$$
$$- \; - \; \mid \;\; \cup - \mid - \;\; \parallel - \mid \cup \cup \cup \;\; \mid \; \cup \; - \; \mid \cup \; -$$

It has been said that "the tribrach is never allowed in the sixth foot" (Sidgwick); and we all know the rule that if there is a break before the final cretic, the fifth foot must be an iambus. The second of these two injunctions is violated by Aeschylus (*Pers*. 321, which ends with the two proper names Ἀριόμαρδος Σάρδεσιν), by Sophocles (*Phil.* 21), and by Euripides, the first line of whose *Ion* ends νώτοις οὐρανὸν (this word οὐρανός at Manchester I was blandly allowed to pronounce, uncorrected, with the second syllable long), a reading accepted by Wecklein (Vol. 10, 1912), by Verrall (1890), and by Murray (OCT, Vol. II, 1913), though he, lacking the intrepidity of Verrall, marks νώτοις . . . μιᾶς(1–3) as corrupt; the former frequently by Aristophanes, as we have seen already. Classical scholars who have learnt these prohibitions in their youth simply reject everything that conflicts with them. It is a rare Rogers (a barrister-at-law) who admits (*Frogs* 1203) that "nice customs curtsey to great" necessity, while Porson, drunk or sober, considered the line hopelessly corrupt.

Scholars, above all, those who deal with dead languages, have invented an imaginary world of perfect linguistic order; lawyers and linguists, above all, those who study language as current usage, are familiar with anomaly, where the hypergrammatical make a fetish of analogy. *De minimis non curat lex* is a maxim which *lingua* would suit equally well. It is the same story in prose. Take for example Plato 190C οὔτε γὰρ ὅπως ἀποκτείναιεν εἶχον. Sense requires the potential (not the indirect) optative; but the potential optative "requires" ἄν—unless anomaly is admitted. Now there would be ample evidence for the anomaly if editors had not removed it. It is barely possible that ἄν may have been dropped after ἀποκτείνειαν (-ειεν is the reading of W), but that still calls for "emendation"; as Gildersleeve[7] puts it, "the tendency is decidedly towards the norm," that is, to refusing to admit the optative without ἄν. Yet Gildersleeve, who had read widely and attentively, and who believed that "the study of syntax is of the utmost importance for the appreciation of literary form," without making collections intended to be exhaustive, was able to quote no fewer than half a hundred places, and Slotty more than seventy (only ten or so from Homer), in which the text shows ἄν, if at all, only through the interference of hypergrammatical editors. Those editors and writers of Greek grammars who put the cart before the horse

---

[7] *Syntax of Classical Greek* 1, 1900, pp. 180–182; Slotty, *Der Gebrauch d. Konj. u. Opt. in d. gr. Dialekten* 1, Göttingen 1915, pp. 140–142. Cf. Schwyzer-Debrunner, *Gr. Gram.* 3, 1950, p. 325.

when they declare that ἄν is "omitted" are hardly more sensitive
to the ways of language than the editors who do not hesitate to
insert ἄν. But ἄν was not omitted; it had never stood in the
author's original. Instead he had used the simple optative in a
legitimate and, as Schwyzer saw, ancient, potential sense. The
statemental indicative, past or present, stands in opposition to
the subjective warning or prohibition of imperative and injunc-
tive, or of anything else (subjunctive or optative) that is futur-
istic. The technique of oppositions or contrasts, it must be made
known to those who do not know it, is fundamental to all linguistic habit—the meanings of grammatical features, even of
words, are best discovered and chiefly conveyed by this very
means.

Analogy, then, has often been dragged in, as it were, by the
scruff of the neck, to be a scapegoat, to account for those disturbances that violate the regularity of phonematic substitution, or of morphological and syntactic pattern, whenever the
historian of language can think of nothing else; as a principle it
has been freely recognized ever since Wheeler's day in historical
and comparative linguistics. And the ancient dispute between
the analogists and the anomalists has never really been stilled
among critics. But the appeal made to analogy in matters of
meter and text becomes fallacious as readily as in logic. The
fact is that analogy and anomaly operate by turns. The second
fallacy, then, is this illegitimate editorial appeal to analogy,
under the guise of rule or canon. It is responsible for our modern
corrupted texts; and, if editors take the easy way out, instead of
the laborious one of discovering where anomaly operates and
where it does not, is responsible for introducing and perpetu-
ating error.

Now language does indeed show pervasive orderliness, for
without good order it could not function. Language is a symbolism, a systematic and orderly symbolism; but again and
again it is often anomalous, judged by the standards of grammarians and editors, as every piece of modern literature testi-
fies. Editors of Greek and Latin classics have undertaken to

complete, by the broadest generalization, processes which the Greek and Latin languages themselves never did complete. Texts have been edited with an uncritical and undiscriminating criticism. Idle as was the practice of those who continued into the nineteenth century the corruption of ancient texts under the pretense of correcting them, the only fitting judgment upon those who have prolonged these activities into the present century, and teach others to engage in them *in the name of education,* is to condemn their behavior as criminal.

The scientific method is "formal" (i.e., morphological) and statistical. The term "foot" says less than structural types; and these are most accessible to objective observation in terms of frequencies. Verse cannot be a matter of short (or unstressed) syllables grouped around a long (or stressed) syllable, for comparable groupings appear also in prose. Statistically it is necessary to discover the relation between the verse pattern and the speech rhythm, to which the verse pattern frequently does violence. Investigations conducted along these lines tend to show that different authors vary in the degree to which they observe a verse pattern and that *none* observe it with absolute rigidity. Moreover it is clear that no pattern—Sanskrit, Greek, and Latin included—is solely quantitative, but that other factors of accent, pitch, and word structure enter into any verse pattern.

No linguistic phenomena have been subjected to statistical study longer than those of versification,[8] but in an elementary way that hardly goes beyond simple arithmetical enumeration, which fails to appreciate the fact that the object of study is *not the individual case but the total population of possibilities,* and the degrees of variation which any form of human conduct, even the composition of verse, must inevitably show, notwithstanding its concurrent high degree of good order *as verse.* Leave what the author will as limping prose, his "toil is vain, critics . . . make it verse again."

---

[8] *Bibliographie critique de la statistique linguistique,* Publications du Comité de la Statistique Linguistique for the Comité International Permanent des Linguistes, Spectrum: Utrecht and Anvers 1954, pp. 18–28.

Now no observational record, no matter how detailed, can completely specify any human activity, no matter how orderly. Poetry, like the yield of wheat, demands the study of variations. The understanding of variable phenomena, all the way from agricultural production to the intellect of man, calls first of all for examination and measurement of such variations as present themselves.

"The proper study of mankind is man." Very well; but what is the proper form and procedure of this proper study? How am I to justify my work in my own eyes? Not, I trow, by writing facile apologias on the "value of the Classics" or of this or that Greek or Latin author, such as some of my own teachers and their contemporaries produced forty years ago for the edification (God save the mark!) of narrowly educated youths and their just as narrowly educated schoolmasters. Thirty years ago it would hardly have occurred to me to ask the question, Is my time wisely spent? I was positive that I knew all the answers to such a question; that textual criticism and all the rest of it was above all criticism, the finest pursuit to which my intellectual gifts could be devoted. So passionate a pilgrimage inexorably comes to disillusion:

> The critic Eye, that microscope of Wit,
> Sees hairs and pores, examines bit by bit:
> How parts relate to parts, or they to whole,
> The body's harmony, the beaming soul,
> Are things which Kuster, Burman, Wasse shall see,
> When Man's whole frame is obvious to a flea.

It was perhaps all a mistake. This youth had left school, one of the cheap new secondary schools, founded a bare two years before he entered it, with prizes in Mathematics, Latin, History, and "First in Sixth Form"; and with a scholarship for Mathematics or Latin (which meant Classics, though he knew no Greek) at the local University: but not both Classics and Mathematics, not in those days, and not in England. A "pass" course would have been better. He was told, therefore, to write essays on "The Religious and Moral Ideas of Aeschylus," or "Vergil's Philosophy of Life and Death" (though he knew nothing of either); for the Professor of Latin had literally "nailed" him—the saintly mathematician Horace Lamb had not cared either way. So he read and wrote about "soft echoes of sound" or "the resourcefulness of Vergil's imagination," at the same time as hearing Horace and Livy interpreted almost as if it were in defense of the British Empire. Yet a question addressed to the Professor of Greek about logaoedic verse the professor could not answer. What disturbed him more was the discovery that he read and consulted a good many books about books, not always the ancient authors themselves, and never enough of them: that came later.

The one ray of light in this darkness was what was called Comparative Philology. But on migration to Cambridge he found that there this light shone with dim effulgence. He had been advised that he might patronize the then Kennedy Professor of Latin; but Ridgeway was to be his chief inspiration. All this was bad advice. He went nevertheless to Giles, and found him dull as dishwater:

> More had he spoke, but yawn'd—All Nature nods:
> What Mortal can resist the Yawn of Gods?

Conway, whose knowledge stopped at 1893,[9] the maturing student had long since outgrown.

"Pure" scholarship began to emerge as fudge. There was a quasi-scientific air about Comparative Philology that appealed strongly, and his mind was constantly occupied with the problem of introducing quantification into the study of language. Meanwhile archaeology had extended a beckoning finger: here at least was something objective upon which to seize. But a "melting," as they say in Scotland, for science was never stilled. At Bangor in North Wales (1921–1925) E. V. Arnold's statistical work on *Vedic Metre* (1905), and similar work on Plautine meters on which Arnold was still engaged at his death (19 September 1926), impressed me strongly.

[9] Witness his review of Meillet in *CR* 18, 1904, 465. As late as 1919 he had not heard of Hittite, or even of Tocharish.

It was at Harvard in 1927, in September, that the late George Kingsley Zipf[10] came to see me about graduate study in Linguistics. Zipf, after having taken honors in English (S.B., Harvard 1924; *summa cum laude* as of the class of 1923; not A.B., since he had done no Latin in college), had spent the intervening three years (1924–1927) in Bonn and Berlin, and had become acquainted with the doctrine, then just being developed in Prague, of the phoneme and of "efficiency" in the use of phonemes. He was discouraged at Harvard from continuing graduate studies in English—indeed he had little interest in the requirements imposed by the Harvard Department of English. His ideas struck me as new and important, and he set about the study of historical and comparative linguistics with a will. His dissertation dealt with these new ideas. It seemed so valuable to his examiners, and to the editors of the *Harvard Studies in Classical Philology*, that it was printed in full, a rare distinction, in *HSCP* 40, 1929, 1–95. Zipf at once received a subvention from the Harvard Humanities Fund (which had been established by the General Education Board), and the results of his work, supported by this means, were published as a series of studies by the University Press in 1932. There were certain irregularities of procedure in the publication, of which it is not necessary to say more here than that the mistake (on the part of the Press) was admitted at the time. But later books by Zipf had to be brought out elsewhere.

The essential correctness of Zipf's general theory I have steadily maintained, and it is now widely conceded; some of his applications of it I have never accepted. In 1936, at Copenhagen, the opinion of Trubetzkoi was sought. He pronounced Zipf's work "one-half pure genius" (*echt genial*), the other half erroneous. This agreed with my own judgment.

We were mere babes in the woods in using simple arithmetical enumeration, and in time Zipf turned to statistical methods. To

---

[10] He was out of college 1921–22, and repeated his Junior year 1922–23; A.M. 1928, Ph.D. 1930, both in Linguistics (or, as it was then called, Comparative Philology); Instructor in German, 1929—; died 25 September 1950. Miss Selma König, who taught him German at Freeport, Illinois, has told me much of his youthful brilliance.

me the rapid development, in recent years, of what may now be called the beginning of mathematical (as distinguished from mere descriptive) linguistics has been a deep satisfaction. It is, I believe, a promising new approach not only to many linguistic problems but to some problems of interpretation, and of literary criticism.

In general, literature has always been open only to subjective interpretation. The very training in which the critic has been himself brought up has made him likewise prone to exercise subjective judgments. A new, more objective attack, if it fulfills even in part the claims made for it, will be an important step forward in the understanding and appreciation of literature, in which a linguist also may be allowed to take delight, both for its own sake and because at the same time his own special interest— in language—is advanced. For, as Hilbert said ("Axiomatisches Denken," *Math. Ann.* 78, 1918, 405; quoted by von Mises, *Positivism*, 1951, p. 112): "everything that can be an object of scientific thought at all, as soon as it is ripe for the formation of a theory, falls into the lap of the axiomatic method and thereby indirectly of mathematics."

Yet language and literature are inseverable. Any literary text must from time to time raise linguistic questions; and these questions must be answered, and by linguistic criteria. This is self-evident. What is not so obvious is that a scholar who has both strings to his bow is well equipped. At Harvard all candidates for the doctorate in Classical Philology must take courses in comparative and historical Greek and Latin Grammar. A linguist who does not know his languages well enough to read continuous text for himself is halt and maim; so is a scholar who does not know a great deal about language, and in particular the history of the Greek and Latin languages.

In its most recent form our problem is stated as follows: in any sample of literature, a poem, or a play, we have a message or series of messages purposively produced in such a way as to be decoded word by word in the most economical fashion, i.e., most in accord with the economy or structure of the language

in which the piece is composed. This implies a matching of mus-
cular, neural, and cerebral activity. Moreover, the appearance
of any particular word is guaranteed by the sequence in which it
appears, i.e., there is goodness of fit. Presumably, critics have
dimly perceived something of this sort, without being able to
give any proof of the processes which they must have assumed
to exist, though they do not say so, underlying their preference
for this or that wording or interpretation. We have now a mathematical deduction that proves the complete compatibility of
structure or sequence, the decoding (or encoding) of "in-formation," and the economical criterion of matching which links
these two.[11] There is a high degree both of order and of selec-
tivity in sequence, within the variables of state. The utterance
is built up out of sequences of epilegmata which conform to a
statistical distribution law for relative frequency of occurrence,
rank, length, and variation of meanings.[12] The message is
"matched" (i.e., each symbol with its referend) since the encoding or decoding is properly (and originally, where ancient
literatures are concerned) automatic—any comment or interpretation interferes with this, or prevents the original message from
ever being entirely recovered without disturbance. The entire
utterance, no matter how long, is a sequence of entities, an
estimation of the probabilities of which is identical with the
actual probabilities of occurrences of words, notwithstanding
the large number of possibilities of free variation; the symbolism
is systematic. The interpretation of the formula (or graph, a
slope of -1, with its parameters) is quite simply *selective variation*, both within a closed system (status) and historically (as
in literary forms). See the following page.

   And the literary critics? What I am about to say may sound
like heresy to scholars who have learnt nothing since they grad-

---

[11] B. Mandelbrot, *Publ. de l'Inst. de Statistique de l'Université de Paris* 2 i, 1953;
Word 10, 1954, 1–27. I was able to give some account of Mandelbrot's work at the
Bloomington meeting of the Linguistic Society of America on 2 August 1952 (see Bulle-
tin no. 26, supplement to Vol. 29, No. 2, Pt. 2, of the journal of LSA, April-June 1953,
p. 6).
[12] P. Guiraud, *Les Caractères statistiques du vocabulaire*, Paris 1954.

uated as doctors of philosophy. But there is an unsuspected amount of self-deception in the arguments used by critics to defend their preoccupation with problems of authenticity, of "restoring" or "emending" a text, or the like, even of interpre-

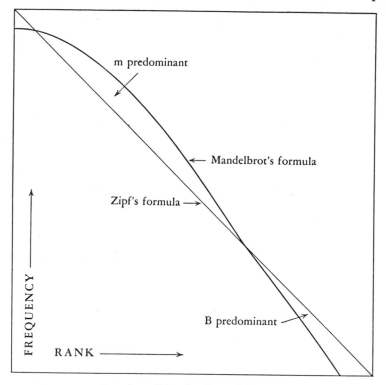

Graph 1. Distribution of Forms.

tation, which a disinterested observer finds repellent. Exposure to Homer, to Dante, or Grillparzer, even to T. S. Eliot, may, or may not, be a major experience: that depends. But if and when it is, its majesty is greatly diminished or even destroyed both by translator and by critic. If this be heresy, make the most of it. Do we not all remember how Shakespeare was mangled by our teachers in school? Fortunate are the few who escape. One summer, some fifteen years ago, a Harvard professor read the Authorized Version of the Bible, now become a unique "original," aloud, from Genesis to Revelation, with his family; and a little later, most of Shakespeare, each of us taking his turn as verse or speaker changed, so that everybody got a chance at each character. No comment or stopping to explain— that each of us can do for himself later on, when he is mature enough for it: the experience was pure delight, a schoolgirl of fifteen rejoicing in becoming Lady Macbeth for half an hour. A freshman class, after one year's Latin, read with me some Catullus, and then Tennyson's echoes of Catullus, and declared, "We had no idea a Latin poet could so move our hearts, as well as our minds." Letters, like music and the fine arts, are to be savored and then digested, not regurgitated: surely the meaning of "ruminate" took a false turn when "great books" fell into the hands of tutors who themselves behave more like sheep or cattle, passing a line or two of cud at a time through the three or four chambers of their stomachs—it would be flattering to say their brains—one after the other. A poet is to be absorbed into the understanding mind at his creative highest and best. Once poetry gets into the hands of the translator or professional critic, its message is reduced, twisted, and impaired. In the course of my work I have often had to consult the elder Pliny, but I have never read his *Natural History* through from beginning to end. And I have never consulted a translation of it. To do that would have been to prevent all possibility of understanding, by importing inescapably a North American milieu of the twentieth century into a work written nearly two thousand years ago at a place more than three thousand miles away. How much more disabling is a translation of Plato or Aeschylus or Homer! The truth of what I say has often been perceived before now, and sometimes stated unequivocally. "The simple basic fact that the meaning of every linguistic expression depends only upon incomplete, uncertain, and temporally shifting convention within a community of language has as its necessary consequence that equivalent reproduction of a text in a foreign language is *impossible*." We shall see in a later lecture that a statistical in-

propose to consider in a later lecture (vii, "Order and Disorder"), in which I shall develop the thesis that literature, by introducing its own "messages," provided always that the language in which it presents them is neither translated nor explained (by way of commentary, for example), maintains its own good order (negentropy); but that, by the same token, it is subject to the entropy of transmission if it is translated or "explicated." Language is a form of order, the formula of which was proved in 1948 to be identical with that of the perfect gas of thermodynamics. But transference into a different language is into a different code, which upsets the encoding and decoding of the original; and comment, or additional messages, can never contain more information than the original message. The first language preserves its own order (negentropy), a second language (of translation) causes disorder; commentaries change from the original by addition. But an original thought, an original contribution of literature, or science, is itself (nothing more), its own author (none other), and its own justification. This is where literature is important in its own right, e.g. Shakespeare or Milton, just like science, e.g. Newton or Einstein.

What we are concerned with in the composition and reading of literature—and this is what the literary critics do not know, or fail to understand—is the *mechanism* of language, its economy, what I have called elsewhere (*Language*, p. 199) "Glossodynamics." The capacity of human beings to behave in this peculiar and highly regulated fashion is inborn. Writers of genius—your Plato or Shakespeare—possess the power not only in great degree, but also with unusual refinement. However, the details of this behavior, in their initial, that is, childish, stages are *learned* and *imitative*. It is not a matter of inheritance (except the capacity itself), but of learning the particular code or pattern of the environment, and then of elaborating it when learnt. So-called "information" theory refers not to the actual information contained in a particular message, but to the maximum amount of information a particular line of communication might transmit. Now a translation line is limited, because of the disparity of codes, the impossibility of matching: an impossibility which may yet be overcome by machine translation.

This limitation operates at all levels, phonematic, morphomatic, syntactic, semantic, and behavioral; and as much in men as in machines. In fact it is precisely because all these data have not yet been completely coded for any language, or built into any machine, that machine translation has not been achieved.[13] Even for that purpose the data must be completely available for *both* of two languages, both the target language (into which the machine is required to translate) and the original language. Good interpreters come very close to the requirement; so does, or did, a really good Latinist or Hellenist, men like Jebb,

> you that yesterday,
> From out the Ghost of Pindar in you,
> Roll'd an Olympian,

or Archer-Hind, who translated Mandeville into Herodotean Greek. Archer-Hind, it is true, was good for little else, unless to give an opinion on the nicer points of a vintage; Jebb, however, did represent the University constituency in Parliament for some years. But perhaps the day for such achievements as theirs in composition has gone past, and forever, except in modern languages.

If so, and whether it has or not, the translating machine, when it is perfected, will be quicker and better than the human. Human coding is relatively slow and ineffective. At all events, translation constantly loses, never gains; always changes the original message. Thus the ideal at which a scholar should aim is to *read* Greek or Latin literature *as literature*, in precisely the same way as he reads English literature.

The stream of speech, and this includes literary texts, constitutes a system of probabilities of behavior built up throughout the history of the language. Every possible sequence of pho-

---

[13] The best attack on this problem known to me so far is that of Dr Anthony G. Oettinger, "A Study for the Design of an Automatic Dictionary" (Harvard Ph.D. thesis in Applied Mathematics, Division of Applied Science, 1954).

nemes, morphomes, words, syntagmata, *and of meanings*, has a predetermined probability, which the brain follows, indeed creates, automatically, if its owner has the kind of acquaintance with the language that we have specified—not otherwise. The utterances come without premeditation, however much they may later be polished. This is what the poet does when he writes his poetry, even though he ponder it until his brain is at last satisfied with the result. The task is not so readily, or perfectly, performed, in this year of grace 1955, in reading Greek or Latin authors, who wrote in a very different milieu. But, even if not perfectly performed, it is more than worth the attempt, which, honestly made, is richly rewarded. I speak from experience: it is the way I now try to read Homer or Vergil, Plato or Cicero. These are authors for mature minds. Commentaries and translations I *never* touch, the dictionary only as a desperate last resort: for then the line between the source and the terminal is filled with "noise" (to use the technical term), and the message is distorted, even dissipated completely—above all, in the lecture room.

What I have just been saying is true both of spoken and of written utterance. The Classical authors may be read aloud—particularly, Greek epic and all drama are better declaimed, even to yourself—or silently, which is, I suppose, the usual practice. But the principles involved are not a whit different: the receptor is the eye, not the ear, that is all, when we read. That is to say, we then have to do with visual language, with graphemes, instead of with phonemes. There is some evidence to suggest that, after the initial stage or stages, the brain decodes (or in composition, terminating at the hand, instead of at the mouth, encodes) the stream of utterance identically in both situations as the semantic value is reached. Here memory, which depends on input, output, and feedback, plays a large role, even in creative writing. It uses chiefly the existing pathways and switching points; in original composition it creates new ones, which the reader or hearer will decode. All the evidence thus far available tends to show that this is done word by word,[14] not, as might superficially have been supposed, in groups of words or idea by idea. New investigation may compel a modification of this statement; but the best research so far conducted views unfavorably the notion that we receive language, physically speaking, by "ideas" rather than through the words which infer them. When this level is finally reached we have the true behavioral level of language, at which meaning itself has become true goal-directed activity.[15] The written language is, or, I believe, some day will be, demonstrably the internal thought of the author, but it is probably always less "information," as received by the reader, than the actual output of the writer. This follows from the discovery that "information" obeys the law of entropy, that is to say, is "only true if at each stage we regard the 'information' transmitted as the maximum 'information' that could be transmitted with an appropriately coded receiving system,"[16] namely, the brain of a contemporary, intelligent, and well-informed reader—formerly, we may say, of a contemporary of Plato or of Cicero, as the case might be. There is, perhaps, no way of doing anything like this now, not even by learning to talk and to read and to write Classical Greek or Latin at the critical stage of language learning, namely, the first few years of life.

These basic, fundamental facts have serious consequences. We have arrived at an impasse. Two ways out are possible. We may return to an understanding of a text as penetrating as it can be made, based on intimate, habitual, and intuitive familiarity with the original language, a systematic knowledge of it, and effective ways of thinking in it and about its documents—in short, an understanding based on *noumena*, not *phenomena*; or we may abandon professional exegesis of literature entirely in favor of reading it solely *as literature*, even imperfectly. This is something which each generation will have to do for itself; and, as I have said, the rewards are exceedingly rich

---

[14] See *Language*, p. 171.

[15] See *Language*, pp. 102, 177.

[16] N. Wiener, *Human Use of Human Beings*, 1950, pp. 91–92.

for those who will do it. It is open to question even whether a poet's interpretation of poetry, a dramatist's of drama, a historian's of history, a philosopher's of philosophy, and so on, would succeed. My own experience is that I do better reading poetry, drama, history, philosophy, and the rest for myself. As for what has aptly been called the literary world's, the critic's, "lacy language," the less said the better.

Everything depends, in reading literature, on the amount of "information" that we can get through. To us, as native speakers of English, there is really nothing to prevent complete recovery of modern English literature, if we use all the "information" that we can get, since we have at our disposal a complete repertory of receiving apparatus—provided that we do use it, and provided that the message itself is not mutilated at its source, as in James Joyce's *Finnegan's Wake*, which uses about a score of different and incompatible linguistic patterns, thereby giving rise to a very large amount of "noise." But to get from Greek and Latin writers an amount of "information" at all comparable with what we get from English writers, it is necessary first to acquire a comparable understanding of the languages, and through them to build the line of transmission just as well as we possibly can. Even in ordinary conversation the amount of "information," for one reason or another, is not always the same for sender and receiver; then, as we say, we do not "understand." Translation is a frequent cause of disturbance and loss, perhaps the most frequent. Yet the two different quantities, of "information" sent and "information" received, may be defined in terms of each other.

To obtain satisfactory semantic coding, at whatever level, of words or, for example, of an entire poem, there must be first and foremost a well-established "storage" in the brain of the receiver, what we call memory, built up perhaps over many years, their entire "input." This is not difficult to do for Shakespeare; it is very much more difficult to do now with Sophocles. Attempts are continually being made (I can think of two recent works, good ones as such works go) to help us, to try to tell us what

Sophocles "meant." But I am not convinced, for reasons already set forth, and I prefer to read Sophocles. Whether those who cannot read Sophocles at all should be encouraged to read such books is a question which, I *am* convinced, should be answered "No." Whether those who can read Sophocles imperfectly, or only with difficulty, should read him, is a question that is at least open to debate—the result may be quite incommensurate with the effort. To read a translation, even a "good" one, is quite certainly to get only a distorted message. The true behavioral level of language is a form of action in which "meaning" is less our own thought than a form of goal-directed activity—what you "do" about the situation,—in which what you say or what you understand is also part of what you do.

The result is vastly more complicated by the qualitative aspect of the utterances than by the quantitative, chiefly because the qualitative aspect is not so far known in such a way that it can be formulated in statements of comparable completeness or accuracy. It is either unknown or known only in a vague way. The problem is not of producing behavior by means of the message, but the opposite problem of identifying the message, if we can, by the *structure* of the message. This is what I have daringly called a new approach to Greek and Latin—or any— literature in the subtitle of this course of lectures; the following lectures will attempt, in a modest way, to prepare the ground, and perhaps to take a few steps in the direction of this approach. With all respect to Professor Wiener, the philologist, like the engineer, can tear his "little black box" apart: we can, we must, and we shall.

Moreover, throughout these lectures I shall appeal for the establishment of a common ground, through language, among linguists, philologists, and scientists, not merely because language *is* their common meeting place (since any linguistic norm is found by abstraction from usage), but for the much more important reason that the present disharmony tends toward negation. By this I mean the trend, just now setting in as a strong current, against faith in science and in scientific method. This trend has had considerable support from time to time in the past, and just now is marshaling its forces in a new anti-intellectual movement expressed in clichés such as "soul, not reason," or "spirit versus intellect," or "not formalism, but insight," and "feeling for life" or "the sterility of thought." All this, I need not say, has nothing to do with the matter, except for the harm it does. Nor has what comes next.

To come a little closer home, let me quote, as examples, some statements which seem to me negative. Mackail speaks of Vergil's "language of liquid . . . beauty"; he writes that in Catullus "language . . . is transmuted into air and fire"; Rand's remark (apropos also of Catullus) that "we moderns are oblivious to form" is, as we shall see, nearer the mark (if I may be allowed to write *insensible* for his *oblivious*), but goes on, alas, "and search for spirit." Far worse (I say nothing of his mixed metaphors, which he did not write to sustain any theory of synaesthesia) is his comment on Ovid *Amores* 1.6: "the tone of this poem is parody . . . permeating the substance like a perfume, invisible but appreciable by those who have the sense of smell," with its implication that Rand had, but I have not, this sense of smell. Be that as it may, I have, let me insist, a sense of sense, and of nonsense, and of the difference between sense and nonsense. What Rand said is, "Ovid *Amores* 1.6 smells," and this I do not understand. Such a statement, nonsensical as it is, is meaningless; it is neither connectible with experience nor communicable to others, it evokes no response: for smell has to do with the inhibition of certain enzymes contained in the olfactory organs, changes in the concentration of which are converted into distinguishable neural signals. Education in such meaningless rubbish as comment on the smell of a poem is demoralizing. I know whereof I speak; I know also that it took a quarter of a century to shake myself free of it. Read Ovid if you will, trifler as he was; but do not tell me that any poem is pervaded by perfume. I know, or think I know, what Rand may have meant; but he did *not* say it.

Here are a few other samples: "the sophists . . . those sapless leaves frozen on the tree of knowledge" (Wright); "the poet dexterously imparted an edifying religious coloring to the hero-legend" (Sedgefield, of *Beowulf*); "the shadow of the trial and death of Socrates caused Plato . . . to call forth the vision of an upward road leading to a city set in heaven" (Adam). These statements—I quote from the dead, lest I disparage living colleagues who continue to emit such utterances while changing only the wording, and some of them not even that—these statements have now no discoverable meaning, and have had none since the passing of the age of magic, when it would have been taken for granted that they had something to say. But perhaps it is still too early to say that the age of magic has passed.

No, not criticism or emendation: I am not wedded to νὴ Βελσοῦρδον, or to ὀλβεττήρ—they may be wrong. Nor is it important.[17] No, not antiquarianism either. But reading, reading, and more reading. I too have tried the other ways (e.g. an un-

---

[17] Words that occur once only are in any sample the most numerous, although the larger the sample the proportion falls—with relative slowness—as the sample is increased. Hence the reluctance of scholars to accept a new word in an inscription or papyrus is curious, the probabilities being all in its favor. In criticism they are just as uneasy if the word proposed is not already in the dictionary. This reluctance is irrational, as Haupt implied in his well-known remark about *Constantinopolitanus*, "if the sense demands," a proviso that applies to Βελσοῦρδος, which is not an invention, or ὀλβεττήρ, which is no invention of mine either. Since both are actually attested in Greek epigraphic documents, the probability of their occurrence cannot be zero (i.e., impossible) any more than it can be unity (i.e., certain).

No critic can possibly be more aware than I am myself of the weaknesses of νὴ Βελσοῦρδον and ὀλβεττέρ' ἄρον, or of the absurdity of defending them. All this is done as a sample of twentieth-century triviality in the realm of textual criticism, a veritable *reductio ad absurdum*, however important such things may have been at the Renaissance, or even in the eighteenth century. But it is no longer a man's work; to behold it is like nothing so much as watching grown men playing in a lunatic asylum with a child's box of bricks, above all at a moment when human life is face to face with the possibility, nay the certainty, of new and bright, almost blinding, enlightenment on every hand. Much in these pages will be seen by some as through a glass darkly; for light always casts shade. But behind the glass I see a very bright light by which man may take some few steps forward into the darkness, *lampada uitae tradens*. Anything that lights a ray and carries it forward to dispel the pall surrounding man's understanding of himself, of his nature, and of his total environment, is to be welcomed, however hesitating each step, and even if one or two steps should at first flounder, or occasionally one of them have to be retraced, the better to take the next one forward.

published emendation in Juvenal 10.54–55, which a letter from Housman discouraged; notes on Lucan 4.632 and 7.179–180; an essay on "Aspects of Life under the Roman Empire Illustrated by Metrical Inscriptions"—this published only in part, and only a poor Arabic version; a newspaper column called "A Lesson from Sophocles," or "Antigone at Manchester"; "Herodotus in Bangor," with apologies to R. Y. Tyrrell; and so forth). And when the Classics were my bread and butter, I too could and did preach their "values" (something about which many fine scholars have had nothing to say, unless to declare that they despised the whole topic), in specious arguments alas, as now I see to my shame, up hill and down dale, in season and out of season, against friend and foe. In all that I no longer believe; but in literature for its own sake, for itself. Among great books, however, I count unhesitatingly the *Origin of Species*, or Sherrington's *Man on His Nature*, or Eddington's *Nature of the Physical World*, as well as Shakespeare and Milton, Lucretius and Sophocles. None of these is—no book is—κτῆμα ἐς ἀεί, nor yet *aere perennius*, two ascriptions both of which suggest glacial boulders more than the breath of life. But they all have much to say both as literature (form) and as language (content). To the examination of literary—especially poetic,—scientific, and other forms of discourse, qualitatively as well as quantitatively, we shall turn in subsequent lectures, beginning with Catullus, in the hope of understanding them better.

II

Pudicus Poeta:
Words and Things

The Vocabulary of Catullus

WIGHT DUFF, in his chapter on Catullus, speaks
(p. 325) of the poet's "foul-mouthed abuse," calls him "un-
speakably coarse." As every schoolboy knows, Catullus, like
Martial and Ovid, would have denied the charge; the poet is
pudicus, pius, and *castus,* three interesting epithets. It is refreshing to find Merrill (p. xxvii) understanding the language of
Catullus as "formal, not literal," i.e., structural; but he made
no attempt to explain just what he meant by "formal," or how
the subsumed form was to be discovered: not exactly what we
have called tearing the black box apart, but very close to it.

This lecture deals with poetic discourse. I shall use, for illustration, chiefly Catullus, since his book is compact and makes,
even in its entirety, a sample suitable for examination. But the
method is applicable to larger works in Latin or Greek, or in
other literatures. Distinctions are often drawn between a literature and its language. This seems to me a mistake: for a literature cannot exist without a language, and much that is often
said to be "not literature" is excluded on grounds not strictly
justified. Aesthetic judgments are more open to error still, and
semiotic is both boring and bogus.

It is necessary to distinguish. Of what has come to be known
as "General Semantics" I shall point out here only that it mis-
conceives language fundamentally in two of its tenets. First, by
seeking to reduce language to a purely referential use, taking
notice of its dynamic and emotive and aesthetic values only to
reject them, it naïvely supposes that such a restriction, which
would make language invariable in its responses and therefore

static and totally inadequate to any but the most simple and concrete situations, a restriction which would change the entire nature and use of language, can possibly be imposed. And second, the advice to "delay" utterance (so as to say nothing that is not strictly referential) would reduce a large part of the normal units of utterance to a succession of zero elements. Imagine Catullus full of dashes or asterisks!

Semiotic, the chief distinction of which is a totally unnecessary and extremely involved terminology, has been condemned, and in my judgment rightly, as a pseudo-science.[1] The marks of a genuine science are not hard to see, or their absence. A genuine science does not, for example, pursue red herrings; that is, it does not explore something entirely different from the topic professedly under discussion; it avoids platitudes disguised by technical jargon, elaborate technical devices that after all lead only to empty tautologies or futile results, all promulgated as if *ex cathedra*, with a great fanfare; and it does not present as new discoveries what are in fact matters of common knowledge made to appear other than what they are by being cloaked in a new set of terms. Semiotic, it seems to me, is open to attack on all these counts, and in any event no help to us in our attempt to understand the usage of Catullus.

From these prefatory remarks it will be plain that form is to be my theme. This is not to ignore content. For form and content are no more to be separated than language and literature. There is one preliminary caution I must make at this point. There are, in Catullus, written down for all to read, some words which we consider coarse, though we do ourselves use such, if not always, or all of us, in mixed company (I have no idea what women say to one another), and some English writers, both in this and in former times, have not shrunk from their use in their writings, or, nowadays, in print—John Donne, for example. If any of you are squeamish about these things, I give you fair warning, and those who will may go now, and have done with it.

---

[1] Errol E. Harris, *Nature, Mind and Modern Science*, London 1954, pp. 343–344.

Catullus, like Ovid and Martial, was well aware of the accusa-
tion to which he was exposing himself and reproves (16.4) those
of you

> qui me ex uersiculis meis putastis,
> quod sunt molliculi, parum *pudicum.*
> nam *castum* esse decet *pium* poetam
> ipsum, uersiculos nihil necesse est.

Ovid (*Tr.* 2.354) confesses that his muse is *iocosa,* but insists
that his life is *uerecunda;* Martial too (1.4.8) declares his life
proba, while admitting that his page is *lasciua.* So Hadrian (ap.
Apul. *apol.* 11) grants to Voconius, and Apuleius claims for himself, that he was *pudicus* in mind, no matter how *lasciuus* in his
poetry. Other such assertions are to be found in Seneca and
Pliny, both cited by Merrill (at Catullus l.c.), and Herrick
writes (*Hesperides* fin.)

> To his Book's end this last line he'd have plac't,
> *Jocund his Muse was, but his life was chast.*

And when Jonathan Swift complained to his landlady that the
sheets were dirty, she retorted that he was the last man in the
world to complain about a dirty sheet, *cacata charta.* If, at the
end of this lecture, it is thought that our author ought to have
been ashamed of himself, well, that is what *pudicus* means. The
word is as old as Plautus, it is classical, and it is in common use.
It is connected with *repudiare* and connotes repulsion, a negative not a positive modesty.

As for *castus* (poeta), also Plautine, classical, and common,
some may recall a remark attributed to another poet, that "of
all sexual aberrations, chastity is the rarest." The word means
both "according to (religious) rules, ritual" and "abstinent"; it
is connected with *castigare* "chasten," again a negative attitude
toward duty, clearly in the related Oscan *kasit* (like Greek δεῖ)
"must" in the sense of "stand in need" (in Latin *caret*), "not to
have, want (in the sense of 'lack,' not 'wish' or 'be willing')."
There remains *pius,* a word of great interest, to which we shall
return in a subsequent lecture. Here I shall only point out that

it also is Latin (as old as Ennius) and Italic, classical, and frequent; that it means "pure in heart" as well as "dutiful, clean in hand and action," and (*u* having been lost) that it is related to *purus* and *purgare*, and therefore ultimately also to *pudicus*.

Literature may be examined in any mass whatever. The largest library in the world contains *x* millions of books, written in *y* thousands of languages. But such mass is far too great for practical study. On the other hand, minimal literary units such as figures of speech are too small.[2] It is better to take a sample of moderate size, as a useful preliminary to postulating any theory of design, in order to form some idea of the whole by examining the whole, and not merely a part. It is obviously difficult to make exact, detailed statements about the entirety of discourse, even of poetic discourse; inferences drawn from a part only will be still more uncertain. We shall aim, therefore, at finding a sound basis for statements which are admittedly, and from the nature of the case, of restricted application. In the humanities in particular we have to deal with factors that are not easy to control, some of which are comparatively large in their effects. It is necessary, therefore, to be able to distinguish between differences that are due to a particular factor under consideration and those that are due to a haphazard influence which induces variation. We need to know the number of individuals in a category, in order to estimate their effect. Frequency and variate then emerge clearly.

For example, if we are looking for the total number of words of unique occurrence in a set of authors or in a language, instead of searching the whole, we may take a random sample to make the actual selection from a dictionary, which is taken as being as full as it can be made, and we shall have representative specimens of the *hapax legomenon* which we can be sure have been selected without systematic bias. There is also another technique, to which I shall come back presently, namely, the degree

---

[2] Compare Yule's criticism in *The Statistical Study of Literary Vocabulary*, Cambridge 1944, p. 113, of Lutosławski's listing and discussion of "peculiarities" of Plato's style; and see now 8A.15 in *BC* (Guiraud and Whatmough, *Bibliographie critique de la statistique linguistique*, CIPL, Utrecht and Anvers 1954).

of determinacy in the occurrence of a particular item of vocabulary at a particular place, and again the variance within the
sample, the extent to which an author is, or is not, commonplace
in the several features of his writings—such as choice of words,
orders of arrangement, and the like.

To read "what Plato said" (or Catullus or any other writer)
is easy; it is not so easy to understand what he wrote. Some students of language hold that we cannot know meaning, even with
all the help of all the dictionaries of words, of phrases, and of
concepts. But it is not so. We are dealing with a form, with an
equilibrium of insubstantial elements, in which an understanding of each of a number of pieces, and of their arrangements,
infers that of the whole: the system is found in the parts, and the
system is, at any given point or status, closed. Think of the
absurdity of compiling, after twenty-nine years of effort, an
analysis based on many thousands of examples from hundreds
of sources![3] Instead I propose, in this lecture, to take a limited
ensemble covering a selection from the activity of one author
only, thus using homogeneous material, limited but complete in
itself. If we took the whole, we should have a statement in
which each important factor in the system would appear with
its coefficient of usage. As it is, we shall have a more restricted,
but not a less certain, statement.

First, an important principle. *Subject matter never affects the
total vocabulary at risk.* Certainly the nature of the field determines the quantities λ which determine (measure) the chances
that one word or a different word will be used;[4] but it does not
render strictly and mathematically zero—not even for obscene
words—the chance that any word known to the author will not
be used. The subject matter determines only the relative frequencies—*any* word known to the author may occur in any work

---

[3] Damourette et Pichon, *Des mots à la pensée*, Paris 1927 et suiv., in seven volumes.
The utterances were collected between 1911 and 1940. Compare the criticisms of H.
Frei, *Le Livre des deux mille phrases*, Geneva 1953 (Société de Publications Romanes et
Françaises, n°. 40), pp. 11, 16.

[4] λ is the ratio of the number of occurrences n to the number N of words at risk
(Yule, *op. cit.*, p. 48, cf. 52, 54, 69).

on any subject. Thus, for obscene words we have two distinct measurements: (1) the proportion in the vocabulary (i.e., of the number of words of this special class to the total number of words in the vocabulary, *a* actual, *b* at risk); and (2) the proportion of occurrences, namely, of words of the special class to all occurrences. Of these measurements the former is independent of the size of sample, and is constant for all sizes of sample; the latter is a function of size of sample, and may be misleading if samples of different sizes are compared; in a very small random sample few (or no) words will occur more than once, but in a very large sample the total stock of words approaches exhaustion.

Now Catullus is of convenient size; and a peculiar interest attaches to his writings because of the high proportion both of "taboo" words and of *hapax legomena* (some of these not occurring elsewhere in the whole range of Latin literature).

However, we are interested in content (that is, meaning) as well as form. But there is one important observation to be made: it is a mistake to assume that there must be a special relationship between content and form, that certain content is impossible apart from certain form—for example, that there is any kind of content peculiar to poetic discourse. The whole of Catullus may be put into prose; the atomic theory of Greek prose writers (Leucippus, Epicurus, Democritus) was put into verse by Empedocles and Lucretius; Dante drew upon sources in prose. We may "feel" that verse is somehow "better" for epic, and prose not so "good." But the "goodness" is a matter of fit, of epic form, not of epic content, and the very use of the terms "feeling" and "goodness" brings us to some serious questions of aesthetics which must be reserved for a subsequent lecture.

Literary form need hardly consider the phonological level of language. But it may not ignore the semantic, visual, and behavioral. Of these the semantic and behavioral are closely connected, for the behavioral aspect is concerned with meaning, and the visual with written, as distinguished from purely oral, literature.

The simplest relation for meaning may be described as ostensive, when it is possible to present a specimen of what is under consideration, say a *table*, and leave it at that. This satisfies most ordinary, day-to-day situations. But it would not satisfy a physicist even for a table, not to mention more complicated problems of meaning. For him a table is a complex structure of events in certain spatio-temporal relationships;[5] and for him a word has a laboratory meaning with which various logical operations of mathematics, or experiments, are performed.

More familiar to most of us are attempts to understand meaning by using other words, that is, definition in a dictionary, either monolingual, like the Latin thesaurus, or bilingual, like Liddell and Scott. This is essentially translation, the weaknesses of which we have seen already. Or we may have dictionaries of synonyms and antonyms. Theoretically these latter imply a sound principle, that a given linguistic unit is either the same or not the same as another given unit. But in practice, while the theory works well enough for the speech sounds, forms, and constructs of words (that is, syntax), it breaks down badly in the field of meaning, and children learn in grammar school that there are no exact synonyms. Etymological definition is usually no better than lexical definition, though it has its usefulness in a tight corner. Meaning in a work of literature certainly cannot cope with the entire universe, any more than lexical meaning; for out of a multitude of unrelated random experiences of a multitude of different human beings a language must sort and classify. Its number of meanings is very large, much larger than the number of words, just as these are larger than the number of forms, and the number of forms larger than the number of sounds, but it cannot be considered to be infinitely large at any

---

[5] "I say, 'I sit at my table.' I ought *not* say that. What I ought to say is this:

" 'One of a certain string of events causally connected in the sort of way that makes the whole series what is *called* a "person" has a certain spatial relation to one of another string of events causally connected with each other in a different way and having a spatial configuration of the sort denoted by the word "table." ' "

I take this statement, assigned without source to Bertrand Russell, from W. M. Urban, *Language and Reality*, London 1939, p. 290.

given linguistic status such as that of Classical Latin or Greek. The increasing numbers, from sounds to forms, words, and meanings, is given by the large number of possible permutations and combinations, and these are restricted by the pattern of the language, the economics of which depends upon a strictly limited actual use of the theoretically possible total: the actual efficiency is much less than 100 per cent—exactly like the performance of an internal-combustion engine.

Besides, we are all biologically individual, and the whole complex of associations that go into the meaning of a single word, except the simplest and most concrete, can never be identical for any two of us. The most recent theory is that a minimum definition of the meaning of a word is given by the structure of the permitted sequences in which it appears; if you like, by context. Context is admittedly one of the most difficult features to control, but it is by no means necessary to despair utterly of rigor of method.

Catullus, then, is our sample of poetic discourse with reference to meaning, not in an attempt to discover an absolute canon, but rather a working hypothesis, an empiric solution, even if not always completely demonstrable.

So far as concerns Greek and Latin literature the correspondence between grapheme and phoneme is close enough to make any question of inequality in their "informational" value superfluous, whatever importance it may have (in special cases) for the text as such. Few moderns, I suspect, take in by ear Greek and Latin authors as readily as they do by eye, and still fewer reproduce them orally at length. James Joyce's "It was so scalding sorry for all, the whole twice two four of us . . ." is less troublesome in print than read aloud, but more trouble in either than $2 \times 2 = 4$. This is the consequence of confused or imperfect control over the entire "network" which computes and governs the transition probabilities in the stream of speech, an utterance or sequence of utterances being, together with their "meanings," from this point of view, a form of goal-directed activity. The process depends upon probabilities that can be

calculated, and proceeds along paths that are statistically determined.

Discourse is compounded of utterances, which fall into words,
forms, and speech sounds; the totality of discourse makes up a
language, which must be distinguished from language in the abstract and this from speech, which is a matter of gross physiological and acoustic features. What we are asking is the question, How does the diction of Catullus, for example, stand with
regard to that of other Latin authors—or, for that matter, how
does any Latin author so stand?

Previous studies suggested that the rank of an item of vocabulary (for example, the number of words of a given frequency of
occurrence, or the number of meanings of a particular word of a
given frequency) stands in a constant relationship when multiplied by the frequency itself, which may be expressed graphi-
cally as a curve with a slope of $45°$, i.e., -1. More recently it
has been shown that this solution needs correction by the introduction of two parameters (or constants) at the extremes of extremely high or extremely low frequency of occurrence. Even
so, I believe that the curve is to be interpreted as representing
the inherent good order of any kind of discourse, *the preservation, by means of selection, of its form or equilibrium, against the
ravages of variation* that inevitably occur with the passage of
time (the history of the language) and from place to place (i.e.,
dialect areas).

The range of occurrence varies from 1, 2, 3 . . . upwards, but
there is no probability that the occurrence of any word whatever
in the total vocabulary at risk will be strictly zero. Now the
hapax legomenon, the word that occurs once and once only, has
a high degree of conspicuousness; for the same law applies, that
frequency varies with conspicuousness, and that their product
is constant. But the *hapax legomenon*, although statistically it
hardly differs from a word of very low occurrence (say twice or
three times), is nevertheless anomalous, just like the scazon in
Greek comedy. Think, however, of the ridicule that would greet
or ought to greet the editor who attempted to remove a *hapax*

legomenon from Catullus on the ground not that the form is inde-
fensible, but that it never occurs elsewhere in Catullus, or (from
this point of view, a stronger argument) anywhere else in the
whole of Latin literature! Of such are the scribes who wrote
scorpionibus for *sopionibus* at 37.10. The anomaly lies not
usually in the morphological structure of the word itself, any
more than in the metrical structure of the word that gives a
scazon, but in the event; for *hapax legomena* show no departures
in pattern either in phonological or morphological structure:
brillig is not offensive on this ground—it might, so far as concerns form and sequence of sounds, be perfectly good, like *whirli-
gig* or *thingumajig*, or words with *-ig* : *-ic* like *t/d*, *s/z*, *f/v*; but
it just happens not to occur except in Lewis Carroll, and it is
excluded from current usage. In Greek and Latin, a unique
word is taken to be admissible to the dictionary, and often there
will be an ancient gloss. If not, editors are guided by context,
but do not resort to "emendation" unless there is a manifest
copyist's blunder, always a possible source of error in Catullus,
since the text depends on copies of a single manuscript, and for
insidias he at 84.2 of this lost Veronensis most editors write
hinsidias; a better emendation, as I showed in 1941 (*CP 36*,
1941, 410), is *insidihas*. But this is no *hapax legomenon;* it is a
mere variant of a common word and form. There is no cause, as
a rule, to interfere with a genuine *hapax legomenon* provided
that it follows the pattern of language, be the meaning well
established or not. Here at least that subjectivity which is given
free rein in an argument about authenticity, based on vocabulary, is now held sharply in check; it has no good cause for demanding freedom to roam. The anomaly remains, and analogy
is not allowed to dislodge it.

In fact in any simple random sampling, large enough to give
trustworthy results, there is normally a large number of any
class of words (e.g. taboo words) which occur only once in the
sample taken. These, however, usually occur elsewhere, either
in the same or in other authors; but again, not in the author now
under consideration, Catullus.

The characteristic K, a complicated quantity indicative of the concentration of vocabulary, or of the degree to which an author relies on the commoner words of a given class (say nouns)—that is, has a commonplace vocabulary—is remarkably low in Catullus. To put it another way, his vocabulary is anything but commonplace. We can only estimate the total number of nouns known to the living Catullus. But it is probably safe to assume that it was not less than the total number in Harper's *Latin Dictionary*, those nouns which can be shown to have become obsolete already or to have come into existence only at a later date being omitted. This number (W) can be estimated with approximate accuracy. Then the formula

$$10^{-4} \cdot W(K - 1)$$

gives the square of the coefficient of variation of the liabilities of nouns to occur.[6] In Catullus it is quite remarkable that the liability is greater than normal. Let us now examine some of these.

In a sequence the basic principle is that of binary choices. Starting from silence, the first unit may be any word in the language, each other word in the language being rejected (o) except that particular one which is accepted (1), and so on to silence again, subject always to the restrictions imposed by (*a*) conformity with the pattern of the language and (*b*) intelligibility, i.e., meaning. Thus the movements of molecules of water in parabolas, and the other phenomena of tides and breaking waves which are part of the field of hydrodynamics, emerge from a totally different choice of words in poetic discourse, yet a choice made on the same principle, and as a valid part of the unity of knowing in the words of Catullus (31.13; cf. Lucr. 1.8):

> gaudete uosque, O Lydiae lacus undae:
> ridete, quidquid est domi cachinnorum

---

[6] Yule, *op. cit.*, chap. iii.

echoed by Tennyson ("Frater Ave atque Vale"):

  Gazing at the Lydian laughter of the Garda lake below,

and doubtless echoed from Aeschylus (*P.V.* 89–90):

   κυμάτων | ἀνήριθμον γέλασμα.

Lydiae (*lidiae* Ven., *y* cod. G) occurs nowhere else in Catullus, and it has tempted editors to change, from Scaliger to Palmer. We need not stay over the lack of understanding on the part of these critics. The ἀνήριθμον of Aeschylus invites us to consider the arithmetician who assigns, almost arbitrarily, a name *two* to one of a kind plus one of the same kind, taken with another *two*, and writes $2 + 2 = 4$; Asquith, like Housman, would have said the same—"two and two make four"; but the late Honorable Mr Chaplin in the House of Commons would have said, in his Ciceronian prolixity of oratorical discourse:

 Mr Speaker, I have come to the House this morning with the intention, let me say the fixed and unalterable intention, of declaring my conviction, my firm conviction, that if you take the numeral commonly known as two and increase it by itself, the result will be found to be on the one hand no more, and on the other hand no less, than four,

or something like it. Contrast now Housman's

   To think that two and two are . . .
   . . . neither five nor three.

Here again we have a matter of selection.

 When it comes to matters of less certainty than arithmetic or hydrodynamics, matters which the logical positivists would rule out altogether, or declare to be meaningless statements, we find no unity of knowing, but we do find the same principle of selection and choice in poetic diction. Neither Housman's

   Think rather,—call to thought if now you grieve a little
   The days when we had rest, O soul, for they were long

    . . .

   Oh why did I awake? when shall I sleep again?

nor Wordsworth's

> Our birth is but a sleep and a forgetting:
> The Soul that rises with us, our life's Star,
> Hath had elsewhere its setting
> And cometh from afar

can be reconciled with the physicist's account that sees in life the force of negative entropy, a derivation from environment that postpones death. It is curious to note, in passing, that here are relations of order and disorder, both in the structure of life itself and in the structure of language. But what I wish chiefly to emphasize—and examples are numerous (I might point to one that I have developed elsewhere,[7] the scientific discourse of the meteorologist as compared with Shakespeare's description of a hurricane in the *Tempest*)—is the variation in the value of the characteristic K, that indicates a command of more extensive vocabulary and a lower degree of reliance upon the commonplace. To repeat, this is not a subjective impression. It is found by statistical methods and can be stated in precise mathematical quantities.

I come now to the special case of Catullus. Like Vergil he was a "northerner," from Cisalpine Gaul. He is not much earlier in date than Vergil. He has greater variety of metrical form, in a bulk of writing that amounts to about one-fifth of Vergil's. He did not go in for "fine" writing, like Persius, whose bulk is barely two-thirds that of Catullus. There are 150 words in Catullus which occur once only in his writings, and of these more than 70 per cent are rare in the whole of Latin literature, and more than 90 per cent do not occur in Vergil at all, unless the *Appendix Vergiliana* be counted authentic, in which event only 12 words out of the 150 would have to be reckoned also as "Vergilian." The absence of these twelve from the rest of the Vergilian corpus is not against the authenticity of the *Appendix*, or even of those poems in which they occur. What *is* against the authenticity of the *Appendix* (and the *Aetna*), as a whole, is

---

[7] *New World Writing* 6, October 1954, pp. 294–295.

that its vocabulary has a different characteristic (*K*) from the rest of the Vergilian corpus.

The remarkable feature of the words used by Catullus is not in the number used once only, for this is normally large in any literary sample, but in the number of them which are peculiar, or almost peculiar, to Catullus in the entirety of recorded Latin literature. Even in the Basic English version of the Gospel According to St John 24.3 per cent of the nouns that occur, occur once only, but the percentage is usually around 55, though in a few authors it rises somewhat higher, and regularly tends to rise somewhat, the smaller the size of sample. Since a very small number of words that occur frequently may contribute more than one-fifth of the total number of occurrences of words, and since also a high percentage of the total number of words used in a sample occur more than once, the burden placed upon those that occur once and only once is proportionately greater. The writing of Catullus is not peculiar in this respect, nor with respect to the smaller number of words occurring only twice or three times. What distinguishes his once-words is the fact that many of them are ἅπαξ λεγόμενα for the entire corpus of Latin literature.

A casual reader—which means most readers—would hardly distinguish a word that occurs once only in an author from a word that occurs twice or three times in the same author, if the editor of an annotated text did not direct attention to the fact, a fact to which the casual reader again is not likely to attach any significance beyond that of a grammatical or lexical curiosity. It is necessary to distinguish also between genuine and apparent once-words. The true once-word is a coinage that never recurs. The number of them is exceedingly small, for by definition a once-word must eliminate, or at least impair, convention, the very factor that is indispensable to language; and theoretically a word once used may always be used again, and so pass from the class of words used once to that of words used twice, or three times, or any very low number of times. Hence the entire notion of the *hapax legomenon* is something of a mirage,

and unless there is some special feature in a series of such supposed once-words, any given specimen is not really worthy of
notice; it is a mere accident. We may believe that the so-called
once-words in Catullus were well enough known. But not in
writing. Their very appearance in the manuscripts of Catullus
led to the almost complete disappearance of *all* the copies, of
every single copy of the works of Catullus.

Some years ago I suggested in a book review, as a topic for
investigation, the question, How "real" a phenomenon, or
merely apparent, is the ἅπαξ λεγόμενον?[8] Theoretically, I added,
one would expect such words to be polysyllabic; so, in fact, are
the comic jawbreakers of Aristophanes. But the long words of
comedy, and occasionally of other literary forms, that occur
once only are perfectly normal with respect to word formation,
and usually with respect to meaning in compounds; that is, they
function syntactically in a normal way, like the rest of Greek
compounds, or like Sanskrit or other Indo-European compounds.
It is remarkable, but not accidental, that the long Aristophanic
"once-word" fits the pattern of his verse so well.

The curious thing about some *hapax legomena*, therefore, is
their brevity, in itself an indication that they are not after all
genuine "once-words" of the spoken language, perhaps not of
the written language, or of the particular author in whom they
appear. In fact the term "once-word," if it is taken to mean an
absolutely unique word, is a contradiction in terms. A word is
a "free" form, that is, a form that can stand by itself and at the
same time have meaning. (For languages such as Eskimo, of
which it is said that the speakers do not recognize the "word"
as an entity or unit of analysis, the term *epilegma* may serve.)
From another point of view a word may be described as a
bounded unit (that is, it has in the permissible phonematic sequence a clearly marked beginning and end, or, in print, small
pieces of paper left blank before and after it), with strong internal statistical probabilities. But a form is a recurrent feature,

---

[8] The question has been taken up by F. Martinazzoli in a monograph called *Hapax
Legomenon*, Rome 1953; but Part One (all that has yet appeared) is disappointing.

repeated again and again, identically or almost identically (for example, with inflexional or even phonetic variations). Hence by definition (i.e., theoretically) as well as by observation a word should occur more than once if it is to be recognized as a word at all. A true "once-word" (of Lewis Carroll, or Edward Lear, or e. e. cummings) does not get into the dictionary. If truly unique it cannot function as a genuine linguistic symbol, any more than a unique ideograph, or even thousands of unique alphabetic "spellings"—a separate symbol for every single concept is an impossible burden.

But there is another class of words that may not get into the dictionary. These are short enough, usually monosyllabic in English, and by no means "once-words." They are excluded from the dictionary, and from polite letters, or scientific usage, because of a current taboo. Many of them have not always been under a taboo; and though they are now banned, it is not the content of meaning that produces the ban, for euphemistic substitutes are readily found, and constantly used. No, it is the form and especially the association, the habitual context, what I have called "determinacy," or the degree to which the construct, the syntactic string or sequence, guarantees their occurrence, unless they are consciously and deliberately rejected. These are the most obviously apparent and merely apparent of all apparent "once-words," the most shadowy of genuine "once-words." They are also the most affective.

Yet to discover the meaning, for the most part easy enough, is not always the simplest matter. Take *ploxenum*, which I am about to consider; or *salaputium*, which will be considered later. The sequence, or construct of words; the help of glossaries, where it exists; etymological justification; and, where Catullus is concerned, our knowledge of his non-Roman birthplace and youthful environment—all these may have something to say.

Miss Gertrude Stein declared that "poetry is a vocabulary," A. E. Housman that it is "not the thing said, but a way of saying it."[9] Both stress the form more than the content. The content of

---

[9] *Name and Nature of Poetry*, Cambridge 1933, p. 35.

Housman's own poetry is a rather commonplace pessimism that
sometimes rises to a second-rate Stoicism. It is the form, not
even the vocabulary as such, but the disposition of it—the
orders, arrangements, all within the severe restrictions of the
pattern of the English sentence,—that makes his poetry. The
same is true of Byron, whose "Stanzas written on the road between Florence and Pisa":

> Oh, talk not to me of a name great in story—
> The days of our Youth are the days of our glory;
> And the myrtle and ivy of sweet two-and-twenty
> Are worth all your laurels, though ever so plenty.
>
> What are garlands and crowns to the brow that is wrinkled?
> 'Tis but as a dead flower with May-dew besprinkled:
> Then away with all such from the head that is hoary,
> What care I for the wreaths that can *only* give glory?
>
> Oh Fame!—if I e'er took delight in thy praises,
> 'Twas less for the sake of thy high-sounding phrases,
> Than to see the bright eyes of the dear One discover
> She thought that I was not unworthy to love her.
>
> *There* chiefly I sought thee, *there* only I found thee;
> Her Glance was the best of the rays that surround thee,
> When it sparkled o'er aught that was bright in my story,
> I knew it was Love, and I felt it was Glory

are redeemed from sentimentality by the majestic command of
language as form and vocabulary.

The concentrated hatred of Catullus 97 makes the greatest
possible contrast, but its hatred, like Byron's love, also is contained in the language used. I forbear to translate a poem not
commonly read in school or college and even suppressed from
many editions. Here is the text, of which I propose to make a
word-by-word study.

> Non (ita me di ament) quicquam referre putaui,
>   utrumne os an culum olfacerem Aemilio.
> nilo mundius hoc, niloque immundius illud,
>   uerum etiam culus mundior et melior:

nam sine dentibus est: os dentis sequipedalis,
  gingiuas uero ploxeni habet ueteris,
praeterea rictum qualem diffissus in aestu
  meientis mulae cunnus habere solet.
hic futuit multas et se facit esse uenustum,
  et non pistrino traditur atque asino?
quem siqua attingit, non illam posse putemus
  aegroti culum lingere carnificis?

Of the words that appear in this poem, one occurs in the whole of Catullus more than 300 times (*esse*), two (*ego, qui*) between 200 and 299 times; four (*non, hic, in, et*) between 100 and 199 times; seven (*ille, multus, se, facere, atque, si, posse*) between 50 and 99 times; four (*deus, amo, bonus, nam*) between 25 and 49 times; fourteen (*ita, quisquam, putare, -ne, os, an, nihil, uerum, dens, sine, habere, qualis, solere, tradere*) between 10 and 24 times; and there is a tail of twenty-eight words occurring a smaller number of times than 10 in the total work of Catullus. Naturally some of those that occur once only in Catullus and also in this poem (twelve all told) are of special interest, and some also of those that occur twice in Catullus, whether or no both times in this poem. Of peculiar interest are one or two taboo words that, while not at all frequent anywhere, are relatively so in Catullus, and actually make half of their appearances in this very poem. One wonders why Catullus (or Persius) is read by beginners; the purpose cannot be to inculcate a peculiar but rather useless Latin vocabulary, likely enough as that is to be the result.

Thus *culus*, six times in Catullus, three of them in this poem, is, like *cunnus* (line 8, nowhere else in Catullus), rare throughout Latin. Both are obscene words; they shock, by their very presence on the printed page, after having first made unusual demands upon our decoding facilities. Yet the corresponding anatomical or polite terminology would not do. They are in fact just the sort of word which a modern also uses in hatred, consuming hatred, cold or hot, not in anger, but in utter detestation. The choice of these two terms, in a sense automatic, not

that Catullus stopped to ponder each possible word one by one
that he might have used, nevertheless obeys the binary principle, in the sense that nothing else would do, that every other
possibility is considered and given the answer "No," while thes
are accepted and given the answer "Yes." But *meientis* (8),
evoked by *cunnus* in the same line, is a veterinary term. This is
the only place in which that form appears in Catullus; *mingere*,
elsewhere twice (39.18; 67.30), has a more marked overtone of
obscenity, and is (accordingly) more corrupt in the ms. tradition. Both words are rare. So is *gingiua* (line 6), but less so; and
it is almost a scientific term, frequent in medical writers. It also
occurs twice in Catullus, for it is joined both here and in 39
with *meiere, mingere*—the one word called up the other in the
mind of Catullus, along with *dentes* (39.19 and 97.5), and we
now find ourselves in the context of ammoniated dentifrices, the
"science" of advertising accompanied by a slight snigger, especially since Aemilius is compared with something long in the
tooth (97.5)—we shall see what in a moment; something that
also has *dentes sesquipedales* in fact, an adjective found only here
in Catullus, rare in Latin, a technical term, of exact measurement (1½ ft.), even if not to be interpreted of Aemilius, however it may be of the object to which Catullus likened the mouth
of Aemilius, in absolute literalness. The final word of the poem,
in a final line laden with disgust, is *carnifex* (only here in Catullus). This word is not rare, and certainly not free from emotional overtones; but it also, in a strict literal sense, is a technical term, and not free from a certain fascination of horror. In
my boyhood the hangman of the County of Lancaster had seldom any official duty to perform. Murder was definitely a hanging matter, but of infrequent occurrence, however frequent or
infrequent the word. He added, therefore, to an occasional £12
sterling for a hanging, what income he could get from his private
calling as a barber in Rochdale. He used to trim my father's
beard, and we sometimes heard a tidbit of gossip; but we boys
looked upon him with awe, and his business was perhaps not so
good as it ought to have been, his high abilities with comb and

scissors, as well as with gallows and rope, considered. How many of you have *known* a hangman, in the flesh? I think I know perfectly the content of meaning of *carnifex* in Catullus. It is by no means the "rascal, scoundrel" of the dictionary; Jack Ketch is nearer the mark, and his successor, a butcher not a barber; and some recollection of the hanging scene in James Joyce's *Ulysses* will also add to the picture. Hanging, strangling, decapitation, garrotting, electrocution—it makes no matter, all have their peculiar horrors, on which we need not dwell.

Of the words remaining that occur once and only once in this same poem, and once only in Catullus (*refert, immundus, rictus, diffissus, pistrinum, asinus, aegrotus,* and *ploxenum*), or twice only in Catullus (*olfacere, mula, lingere,* and *futuere*), only two call for comment. None of the words that occur from three to nine times is noteworthy. The word *os* (97.2), frequent in Latin, is frequent also in Catullus (17 times). It is startling here in a context so much the opposite of *iucundum* (9.9), a term more appropriate to the writer of love poems. *Futuere* and its cognates or derivatives total seven occurrences in Catullus, a high total for this word; it occurs once in 97 (line 9). However that word began, it went the way of *baiser* in French, a word the early history of which also we shall consider. It is not really frequent in Latin, it is vulgar and in some contexts obscene, its frequency in Catullus (the related words included) being a remarkable indication of his readiness to draw upon the vocabulary of the stableboy and farmyard. *Pistrinum* (1) is a technical term that has taken a pejorative turn which is not peculiar to Catullus.

But *ploxenum* (6) is a different story. It is an absolute ἅπαξ λεγόμενον, for the mention by Quintilian and by Festus is merely an unsuccessful attempt to explain the word in this very place in Catullus, not an independent occurrence. The word was barely corrupted in ms., for its strangeness, its uniqueness, guaranteed careful copying. Even modern commentators are desperately hard put to it to explain the word at all in the line of Catullus

gingiuas uero ploxeni habet ueteris

where the definition of Quintilian, echoed by Festus, seems not
to fit. How can a man, even a filthy man, have the "gums of an
old 'wagon box' [as we might now say, 'trunk case']" in his foul
and diseased mouth, projecting and rotten as his teeth may be?
Indeed, what have teeth to do with a box?

We may begin by observing that there is nothing in the phonematic pattern of the word *ploxenum* that might not be Latin,
except the medial short -*e*- instead of -*i*- that certainly does
point to a dialect source. In fact Quintilian (1.5.8) locates it in
the vicinity of the river Po, and there are possible cognates in
the Raetic *ploum* "plough" (*Prae-Italic Dialects of Italy* [*PID*] 2,
1933, p. 63) and in Latin *plaustrum*, and a variant spelling -*in*-
is recorded (ib., p. 204)—evidently *ploxenum* has something to
do with a wheeled vehicle. Another modern etymology connects
the word with *plectere*, which suits the ancient definition *capsa
in cisio* better. Now *crates stercorariae*, apparently the same as
sirpeae, are known from Cato and Varro as wicker contraptions
used in carting farm manure from the dung pits to the fields. In
the city, cesspools (*foricae*) were emptied by despised contrac-
tors (Juvenal 3.38).[10] Here, I believe, is the answer: *ploxenum* is
a two-wheeled cart carrying a wicker basket used for this purpose; as the basket was worn by use, the broken withies stuck
out as much as half a yard, and the mouth, gums, and teeth of
Aemilius, foul and diseased, reminded Catullus, he says, of a
much used *cratis stercoraria*. Whoever knew the word must have
found it apt, if disgusting: it fits the context perfectly, that is to
say, it is determined by the sequence in which it appears, and,
like the other shocking items of vocabulary in this poem, comes
straight from the farmyard and dunghill.

Cognate with *culus* and *cunnus*, I think, is not only *cutis*, *Cu-*

---

[10] I have had some difficulty in discovering how the Romans dealt with night soil, a
subject on which books of reference are silent. A. S. Pease, to whom I appealed for help,
directs my attention to Cicero *de div.* 1.57 and his note ad loc., with the reference to
Lex Iul. municip. 66–67 (*CIL* 1, ed. 2, 593); both places mention the use of *plostra* for
carrying out *stercus* before sunrise. The *ploxenum* of Catullus is almost certainly cognate with *ploum* and *plostrum*, see *DAG* 2, pp. 63, 204. H. W. Garrod (*CQ* 4, 1910, 202)
thought that *ploxenum* was a sort of "taximeter"!

cull-atus (genius), *cucutium, praeputium,* but also *salaputium* (in Catullus once only, 53.5), as I have explained in *Ogam* (Rennes) 5, 1953, 65–66 (cf. *Zeuss Memorial Volume,* Dublin 1955, pp. 249–255), which appears also as a personal name *Salaputis* (*CIL* 8, 10570.4, 29), a situation paralleled not only by Latin *Verpus* (: *uerpa*) but also by English *Cockshut.*[11] If *genius Cucullatus* (cf. *Cicollus*) introduces also the gods, so too does *deus Verpatus* (Priapus), and the images of *Cucullatus* recall the Greek ὄλισβος[12] (Latin *gillo,* Juvenal 1.40), the Paiute *ma'va'tca,* and English *dildo.* Catullus himself has *Mentula* (sc. Mamura) as a personal name (94.1, 105.1, 114.1, 115.1) as well as a common noun (29.13, 37.3, 94.1, 115.8),[13] a word that has given some difficulty to the copyists or editors, as well as to the etymologists, but not so much as *sopio* (once only in Catullus, 37.10), which they corrupted to *scorpio, ropio,* and even *Scipio.* Of these words *sopio* is definitely colloquial, *mentula* rustic, and both of them rare and obscene for the more usual, but hardly polite, if now quasi-medical *penis* (twice in Catullus, 15.9, 25.3); of these three words the second (*mentula*) is possibly cognate with *membrum,* which Catullus uses as a synonym, the first with *pro-sapia* (*-es*) "offspring, family," and perhaps with Πρί-(σ)απος.

Both *salaputium* certainly and *uerpa* possibly are Keltic in origin. So is *basium* (five times), *basiatio* (once), *basiare* (four times in Catullus) Keltic, but this word was thoroughly acclimatized in Latin, as the derivatives and intervocalic -*s*- show. It appears first in Catullus, is not common, and is defined in ancient commentaries and glossaries as the kiss given to a wife. Either the ancients were more passionate than the moderns, as Italians than Americans, or else Catullus used the word as the equivalent of *s(u)auium* (twice only; derivatives four times). The English *buss,* borrowed from Welsh or Gaelic, reflects Keltic

---

[11] On this and other names in *Cock-* see C. W. Bardsley, *Dictionary of English and Welsh Surnames,* Oxford 1901. Ellis assumed that *uerpa* had stood originally in 6.12, where the mss. are corrupt.

[12] Cf. possibly ὄλισθος "slipperiness," ὀλιβρόν and ὀλίσθημα "luxation" med. (i.e., dislocation)?

[13] It is possible that *mentula* is cognate with *membrum.*

forms like Gaulish *buddutton* "kiss," *Bussumarus* "big-mouth,"
Irish *bus* "mouth, kiss"; but in these Gaulish words the vocalism
($a : u$) is troublesome ($*g\breve{u}s$- : $*g^u\overline{as}$- : $*g^ueH_2$-es-). The word
seems to have become associated with some items from a differ-
ent root ($*\hat{g}eus$- "taste, sample") represented by English *choose*
(OE *ceosan*), Latin *gustus, gustare, degunere*, if not by English
kiss (OE *kyssan*, older *$*kussian$*), as if literally "to kiss" were
"to take a sample." Be that as it may, the word is not only rare,
but has a strongly emotional flavor, verging upon the obscene,
like modern French (*se*) *baiser*, a word now avoided in polite
society, a tendency which the most modern English *kiss*, as a
euphemism for other, less delicate, expressions, is likewise beginning to show.

Tappo (104.4) is said to be named as a scurrilous gossip-
monger. Perhaps we have a common noun *tappo*, "any cheap
gaper"; if it is a proper name (only here in Catullus), then
Tappo recalls that ghostly name in the catalogue of Latin
writers whose works are lost;[14] but it is common in Cisalpine
Gaul (*DAG* 3.138), and appears also in Livy as the cognomen
of a plebeian gens Valeria. The literary activity of a certain
Valerius Valentinus, whose family perhaps came from Vibo Va-
lentia, is said to have cost him the loss of a lawsuit. His facetious,
but improper, banqueting rules have been identified in the prose
poem the *lex Tappula*, a copy of which was discovered in 1882
at Vercelli (Dessau 8761). Its apt characters include *Multiuorus*,
Properocibus, and *Mero*. The name *Tappo* is a nickname of the
same type as the better-known *Macco, Bucco, Pappus* of comedy, with the characteristic doubling of a medial consonant,
and, like many such Latin bynames, points in a half affectionate,
half depreciatory manner to some personal quality or failing.
Our Valerius Valentinus inherited his cognomen from his father,
and hence its literal meaning may not have been obvious to
Catullus and his contemporaries: it means the man who makes
a marvel of everything. It was in all likelihood introduced into
Italy as the name of a character in the farce (ἱλαροτραγῳδία or

---

[14] See *Erasmus* 7, 1954, 229–233.

φλύαξ)[15] of Magna Graecia, to which I assigned ὀλβεττήρ, that is to say, Doric *θᾶπῶν for Attic θηπῶν· θαυμάζων, ἐξαπατῶν, κολακεύων (Hesychius), which must be cognate with the Homeric τέθηπα, ταφών "to marvel," and with the modern colloquial English *dab*, as we say a "marvel, dab" (at Greek, at tennis, or the like). The *lex Tappula* seems to have been an amusing and sophisticated skit, rather like the stuff that gets printed in *Punch* or *The New Yorker* nowadays, good enough to have been inscribed on bronze, but not great literature, and hardly *aere perennius*.

In a suit which Tappo brought against C. Cosconius (victor in the Dalmatian campaign, 78–76 B.C.), the defendant quoted a poem of Tappo in which Tappo boasted the seduction of youth of good family. His vocabulary was perhaps comparable to that of Catullus in 29 (vv. 2, 5), in 21 (vv. 4, 13), and in 16.1, this last the poem in which the *poeta lasciuus* of Propertius (3.34.87) proclaims himself *castus*, *pius*, and *pudicus*.

Whoever will compare the contexts in which Catullus has *castus* (take 16.5; 15.4; 62.23, 46; 64.384; 66.56, 83), *pudicus* (16.4, 8; 21.12; 76.24), *pius* (76.2; *pietas* 76.26) with those of *impudicus* (29.2, 10) and *impius* (14.7; 30.4; 64.403–04; 67.25), using the method of contrast, and then reflect on some of the items of vocabulary which we have been exploring, must, I think, look for some other explanation than the familiar apology: the words "are here not to be understood in the literal sense, but only as conveying vague threats, in the gross language of that day" (Merrill on 16.1), or (id. p. xxvii) "virulence of language in invective, especially in the use of terms applied to sexual impurity, was by no means accompanied among the ancients by corresponding intensity of feeling." I have found no good arguments to sustain these apologetic, and in themselves implausible, assertions: Catullus meant what he said. The reverse problem is presented by the use of *pius* in Latin generally, and especially in Vergil; to it I propose to return in a subsequent lecture (III). Here a tentative answer to the question will be suggested, to be developed more fully toward the end of the series

---

[15] See my *Foundations of Roman Italy*, London 1937, pp. 391–392.

(lecture VII). It is, in brief, that increasing affectivity of content varies inversely with frequency of occurrence. The words we have chosen for consideration in Catullus are rare, some of them genuine "once-words," as that term is usually understood. They are almost unpredictable, and "information" is high. The pedestrian and trumpery trash that passes as "original composition" for presentation in the so-called "mass media" of communication of our day can be and is readily anticipated, like the *clausulae* of the Roman orator too banal for his audience, by the most feeble-minded listener, word by word and line by line, once the cue is given; a machine easily does far better, in fact it produces something more like Gerard Manley Hopkins than the bathetic inanities of a popular but bad composer such as (if I have the name correctly) Mr Eddie Visher. No wonder my beginner's Latin class of 1945 was stirred by Catullus.

To end here *would* be bathos, even for me, who make no claim to have any feeling for the stuff of poetry. I do recall most vividly that in that year a group of tough young men, many of them already war veterans, who had begun Latin with me nine months before, were deeply moved, and said so, by the reading of Catullus 31:

> Paene insularum, Sirmio, insularumque
> ocelle, quascumque in liquentibus stagnis
> marique uasto fert uterque Neptunus,
> quam te libenter quamque laetus inuiso,
> uix mi ipse credens Thyniam atque Bithynos
> liquisse campos et uidere te in tuto.
> o quid solutis est beatius curis?
> cum mens onus reponit, ac peregrino
> labore fessi uenimus larem ad nostrum
> desideratoque acquiescimus lecto.
> hoc est, quod unum est pro laboribus tantis.
> salue, o uenusta Sirmio, atque ero gaude:
> gaudete uosque, O Lydiae lacus undae:
> ridete, quicquid est domi cachinnorum

and even more, in that year of brothers still daily facing violent death, of 101: *Multas per gentes et multa per aequora uectus;* even though no version, prose or verse, was attempted. And it takes little acquaintance with the structure of language, the Latin language, or with the structure of the life of men, to understand the impact of 76, in which stand *pius* (of Catullus himself) at beginning and end, the unique *animo affirmare,* the unusual *puriter,* and above all (line 24) the unattainable quality—no, not *pudicus* (for it is not Catullus), but *pudica,* which Lesbia did not, could not, even wish to be—and therefore to see in this poem communication ("information"), form, and content, at their most successful.

> Siqua recordanti benefacta priora uoluptas
> > est homini, cum se cogitat esse pium,
> nec sanctam uiolasse fidem, nec foedere in ullo
> > diuum ad fallendos numine abusum homines,
> multa parata manent in longa aetate, Catulle,
> > ex hoc ingrato gaudia amore tibi.   [possunt
> nam quaecumque homines bene cuiquam aut dicere
> > aut facere, haec a te dictaque factaque sunt,
> omniaque ingratae perierunt credita menti.
> > quare cur tu te iam amplius excrucies?
> quin te animo affirmas atque istinc te ipse reducis,
> > et dis inuitis desinis esse miser?
> difficile est longum subito deponere amorem.
> > difficile est, uerum hoc qua lubet efficias:
> una salus haec est, hoc est tibi peruincendum:
> > hoc facias, siue id non pote siue pote.
> o di, si uostrum est misereri, aut si quibus umquam
> > extrema iam ipsa in morte tulistis opem,
> me miserum aspicite et, si uitam puriter egi,
> > eripite hanc pestem perniciemque mihi,
> quae mihi surrepens imos ut torpor in artus
> > expulit ex omni pectore laetitias.
> non iam illud quaero, contra ut me diligat illa,
> > aut, quod non potis est, esse pudica uelit:
> ipse ualere opto et tetrum hunc deponere morbum.
> > o di, reddite mi hoc pro pietate mea.

It may appear to some readers, especially to those who might be tempted by prudery or by priggishness, however subconscious, that I have deserted Catullus, *pudicus poeta*, and left him *lasciuus* instead. But whoever will read to the end of these lectures, and in particular will read the pages in which I return to *castus*, *lasciuus*, and *pudicus*, will see that the threads that I have begun to follow in the argument so far are finally tied together into a stouter line that effectively rescues Catullus from the implied charge.

III

The Ancient Mediterranean: Area and Language

From Linear B and Homer to Vergil

NOTHING is easier for the ill-informed than to proclaim as new something of which they had no previous knowledge. During the war, as we all know, a number of "new" specialized programs of study (ASTP) were set up under the auspices of the armed forces, called "Area and Language" programs. The purpose was to give men in the Army, or Navy, or Air Force, rapid and specialized training in the language or languages of some area in which it was expected they would have to serve, together with a rather hasty survey of the history, civilization, and general characteristics of the people who lived there. This is not the place to attempt any opinion or judgment on the worth or effectiveness of these programs, or on the relationship between the announced objectives and the possibility of achieving them under the conditions which obtained at the time; still less on the relationship between the claims made for the programs and the degree of success actually won. What I wish to consider now is the Mediterranean area in ancient times, in the light of its linguistic make-up, and for the purpose of continuing our study of some of the ancient writers, and how to understand them.

It is, however, of interest, I think, to point out, if only in passing, that the Ancient Mediterranean does constitute an excellent domain of "area and language" study. It is a compact and well-defined geographical region; there are in it a number of well-understood languages, some of them with extensive and important literatures, and such things as material remains, eco-

56

nomic conditions, colonial expansion overseas, imperialism, or the historical, philosophical, religious, and cultural backgrounds, are copiously attested. The whole may be approached dispassionately, without risk of accusations of bias or propaganda. Not many, I believe, should devote their entire lives to this study, but it is a good training ground for some of our youth from which to move into other fields of endeavor—like, for example, a young student of my acquaintance, who, moving from the Greek and Latin of his undergraduate years, is now applying himself to the study of nuclear physics.

Classical scholars are apt to think chiefly of Greece and Rome in their map of the Ancient Mediterranean. In addition to those two preëminent units, there was, however, a host of less well-known peoples to whom, and their languages, only incidental reference is made by ancient historians and geographers. Of these languages some, like Greek and Latin, are what we call "Indo-European"; others belong to different classifications. Obviously there are the Hamitic languages of the southern shores of the Mediterranean, and the Semitic languages of its eastern end, of Cyprus, Carthage, and one or two other places.

It is an obvious question to ask first of all, What is the relation between Indo-European and non-Indo-European languages—at least in the northwestern quadrant of the Old World? Most of us think that we speak exactly like our parents; and, therefore, like our grandparents, and like our great-grandparents; and so on, it might be supposed, back to Adam and Eve. But one need only look at a page of Spenser or Chaucer, not to mention King Alfred, to realize that that is very far from being the case. We then see that the further back we go, the less the similarity is, between, say Modern and Middle or Old English and still less between Old English and Gothic; or between Germanic and Indo-European itself.

Naturally the question arises, sooner or later, how far one can go back, arguing in this way. Must not Indo-European itself go back to some still older source, and, if so, what? Again, is not the situation the same with regard to all the other well-known families of languages on the face of the earth? The theory, indeed, has been seriously advanced that all languages of the globe, past and present, do go back to one common source. If ever the anthropologists satisfy themselves, and the rest of us, that man evolved at one place and one only on the earth, then it would also follow that there is a single common source of all languages. For language distinguishes man from all the rest of animate creation. No language, no man; no man, no language.

The Ancient Mediterranean is not really so very far removed from the present, if one thinks of anthropological time, not to mention geological or astronomical time. But, clearly, attempts to compare Indo-European languages as such with other groups of languages as such, even if restricted only to the comparison of Indo-European languages with, shall we say, Semitic or Hamitic or Ugro-Finnish languages, cannot hope to succeed. We do not expect, from our present knowledge of the history of writing, ever to get documents of such remote date, especially, shall we say, from neolithic Europe, as would be likely to throw light of any consequence on this problem. But it is proper to apply the comparative method to predialectal Indo-European itself, and similarly to predialectal Semitic and Hamitic; not to the several Indo-European, Semitic, and other languages of the Mediterranean basin, but to the older pattern of Indo-European, Semitic, Hamitic, and the rest, especially in default of written documents of a date considerably older than those which we now have.

We are coming more and more to think of Indo-European not so much as a single homogeneous language as, rather, a number of tribal dialects, which, shortly before the dawn of history, were distributed throughout Europe and Asia Minor and the Near East, presumably by migration. It is well known that the conductivity of nomadism for the diffusion of languages is high, and not nomadism only, but any kind of mobility of mankind. That is clear so far as concerns both Semitic and Hamitic. In the spread of the Indo-European languages it was not nomadism, or seafaring, not at first anyway, but the domestication of the horse, the invention of the wheel, and the use of the wagon, which played a considerable part. So soon as those were available, one of the chief objects of export, if one may put it in that way, had become man himself, and with him his language. At the same time, the evidence of culture has been used to show both actual links or contacts between peoples who early spoke Indo-European and the possible line of migration which they followed. Indeed, it has been argued that there is a cultural line, of late neolithic date, stretching all the way from Central Europe, away across Asia, to the Far East; but obviously this argument, if correct, would not also prove linguistic relationship.

There have also been repeated attempts to give the most minute attention to the recorded details of the early Indo-European languages, with the idea of discovering something about their place of origin. This appears to me unlikely to be fruitful without much new documentation. It reminds me of nothing so much as rearranging the contents of a postage-stamp collection. Anything further in the way of classification of details is not likely to lead to further knowledge. There is small chance of obtaining additional written materials of neolithic date from Europe north of the Alps and the Caucasus, without which minute study of known details is unable to take us any further in penetrating the question of origins. Comparisons made so far between Indo-European and Ugro-Finnish, or Indo-European and Semitic and Hamitic, are not very convincing, and it is essentially for the same reason, but in still greater degree, that recent comparisons of Indo-European languages with certain Far Eastern languages, notably Korean, must be condemned as failures. I see the same objection—lack of comparable materials—against a proposal to connect Indo-European with the Indonesian languages.

On the other hand, comparisons with Semitic such as began in the last century have recently come to be very much more hopeful, largely as a consequence of a different method of approach, inspired in its turn by the discovery of Hittite. In the last century Ascoli attempted to establish relationships between

Indo-European and Semitic, but without success. In this century (1906, 1909, and 1917) the Danish scholar Möller insisted that there was a fundamental structural relationship between Indo-European and Semitic. This preceded full knowledge of Hittite, which has given an entirely new aspect to the whole problem. More recently still, the French scholar Cuny advanced his theory of what he calls "nostratic languages," that is to say, languages of the Ancient Mediterranean basin which would be, on his view, the ultimate source from which Hamitic and Semitic and Indo-European all alike have come. To Cuny, as to most other observers, Hamitic and Semitic run somewhat closer together and stand in contrast with Indo-European, so that the underlying classification would be twofold, not threefold.

The new theory was inspired by the discovery and interpretation of Hittite, and therefore satisfies one of the conditions that I laid down as necessary, namely, the discovery of additional, and also older, material. Moreover, certain new concepts are involved, some perhaps a little hazardous, but at least they push back comparison to predialectal patterns. In particular, much play is made with actual or possible alternants, both of vowels and of consonants. Second, there is the concept, originated by Benveniste, of the Indo-European root, namely, that it regularly took the shape consonant + short vowel + consonant (CvC), which might be extended by a suffix which had the shape short vowel + consonant (vC). In the third place, structural comparisons (including syntax) between Indo-European and Hamitic and Semitic also play a considerable part in the argument. Finally, the principle of selective variation, combined with the concept of linguistic patterning, is highly important and fruitful.

It is the common practice nowadays to insist upon a sharp distinction between synchronic (or descriptive) and diachronic (or historical and comparative) linguistics. This is fallacious. Language is a continuum, unless it is completely suppressed and becomes extinct; not merely the stream of speech at a given time, for a single speaker or a number of speakers, but as one passes from one generation backward or forward to preceding or succeeding generations; and likewise in space from one area to another of related dialects. I admit that the distinction between descriptive and historical or comparative grammar is practically useful. Synchronic grammar nevertheless involves a fiction, a convenient one, no doubt, for descriptive purposes; but it should not blind us to the fact that there is, strictly speaking, nothing static about a language so long as it is spoken. That is axiomatic. No doubt one may suspend the axiom for the purposes of a descriptive grammar; but one should always remember that then there is necessarily some distortion of the facts.

There is another point to be stressed, and that is the distinction between derivational (*man-ly*) and relational (*hominis* : *homo*) procedures in language. By derivational it is meant that complex forms (*man-ly*) may grammatically serve the function of a simple (*brave*) utterance; by relational, that a given complex (*hominis*) form does not function grammatically as a simple (*homo*) form in the language concerned. Now the derivational process tends to lead in the direction of polysynthesis, as, for example, some of the long compounds of Greek or Sanskrit; whereas the relational process, as in inflexion, tends to lead in the end to analysis and extraction.

So far as Benveniste's theory of the root is concerned, the simple statement of the root CvC needs to be amplified to this extent. The single initial consonant may be preceded by an initial *s*, an initial consonantal *u̯*, an initial *d*. Or again, there is always the possibility of an initial alternation between *tu̯* and *t*, or between *su̯* and *s*. Further, we know that when an Indo-European root begins apparently with a vowel, actually it was invariably preceded by a laryngeal consonant which colored the quality of the following vowel before it disappeared, that is, with the exception of h_1, which disappears everywhere except in Hittite, and even there disappears unless it is followed by a consonant;—but when h_1 does disappear, it does so without affecting the quality of the following short-*e* vowel. Then, in addition one must always be prepared for the presence of infixes, and of alternations such as Latin *tremo* (with *m*) beside *trepidus* (with *p*) and Sanskrit *trásati* (with *s*), in which you have the root *ter* followed by an extension *em* or *ep* or *es*: here the *m* and the *p* and the *s* have no discoverable semantic value, and *tremo, trepidus, trásati* do not differ from one another so far as the root meaning is concerned. There is a similar alternation between *r* and *n* in such heteroclitic stems as the Greek ὕδωρ, ὕδατος or ἧπαρ, ἥπατος; Latin *iecur, iecinis*; Sanskrit *yakr̥t, yaknás*, and perhaps in the Latin gerund *regendo* side by side with the Latin infinitive *regere*. There is a weakness in this last suggestion, insomuch as *esse, ferre*, and *uelle* point to an older *s*, not *r*. We have, then, the following rules: (1) the Indo-European root is of the shape CvC, e.g. *i̯eu̯-*; (2) among Indo-European roots there are none of the type *kek* or *lel*, i.e., a root may not begin and end with the same consonant; but *kel* or *lek* may occur. Similarly, the situation never occurs in which both breathed plosive and voiced aspirate appear: *kebh* or *ghep* do not occur, but *ghebh* does occur (for the moment we may ignore the laryngeal problem here); (3) the root may be extended by a suffix *vC*, so that side by side with *i̯eu̯-* we find also *i̯eu̯-eg-*. With ablaut relationships this gives *i̯eu̯g-* as in the Greek ζεῦγος, or *i̯ueg-* as in the Sanskrit *yunákti*, and *i̯ug-* as in Latin *iungo*; (4) the root and its suffix may be extended by a further formant, e.g. *i̯eu̯g e/os-* in the Old Latin *iouxmenta*, *i̯eu̯-n-eg-* in Sanskrit *yunákti*; *per-ek̂-sk̂-* in the Sanskrit *pr̥ccháti* or the Latin *posco*, which thus stands for an older **pr̥k̂-sk̂-ō*; (5) anything further added results always in a substantival form. Accordingly, if you take the root that occurs in Latin *seco* and extend it with *eH̥* and insert the nasal infix, and then add to that a *d*-formant (or, as it is now regarded, a phonematic pattern with *d*) plus the *tó*-participial ending, you will necessarily get a substantival form, namely *scissum*, side by side with *scindo*. Where no such suffix is added, the Latin supine is wanting; there is no supine, for example, to *posco*; (6) there is always a possibility of an initial *s-*, e.g. Greek στέγος side by side with τέγος; (7) observe that no Indo-European root ever begins with *r*, with the result that for Sanskrit *rudhirás* as compared with the Greek ἐρυθρός we postulate the root *h̥₁er-*. This fact is a very

curious one, namely, that Indo-European roots never begin with
r, insomuch as the situation appears to be the same also both in
Iberian and in modern Basque. Accordingly, we now say that
the root of the verb "to be" is h_1es- (cf. Hittite ašanzi, and now
Linear B έενσι, 3 pl. "they are"), and that the root of the Latin
ago is not ag- but h_2eg-, which would be exactly like the roots
sed- "sit," teg- "cover," and this is confirmed by Hittite ḫanti as
compared with the Greek ἀντί or the Latin ante, and, again, by
the Hittite ḫastai side by side with the Greek ὀστέον and the
Latin os "bone," where h_3 (the o-colored laryngeal) will be involved.

Now, quite apart from the extremely important fact that the
Indo-European root plus suffix, when devocalized, gives CCC,
exactly like the triconsonantal roots of Semitic and Hamitic
(though some of those may go back ultimately to older biconso-
nantal roots), the comparison of the laryngeal with the 'alif-
hamza of Semitic at once claims attention. For it would appear
that the coloring of the vowels in Indo-European, e : o and a : o,
depends, at least in part, upon vibrations in the larynx, and not
merely on the configuration of the vocal cavity.

It is not necessary here to go into the theory as it affects details of Indo-European ablaut, or to attempt to consider the
nature of the various laryngeals, except to say that it is possible
to operate with three of them instead of Sturtevant's four or
Cuny's five, and that Pedersen's two laryngeals seem inadequate
to explain all the facts. The three laryngeals generally recognized are: h_1, a voiceless glottal stop, regularly written double in
Hittite; h_2, which gives a vowel the a-color, a voiceless glottal
spirant, again written double in Hittite; and h_3, which gives the
vowel the o-color, presumably a voiced laryngeal spirant. Now
not only may h be vocalized in Indo-European ablaut; it seems
also to account for certain phenomena of voicing and aspiration,
e.g. Sanskrit píbati beside Latin bibo beside Greek πῶθι and
Faliscan pipafo; or Sanskrit pṛthivī side by side with Greek
πλατύς, jívathas side by side with Latin uiuidus; or Sanskrit
tiṣṭhati side by side with Greek ἵστᾱτι (Doric). Alternations of

these several types have long plagued students of Indo-European. A similar problem is presented by Greek ὀκτώ but ὄγδοος, Latin *quattuor* but *quadraginta*, Greek νέφος but ὄμβρος and ἀφρός, πυθμήν but πίνδαξ. Moreover it is clear, in Indo-European as in Semitic, that vowel alternations do not affect the lexical meaning of the root; they do affect relational, but not lexical, meaning, and to that extent this feature of vocalic alternation in Indo-European and in Semitic is not really so different in principle as it may appear to be at first sight.

Now Cuny, in his appeal for the comparative study of Indo-European and Hamito-Semitic, sets up for his "nostratique" or Mediterranean stratum of languages a very large variety of occlusives; for example, for the dentals alone he distinguishes not merely between the fortis and the lenis but also between an emphatic fortis and an emphatic lenis, and similarly for the spirant he gives both the emphatic fortis and the emphatic lenis—that is to say, he roughly doubles the number of types of consonants; in this particular case, eight instead of four;—and he does the same thing with the palatals, the velars, the labio-velars, and the labials. Doubtless the alternants arose as positional variants, not as distinctive phonemes, of which the number would then be far too large to be likely—if possible at all; however that may be, it would seem that this is a constructive suggestion, because it gives us a satisfactory account not only of alternations such as *pibati* and *bibo*, ὀκτώ and ὄγδοος, but also, for example, of πρᾶγμα and πρῆχμα, πτόλις and πόλις, that is, such combinations as κτ and ττ, φθ and χθ, some relics of which remain; granted that for the most part such variants were wiped out by analogical patterning. But so far as the Cuny theory is valid, then it will be both possible and justifiable, as Cuny himself suggested, to make a number of rather telling lexical comparisons between Semitic and Indo-European. Juret has gone very much further than Cuny goes; but Juret seems to have burnt down the house in order to roast the pig, and in his etymological dictionary we now have nothing at all except a large number of roots, about 800 (which is still too small), all of which begin with h_2 followed by $k, l, m, n, p, r, s, t, u,$ or i! That means that there is very low phonematic efficiency, and indeed hardly any variety of utterance whatever. I do not see how such a pattern can have served as a means of communication at all.

On the basis of phonetic comparisons alone, the theory is promising; but it is not only a matter of phonology. There are also questions of morphology and syntax to be considered. Everyone remembers the old-fashioned ideas that language began with a series of monosyllabic roots, or else with long polysyllabic utterances. The notion was that from the positional method language proceeded to agglutination, from that to amalgamation, from that to polysynthesis, and then back again to the isolating method. This view is generally abandoned; in its place I suggest that out of primitive fluid and vague linguistic material selective variation led to the characteristic features of different language groups and of languages, together with growing precision of denotation, instead of an attempt to use separate terms corresponding to changing concepts of something or everything within the visible horizon.

In order to function at all, a language must have a recurrent and regular pattern, a status. Accordingly, certain devices are, as it were, selected and used consistently. A language may have the derivational process leading to polysynthesis, or it may have the relational process leading to inflexion, and subsequently, through extraction, to the analytical method. But whatever procedure is chosen, it is used consistently. It is on this basis that the best explanation of structural varieties in language is to be sought. It is reasonable also to suppose that there exists a possible genetic relationship when contiguous languages use the same devices at the same date. Both early Indo-European and early Semitic show a number of agreements: the triconsonantal root and a poor vocalic system; grammatical gender, the category of case, three numbers, the categories of mood and of aspect; the devices of suffixing and prefixing, and, to a certain extent, reduplication also.

As for syntax, there are clear traces of comparable treatments

of certain features that present themselves in the spatial and
temporal world and that must find some expression in all languages. In particular one notes in ancient Egyptian a preference
for the nominal over the verbal form of expression. But in Indo-
European, on a strict morphological analysis, there is historically no essential preëminence of predicating over denominating
features. The differences are brought out rather by inflexional
devices, not by a divergent lexical core, of one type for nouns
and another type for verbs. There are also clear traces of the
passive yielding to an active form of expression, again a procedure characteristic of Hamitic, which shows a marked preference for the passive, accompanied by an ergative case. Again
note the lack of differentiation morphologically and syntactically between adjective and noun. In Indo-European, the so-
called passive participle in -to- had originally no inherent temporal notion; *tacitus, pransus, potus, barbatus,* all show that very
clearly, like Vergil's *stat ductis sortibus urna,* or *sidera tam nobis
seruanda quam quibus . . . per aequora uectis* where *uectis* trans-
lates the Greek φερομένοις, or Cato's *arant iacto semine.* Similarly
the so-called internal accusative has to be explained on the basis
that the participle is essentially neither active nor passive:
oculos lacrimis suffusa, perculsi pectora Poeni, are exactly like
the Greek ἐπιτετρεμμένοι "being entrusted with," or, in English,
"the boys found fault with by the neighbors," or, "Mother,
whatever did you choose this book for us to be read to out of
for?"

The ancient form of Egyptian verb was built around the
passive participle, as if, for example, "they were on-hearing"
in the sense of "they heard." This is very much like the Middle
English construction, as in Robert of Brunnen, "the church was
on building," or in Holinshed, "he fell on sleeping" in the sense
of "he fell asleep," which again is exactly like the Latin *soluendo
esse,* literally "to be for paying," that is to say, "to be solvent."
Observe also the construction with the predicative adjective,
common enough in early Indo-European, and still to be found
in modern Russian, as in classical Greek ὁ ἀνὴρ ἀγαθός, and in

early Germanic, where a definite distinction is made between the predicative construction and the attributative by means of the devices of the definite article and the weak adjective. Semitic has this construction, common in modern Arabic to this day. So in Hamitic you would say "beautiful-he" in the sense of "he is beautiful."

As for comparisons of vocabulary, at least if one takes into account possible consonantal alternations, one has, for example, Sanskrit *tamasi* : Latin *temere* (which means literally "in the dark") beside Arabic *dāmisu* meaning "obscure," Ethiopian *dāmus* "obscure" or "cloudy"; Semitic **babar(a)* meaning "he broke," compared not only with Arabic *babara*, the Hebrew *šaβar*, the Akkadian *šabaru*, but also (at least according to Cuny) with the Latin *ferire*, *frango*, and the Gothic *brikan*, though this is difficult if we are to postulate an initial *bh-* for the Indo-European words. Finally, the strong probability that an Indo-European objective conjugation is to be recognized in certain verb forms, notably weak preterites, invites comparison with languages of the most ancient stratum known in the Mediterranean basin.

The hypothesis of a proto-Indo-European stratum of languages, to which various Anatolian tongues, and, more distantly, Iberian (with its modern descendant Basque), Eteocretan, Vannic (Urartaish or Chaldish), and perhaps Lemnian and Etruscan, are to be related, has never been completely established, for want of sufficient and convincing evidence. But neither has it been put out of court; who is to say that Linear A may not be it? A link between proto-Indo-European and Anatolian may also point the way to a link between these and Hamito-Semitic. Now that comparisons have gone far beyond those of mere names, it is not unreasonable to see a chain, with some missing links to be sure, that runs from Iberian through Etruscan and Lemnian to Anatolian and thence (with chronological agreement so far as concerns Etruscan) to Urartaish and the eastern highlands of Asia Minor and the upper Euphrates. Here we have characteristically an ergative case (or a transitive subject) instead of a nominative case; and the same feature, so it is said, occurs in Caucasian and in Iberian as well as in modern Basque. Once more we have the Etruscan preterite in *ke* side by side with the Greek κ-perfects, which are often, characteristically enough, intransitive; a nasal termination equivalent to the objective case both in Etruscan and in Indo-European, contrasted with the *s* in the nominative case; whereas Basque has a corresponding *k* which may well be connected with the κ-perfect (intransitive). Brugmann himself was always prepared to believe that in some situations the active verb in Indo-European had arisen from an older passive. Here is an example of the way in which selective variation works to give rise to characteristic patterns in a language. Voice in the verb corresponds to animate and inanimate gender in the noun; and the distinction essentially is one of a generalizing statement (*datur*) rather than a particularizing (*dat*); in other words, it is purely syntactical. There is no distinction semantically between *donum datur* and *donum dant*.[1]

It all seems to mean this: that after the last retreat of the ice, there moved northward from the Mediterranean basin a human group who took with them a language which may be said to have been cradled there, in the Mediterranean basin, not altogether unrelated to Semitic and to Hamitic; and that this language later on had developed, by the middle of the third millennium B.C., into what, if we could hear it, we should recognize as an early Indo-European language. This was already not a single homogeneous language, however, but rather a number of tribal dialects, many of which were subsequently distributed pretty much over the areas in which we find them at the dawn of history.

In historical times the linguistic situation in the Mediterranean was at least as complex a map as this sketch of its evolution paints. Proto-Indo-European remnants, Indo-European, and non-Indo-European elements must all be taken into account. Asia Minor and, in less degree, the mainland of Greece

---

[1] The relationship of -*n*- (e.g. not only in *dant* but also in *danunt*) to acc. -*m* (sg.) and -*ns* (pl.) as part of an objective conjugation deserves consideration.

and the Italian peninsula partake in this complex picture, into which we shall now proceed to fit not so much the figures of Homer with his counterpart Vergil, and Hipponax the counterpart of Catullus, but rather the patterns of their poetic discourse.

The scazon, of which something was said in the first lecture, is reported to have been the invention of Hipponax. The contrast between long and short vowels and syllables is so pervasive in the early Indo-European languages that it must be regarded as basic and inherent to them. In its simplest form it is the mere sequence of short and long, like the sequence of weak and strong (odd and even moras) in Southern Paiute. The orators[2] do not avoid this sequence altogether, and it was natural to dialogue. To reverse the order ∪ – will apply a brake and bring the sequence to a stop, in the Latin clausula – ∪ – – ⌣ no less than in end-stopped scazons in Catullus.

$$\text{homo est uenustus et } dic\bar{a}x \mid \overset{\cup}{e}t\; \bar{u}r \mid \bar{b}an\overset{\cup}{u}s.$$

That a constant or prolonged sequence ∪ – is impossible or monotonous, in any Indo-European structural pattern, is axiomatic. The alternants ∪ ∪ ∪, – –, – ∪ ∪, and ∪ ∪ – could not be avoided, though their appearance is regulated and limited, and absolutely pure iambics turn up only as a *tour de force*. The rhythm cannot but have been familiar and popular, if less strictly regulated in form, long before its appearance in the written literature in the middle of the seventh century B.C.

The epic meter, which is part of epic form, characterizes epic poetry at least as much as content does. The scazon also, viewed as form, suits the everyday content and vocabulary, words picked from the slums of Ephesus or Clazomenae, an Ionic Billingsgate; Hardie (*Res Metrica*, 1920, p. 101) calls it an "adaptation of form to theme or substance"; rather, without verse, the writing of Hipponax would have been indistinguishable from prose, prose of the fish market at that. As it is, "Hipponax was neither an anticipator of metrical licences used first

---

[2] Cicero *Orator* 189, 191; Quintilian 9.4.139.

in the Attic tragic or comic drama, nor an incompetent versifier" (Knox, p. 13). The fitness of the choliambic form for colloquial topics made it fit also for lampoons and epigrams, and the influence of iambic writers on Old Comedy is as clear as the influence of the meter in the writing of Catullus—abusive, personal, and critical, but hardly "poetic" (as the word is usually understood) in more than mere form.

That the verse of Hipponax found occasional admission in Old Comedy has been urged above (in chap. i); the pedestrian, prosaic nature of the line made it apt enough, almost to be expected, if not quite inevitable, in an oath, as in the

ναὶ μὰ τὰς Νύμφας

(Eupolis), a parody that clearly echoes Hipponax (37 B.)

ὁ δ' ἐξολισθὼν ἱκέτευε τὴν κράμβην[3]

and [Ananius] (4 B.)

ναὶ μὰ τὴν κράμβην.

Notwithstanding the assertion of the versifying medico Nicander, who, according to Athenaeus, ascribed a prophetic quality to cabbage, it is more likely that μὰ τὴν κράμβην (or τὰς κράμβας) avoids a sacred name, perhaps no more Greek than the Keltic -δουλον "leaf" (113 B.) which -φυλλον has displaced in [Ananius] —of this more below; or no more than the Σάβαυνι (Hipponax 49 B.) or Σάμορνα "God help us" (M. Schmidt on Hesychius s.v. Σαμονία) which displaced the equally non-Greek Ἔφεσος. "By the cabbage," if not mere parody, must be a substitution of a profane for a divine oath, or stand to a genuine oath much in the same way as "oddsbodikins" to "God's body," or the Plautine *dierectus* "accursèd" to whatever original it burlesqued.

---

[3] Cf. chap. i, p. 2; δὶς κράμβη θάνατος schol. ad Juv. 7.154. The other explanation is that oaths such as ναὶ μὰ τὰς κράμβας, or νὴ τὸν κύνα, imply a belief that there is a common soul animating everything that lives. Cf. Plato *Apol.* 21E (with Adam's note), *Gorg.* 466c.

The editions of Hipponax by Bergk, Diehl, and Knox are indicated by the abbreviations B., D., and Kn. respectively; but A, a, b (e.g. 55A, B. or 14A, D. or 14a, D. or 14b, D.) are references to particular fragments.

We shall presently examine some of the items of the vocabulary of Hipponax, for comparison with those of Catullus. But first it is necessary to examine his linguistic setting. He was an Ionian Greek, to be sure; Clazomenae, however, had been Aeolic before it became Ionic. Moreover, both Ephesus and Clazomenae, though occupied by Greeks, had a pronounced substratum of non-Greek-speaking people—Lydian, Carian, Phrygian, and others, as well as of still more remote linguistic strata, both Indo-European and non-Indo-European. In brief we have (1) a pre-Indo-European stratum, marked by proper names and some common nouns in -ss- and -nt-, or variants of these suffixes, which are found both on the mainland and in Asia Minor; (2) Hattic, the non-Indo-European language which preceded Hittite, and which may itself belong to the pre-Indo-European stratum; (3) other non-Indo-European remains, of still later date, the Aegean "outcrops" of Eteocretic, Etruscan, Lemnian, including certain items of vocabulary and word formation in Greek itself; (4) proto-Indo-European, again reconstructed from fragmentary evidence more than recorded in actually identifiable shapes. This proto-Indo-European is the source not only of the well-known and fully recorded Indo-European languages of the full light of history, the traditional canon from Indo-Iranian to Balto-Slavonic, but also of Tocharish, of Hittite (including hieroglyphic Hittite), and other Anatolian languages (Luwian, Palaic, and perhaps Lycian and Lydian), of Phrygian, and of Greek itself; Keltic and Illyrian are latecomers in Asia Minor, but must not be overlooked. The Achaeans, the first of the Greek-speaking tribes, had reached the Mediterranean by the first half of the second millennium B.C.

It has been shown convincingly that there are some Greek and other Indo-European as well as non-Indo-European elements in the Praesos inscriptions, and therefore presumably in "Cretan" (broadly so called), whatever Eteocretic (or Cretan proper) may have been—most likely an "Aegaean" fragment. As for the Triballoi, who lived on the lower Danube, their dialect is generally considered to be related to Thracian, though it shows some

Illyrian elements, and some that have been alleged to show features found also in Scythian, in Anatolian languages, and Greek itself. Thus if σαῦ νάκα βακτᾶρι κροῦσα (*Av.* 1628: cf. 1678–79) is to be interpreted as the equivalent of Greek σοῦ νάκην βακτηρίᾳ κρούσω, we have no real quotation here from Triballic, but simply a bit of garbled Greek. But there seems to be some evidence that shows *a* for *o* and monophthongization of *au* (to *a*) and *eu* to *e*; of alternations of consonants (notably π : φ, β : φ, and δ : τ); of *z* from ĝ and of ζ : δ (e.g. Σαϝάζιος : Σαβάδιος); possibly of ξ : ζ (σ ?) and of consonant gemination. Ζιβελεῖζις (*REG* 26, 1913, 253) presents a problem not easy to solve in view of the suggestion of Rhys Carpenter[4] that this divine name is that of a bear-god, and that the Thracian alternation μ : β justifies the interpretation of βελ- as μελ- (and hence *Beleïzis* as "honey-eater"). Either Ζι- is a prefixed (intensive?) particle or an abbreviation of some word meaning "god" (with ζ : δ), or of the divine name *Zeus*. On the other hand, Ζιβελ- might correspond to Γεβελ-; and, if so, Ζιβελσοῦρδος (*REG* loc. cit.) would put Βελσοῦρδος entirely out of court. And there are other variants too: Ζβελσοῦρδος, Ζβελθιοῦρδος, Ζβερθοῦρδος, Ζβερθιοῦρδος, Ζλεθοῦρδος, *Zberturdus*, and *Zbertiurdus*, which tend to weaken the form Βελσοῦρδος. But I have indicated already that I do not insist on Βελσοῦρδος, disbelieving as I do in "textual emendation"; with the reservation, only and always, that a text must make sense, and that therefore (in this particular verse of Aristophanes, *Aves* 1615) a divine name is required. Understanding and good linguistic order go together. Triballic, then, goes with Indo-European, not with any imaginary "Minoan."

Too great a faith in the ancient tradition, and in the dogma that the language of Cretan scripts could not be Indo-European, undoubtedly delayed progress in interpretation. But it has long been conceded that Greek must have been the language of the

---

[4] *Folk-Tale, Fiction, and Saga in the Homeric Epic*, Berkeley and Los Angeles 1946, p. 124; cf. *Language* 30, 1954, 401. I do not think, however, that *Zalmoxis* (*Sa-*), *Zamolxis*, can imply either "honey" or "milk"; cf. rather Thracian ζαλμός "bearskin," Skt. *śárman* "hide."

inhabitants of southern and central Greece before the middle of the second millennium B.C., perhaps even near its beginning, and this view has finally been confirmed by the decipherment of the "Linear B" scripts of the mainland (Pylos, Mycenae, and elsewhere) and of Knossos, and the dialect is being called, at least provisionally, "Old Achaean."[5] Two factors are now clearly seen, one or other of which has been in dispute or even flatly denied purely *ex silentio*: (*a*) speakers of Greek were in the Balkan peninsula from the time of the Middle Bronze Age; (*b*) they had a script by the time of the Late Bronze Age.

So far this lecture has been concerned with establishing the setting in which early Greek poetry must be viewed, especially when it is seen as form. An iambus in the place of a spondee in the sixth foot of the dactylic hexameter is every whit as much an anomaly as a spondee in the place of an iambus in the sixth foot of the comic trimeter. Yet critics who are tempted to boggle at the latter, book text or no, may fairly be asked why they do not turn a hair at the former, except only Brandreth, who boldly substitutes ὕδρον for ὄφιν at *Iliad* 12.208. (The explanation that φ is an affricate, i.e. πφ, will not hold water; this is a phenomenon of far later date than Homer.) The word ὄφις occurs only once in Homer, and the metrical difficulty occasioned the quotation of Hipponax (49 B.) which ends

αὕτη γάρ ἐστι συμφορή τε καὶ κληδὼν
νικύρτα καὶ σάβαυνι τῷ κυβερνήτῃ
ἢν αὐτὸν ὄφις τὠντικνήμιον δάκῃ

and here again ὄφις has the first syllable long. In the preceding line σάβαυνι or σάμαυνι, if that is the correct word, is still a riddle (perhaps Carian σαμωνος defined as πρόθυμος, P.-W. Suppl. VI,

---

[5] It is now proposed to abandon "Old Achaean" in favor of Mycenaean (*Bull. Inst. Class. Stud. Lond.* 1, 1954, 10); and Chadwick is reported (*New York Times*, 14 October 1954) as tracing "Homeric sources" to Crete, a report difficult to assess in its present sketchy form. The recognition of a number of local names (*Bull.* loc. cit. 19–20) *Daminio* (: Epi-damnos?), *Ekomeno* (: Orchomenos, Erchomenos?), *Ewiripo* (: Euripos), *Korito* (Korinthos), *Korokuraijo* (Korkyra), *Posidaijo* (Potidaea), if correctly identified, seems a more promising venture.

142.66; the local name Σάμορνα = Ephesus, Hesych., from "Semitic" [?] is perhaps better compared with Cappadocian *Samuha*, but it has also been taken as Lydian, and identified with Smyrna, P.-W. XIII, 2150.65); νικύρτας, however, is explained by Hesychius as δουλέκδουλος, without any hint of its linguistic source (Lydian?)

There is no serious difficulty about ὄφις, anomalous as φ (before ι, for the expected θ) and the Homeric lengthening are. The φ is "Aeolizing," and ὄ points to h_3, which may supply a reason both for the lengthening of the syllable and for the aspiration.[6] Of the three words ὕδρος, δράκων, and ὄφις, the last-named is perhaps the least prosaic, i.e., the least likely to be predetermined in the sequence in which it occurs. It stands in contrast with ὕδρος, but δράκων is a substitute. The νικύρτας of Hipponax, and perhaps also his σαμαυνι (σαμωνος), are to be regarded as proper to the non-Greek substratum of Asia Minor, and evidently Hipponax expected his readers to understand them. I would go so far as to say that his dialect is closer to that spoken day by day at Ephesus and other Ionian cities in the sixth century B.C. than was the Greek of Herodotus in his day; the νικύρτας of Hipponax is like the *ploxenum* of Catullus, no puzzle to his own contemporaries and country.

At an earlier date Homer (or at a later date, his editor) is his own glossographer. Hipponax had felt free to introduce everyday Anatolian words into his colloquial verse, but Homer rejected them as vulgar, with few exceptions and with a curious convention. It seems that in the cities of Asia the poet or the singer realized that many in his audience would not understand the more elegant Greek expression, and so Homer invented the device of human and divine names for the same object. The non-Greek word is the native Anatolian or popular—that is to say, the "human"—term; the Greek is the word of the superstratum, the upper crust, the "divine" term, just as in Hindu tradition Sanskrit is the language of the gods. Homer's heroes (and the

---

[6] See *AJA* 52, 1948, 45–50.

gods) talk the "Old Achaean" which Ridgeway imagined and which Ventris has in part revealed.

A fragment of Hipponax (Bergk 66) reads

$$\text{ἔκρωζεν} \dots \text{κύμινδις ἐς λαύρην}$$

in which κύμινδις is the name of a bird (perhaps a raven),[7] specified by Homer as its human name, corresponding to the divine χαλκίς (Il. 14.291). The popular (or "human") term is evidently Anatolian, with its characteristically Anatolian -νδ- element. Other such Homeric pairs are νέκταρ : ἀμβροσία, Αἰγαίων : Βριάρεως, Ξάνθος : Σκάμανδρος, Βατίεια : σῆμα Μυρίνης, while μῶλυ, πλάγκται, and ἴχωρ are given or implied as divine names, like θυωρός (Diog. Laert. 1, 119). It has been suggested[8] that νέκταρ is a Tocharish word (näkt "god"), borrowed through some Anatolian intermediary; βριαρός and ξάνθος are obviously involved in Βριάρεως and Ξάνθος, σῆμα (Μυρίνης) is Greek, like πλαγκταί, while ἴχώρ (cf. Hitt. eshar) and μῶλυ (cf. Skt. mūla-m) may be Greek.

It is usual to compare λαύρη, which again is Homeric, with λᾶας "stone," which is semantically inappropriate. The meaning of λαύρη "winding passage" (and hence in Hipponax "privy") suggests rather λαβύρινθος, admittedly Anatolian (or at least Aegean) and the meaning, peculiar to Hipponax, a vulgar but easy shift.[9]

The so-called Strasbourg Epode is not with certainty attributed to Hipponax,[10] nor are its fragmentary lines convincingly completed. Its ἔβρυζε, σάννας (?), γυναικ[οπί]πην had better, therefore, be passed by. If actually the work of Hipponax, its chief importance is its clear showing that Hipponax did compose in true iambics as well as in scazons.

---

[7] The interpretation of κύμινδις as "perhaps a raven" (sc. in Hipponax) is suggested by ἔκρωζεν. But Professor H. R. W. Smith tells me that on coins of Chalcis, with a "punning" type, there is a bird (holding a snake in its mouth) interpreted to be a hawk or an eagle.

[8] Kretschmer, Anz. phil.-hist. Kl. Öst. Ak. Wiss. 1947.4, who demolishes the contrary view of Wilamowitz and others that the non-Greek words are divine.

[9] On 92 Knox see K. Latte in Hermes 64, 1929, 385–388 (who makes it probable that Petronius had read this piece, Sat. 138). For -νθ- cf. βόλυνθον (Hesych.)· βόλιτον.

[10] Masson, REG 59–60, 1946–1947, 12 ff. and 62, 1949, 300 ff.

I propose now to examine some of the items of vocabulary, either *hapax legomena* or rare, and either peculiar to Hipponax or not in general use. We shall find, as in Catullus, that they fall into definite categories, especially of taboo words. There is some reason to doubt that Hipponax used ἀνασεισίφαλλος (110–111 B.), for his form is φάλης, not φαλλός, but (ib.) ἀνασύρταλις (not ἀνασυρτόπολις) "a lewd woman" seems to be his and peculiar to him. The impossible βασαγίκορος· ὁ θᾶσσον συνουσιάζων (107 B.) has been cleared up (14A, D.) with the help of other glosses in Hesychius, in particular κρολίαζε· πλησίαζε θᾶττον and βαστιζα-κρολέα· θᾶσσον ἔρχου· Λυδιστί, from which βασγ[ικορλαζε is now read in 92.1 (Kn.). It is generally supposed that βάσγι is βάσκε, that isolated "imperative," and that the verb is Greek and cognate with βαίνω. The glosses in Hesychius might be interpreted to mean that βασγι is a Lydian word for "quickly" or "near," which makes better sense of Homer's βάσκ' ἴθι. At all events, κόρλαζε (κρολίαζε) is Lydian, meaning "approach" (sens. obs.) and perhaps even not a euphemism. Βέβρος (64 B.), and a variant βέβροξ, if Indo-European, seem to be the opposite of taboo words, i.e., they are noa words; literally "brown," it would mean "bear" or "beaver," and be Keltic,[11] cf. Gaulish *biber* in *DAG* 180, Βέβρυκες (ib. 80), hence "stupid" or "soft, gentle," not "arrogant." The ending *-x* suggests numerous names of animals—*esox, camox, ibex*, as well as other types: μῶλαξ "wine" Lydian (Hesych.), κόλλιξ, θρίδαξ, and καύηξ (2, below). But the word may have come from some other Anatolian source than Galatian, e.g. the identical Bithynian ethnicon (P.-W. 3.180, 52).

There follows a list of other noteworthy items of vocabulary in Hipponax:

---

[11] For another Keltic item that has been misunderstood, namely τριγέρανος, see *CP* 37, 1942, 97 and observe that γέρανος was the name of the stork dance in the Labyrinth (p. 129). In Homer φίλος "own" is Lydian, ib. 98 (cf. *Indg. Forsch.* 45, 1927, 267–271). As for χρή and χρὴ ὄν, see *CP* 50, 1955 (after Redard). The extraordinary vocabulary of Hipponax, as compared with other Greek writers, perhaps finds its nearest literary parallel in the language of Villon. On βρύσσος see now also Masson in *Parola del Passato* 5, 1950, 71–73 (P. Oxyr. 18, 19), *REG* 62, 1949, 312–319, Diehl 39.7, p. 92.

βέκος "bread" (82 B.), Phrygian.

βρύσσος, apparently γυναικὸς αἰδοῖον, see O. Masson, *Parola del Passato* 5, 1950, pp. 72–73; cf. Diehl 39.7 (p. 92), where ancient authority is cited for Ionic ἐπιβρύκων instead of ἐπιβρύχον. This is simply back to front. Ionic has aspirate variants (πρῆχμα, μείλιχμα) for Attic non-aspirate (γ), but Attic has πέπραχα as well as πέπραγα (in different uses), and the contrast has something to do with old laryngeals (see p. 63).

γρόμφις (ἡ) "sow" (onomatopoetic).

ἐγγαστριμάχαιρα (85 B.): *hapax legomenon*.

ἑπτάδουλος (113 B.) is erroneously ascribed to Hipponax (75 B.); it is actually Herodas 5.75. But Hipponax does use ἑπτάφυλλον according to Athenaeus, followed by modern editors. The solution of this riddle, I believe, is to write (for ἑπτάφυλλος)

ἑπτάδουλος "seven-leaved" at 37.2 B., a hybrid, -δουλος "leaf" being Keltic, see pp. 70, 71, 74, 76 above (*DAG* 178), Irish *duille*. Hence the curious blunder ἑπτάβουλος (113 B.); a further distinction to be made is δοῦλος· οἰκία (Hesych.) or "lupanar" (id., 69 Kn.).

ἔρπις "wine" (Egyptian, 51 B.); in fact some texts have οἶνον instead of ἔρπιν, exactly like ἑπτάφυλλον (37 B.) instead of ἑπτάδουλος (supra).

ἡμίανδρος "eunuch" (114 B.), perhaps an invention of Hipponax.

θεῦτις for τευθίς (115 B.) "squid."

θήπων (14.1 B.), cf. p. 51 above.

θυμός (or θύμος ?) in 9 B. (ῡ ?) is explained by Schol. A as τὸ ἄρρεν αἰδοῖον!

Κανδαύλης Lydian for κυνάγχης (1 B.); -(ϝ)αυλης may be cognate with εἰλύω, *uoluo*, Goth *walwjan*; Lydian *valves* num. *JHS* 46, 1926, 36–41.

κασωρίς (117 B.) "whore," and (?) adj. κασωρικός (74 B.). The source appears to be unknown. Perhaps not Indo-European (*qā*- [?] Walde-Pokorny, *Wörterbuch* 1.325), but Anatolian?

καύηξ (2 B.) "priest," cf. Lydian καύειν (acc.), a title of the priestess of Artemis at Sardis, *IGRom.* 4.1755; *AJA* 17, 1913, 362 *kaves*; καύηξ is glossed as λάρος ("mew, gull, cormorant," cf. *gauia*, *DAG* 158?), but so also is κίκων (2 B.) as ὄνομα μάντεως.

⟨κέ⟩ρ⟨κ⟩ον (acc.) at 14.3 B. (ἄρτον codd.) "penem" appears to be justified by the preceding δυσώνυμον, cf. τὴν ἀνώνυμον κέρκον Herodas 5.45; if so, read τὴν for τὸν in 14 B. Properly "tail," but sens. obs. also in

Aristophanes and Herodas. Presumably Greek, but the etymology is uncertain.

κνίζων in the same line will take its meaning from κέρκον if that be read.

κολάψαιε⟨ν⟩ 14b, D.; κολάψασα is conjectured by Knox (3), who renders it "exsucta mentula."

κόλλιξ (35.6 B.) "roll of bread," also (med.) of honey, soap, and other substances. Source unknown. Assigned to Phoenix (frag. 8) by Knox.

? κολόβια or κολοβά 122 B., who cites from Hesych. (Schmidt) κολοβὸν τὰ αἰδοῖα, cf. Skt. klībá- "impotent." But Hesychius has (s.v. κυλλήβδην) κολοβόντα· οἱ δὲ κολόβια παρ' Ἱππώνακτι, and κολοβὸν τὰ αἰδοῖα is the proposal of Schmidt. Note also Hesychius κολοβὸς . . . νομός τις κιθαρῳδικός.

[? κονίσκε, glossed as χαῖρε, Lydian, 64 B.; but the text is very dubious.]

[? κοχώνη "perineum" Bergk p. 500, but this Hipponax is the grammarian; or the medical writer.]

κυλλήβδην cf. κολόβια supra; -υ- for -ο- is Lesbian, -δην hardly characteristic, though common in Hipponax, and -δον frequent in Herodotus.

κύμινδις v. supra, p. 75.

κύψασα 22 D. is "sens. obs." LSc.

λαύρα v. supra, p. 75.

λίς 124 B., or λῖς, a Semitic loan word.

μαυλιστήριον· Λύδιον νόμισμα, λεπτόν τι, Hesych., 126 B.; "bawd's hire" (LSc.); μαῦλις is "bawd, procuress," and may be Lydian. But -τηριον is Greek; and the gloss perhaps says no more than that the Lydian price was low, which is hardly a credible generalization.

μεσσηγυδορποχέστης (127 B.), hapax leg.; this opprobrious name explains itself. So also

μητροκοίτης (14 B.), unless it is magnae matris sacerdos, but still a once-word.

μοιμύλλειν "chew, mumble" (80 B.), hapax leg.; onomatopoetic?

μοιχός (74 B.) generally compared with ὀμείχειν!

μολοβρίτης "beggar, parasite" (77 B.), cf. the Homeric μολοβρός, etymology unknown.

μύξα (60 B.) "mucus (from the nose)," rare; Indo-European.

μυσσωτός (35 B.) "savory of cheese mashed with garlic and honey"; a variant of μασσ-, like English *mash* : *mush*, but clearly colloquial.

νικύρτας v. supra, pp. 73–74.

νηνίατον (129 B.) Phrygian (Pollux); but is it the word or the tune that was "Phrygian"?

ὀμφαλητόμος (33 B.) Ionic for μαῖα.

[ὀπυίω, ὀπυιήτης Herodas; cf. Etruscan *puia* "wife."]

πάλμυς four times in Hipponax, Lydian for "king" (Tzetz.), as a proper name *Il.* 13.792; in Lydian inscriptions *paλmλuλ*, apparently the same as Phrygian βαλ(λ)ήν and "Aeolic" (sc. Alcaeus) πέρραμος, Homeric Πρίαμος; Sayce, *JHS* 39, 1919, 202 (who has *h*, not *p*, for the Lydian +; but *p* may become *h*, and the transcription is not sure).

? πανδάλητος (2 B.), -δη- (5 D.) alii alia; *hapax leg.*, apparently "wicked" vel sim. is the meaning required.

παρακνημόομαι (pass.) "go with difficulty" (130 B.), *hapax leg.*; κνήμη Tzetz. took as κινήμη, but the syncope is most unlikely; better cf. κνήμη "leg."

ῥύβδην (35 B.) "luxuriously;" ῥυφεῖν (for ῥοφ-) not Ionic (Photius), but Aeolic (132 B.), "gulp down," or rather Lesbian (Buck, ed. 3, p. 27).

σάβαυνι v. supra, p. 70, cf. 74.

? σαρκοκύων (133 B.), *hapax leg.*, but the reading is dubious.

σκαπερδεύω (1 B.), -εῦσαι· λοιδορῆσαι Hesych.; *hapax leg.* Cf. σκαπέρδα "tug of war."

σόλοικος (46 B.) lit. "living at Σόλοι (in Cilicia)," hence "speaking incorrectly."

τιλάω (55A, B.) seems to mean "to suffer from dysentery"; it is also a medical term.

τράμις (84 B.) "perineum."

τροπήϊον (57 B.) Ionic (for -εῖον), but perhaps to be read τραπ- ? Apparently only here.

ὑποργάζω (84 B.) sens. obs. (LSc.); a once-word.

φάλης for φαλλός (14 D.).

? φελίζων (15 B.) otherwise unknown; meaning?

χάλις (73 B.) "neat wine"; perhaps pre-Indo-European (Balkan?).

The Aeolic dative plural -οισιν as in διοζίοισιν "twin planks, forked branch (?)" *hapax legomenon* (14a, D.), cf. δυοῖσιν ib. and τριοῖσι (51 B.) is an old observation (Smyth, *Ionic* 1894, § 44;

cf. §§ 45–51), and not important; nor λυδίζειν "speak Lydian"
(14a, D.) except in its implication, nor πυγεών and πυγιστί (ib.),
both "once-words" (cf. πυγή). But κονίσκε (64 B.) is χαῖρε (su-
perscr.) and Lydian (Bergk), Μαλίς (ib.) hard to accept as
"Athena" unless again a word of the substratum, τετρακίνη
(135 B.) "lettuce" (for θριδακίνη i.e. θρίδαξ) said to be Phrygian
(Pamphilus), χλούνης "thief" (61 B.) rare, but not peculiar to
Hipponax, *pace* Debrunner.

Hipponax is commonly believed to have been one of the
greatest of Greek poets. For me his interest is his influence upon
Catullus, his meter, and his vocabulary. Meter and vocabulary
are both form, and as such are equally important elements of
poetry. The types of verse in Hipponax are

$$\cup - \cup - \cup \mid - \cup \mid - \cup - - -$$

or

$$\cup - \cup - \cup \mid - \cup \mid - \cup \mid - - -$$

and perhaps $\cup\,\cup -$ or $- \cup$ at the beginning of the line. In the fifth
foot a spondee certainly is admitted with proper names, and
perhaps (rarely) without; in Catullus the scazon goes

$$\cup - \cup - \mid \cup - \cup - \mid \cup - - \cup$$

with $\cup\,\cup\,\cup$ once in the second, and $- \cup\,\cup$ once in the third foot.
Diaeresis occurs with hepthemimeral caesura.

It has been said that the choliambic was invented (by Hipponax) "to suit the exceptional bitterness of the man." Of his
bitterness there is not a doubt, nor of Catullus', who took his
cue from Hipponax. In both the language is popular, the plain
talk of vulgar people, and the verse is pedestrian too; it has the
flat-footed ending of a clausula. Hipponax speaks the language
of the streets of Ephesus. It is no literary language. Many Greek
writers, to be sure, take the language of one city, but, while
polishing it, keep it an exact and unvarying dialect. There is in
actual usage no "imaginary" or "unreal" dialect, such as some
think they can see in Homer, or in Herodas. The probability for
this is zero (i.e., impossible), which can no more be accepted

than a probability of 1 (i.e., certain) in literary composition, except for the final morphome of a word that cannot be continued, for transitions between words, or absolute pause. As Knox puts it, "in real language, for example, 'doubtful quantities' do not occur. . . . If anyone seriously takes Herodas to be a painter from life they must first make his speech realistic . . . insist that he should . . . write . . . not just as suits his meter . . ." His case is the very opposite, so far as we can see, to that of Hipponax—so far as we can see; for it is almost impossible to form a definite opinion when we have hardly anything of Hipponax but quotations, and for text nothing more than a fragmentary papyrus or two. Yet this (14a, D. = 92 Kn., p. 65) is a convincing proof of all that has been written of Hipponax above, difficult as it is to disentangle the compound of glosses and parentheses that confront editors of Hipponax. Even when they have done their best—or worst—we may be left with (56 D., 1)

$$\text{Μαλίς, κονίσκε· καί με δεσπότεω βεβροῦ}$$

which appears also (71 Kn., 1) as

$$\langle \text{'Αθηνα}\langle ίη\rangle\rangle$$
$$\langle ί\rangle λ\langle ά\rangle σκο\langle μαί \ σ\rangle ε \ καί \ με \ δεσπότε\langle ω\rangle \ βεβροῦ$$

of which the first reading is one-half (μαλίς "Athena," κονίσκε "hail," βεβροῦ "gentle") not Greek—except in inflexion, but Anatolian; the second not Hipponax, but A. D. Knox, and a fine example of insisting on sense (understanding) in defiance of the "principles" of textual criticism.

The principles of anomaly contrasted with analogy, and of binary choices in literary form and poetic discourse, are in ample evidence here. Yet Hipponax represents one city, as Homer does not. The Homeric compound of Aeolic and Ionic is not the pedantic artificiality of a Spenser (or of a Herodas, to descend from the sublime), but the result of a transfer from an Aeolic to an Ionic (and later to an Attic) city.[12] From composite dialect

---

[12] Cf. Smyth, *Sounds and Inflections of the Greek Dialects. *Ionic*, Oxford 1894, pp. 34–35.

such as "Homer's," composite composition must follow; authorship is not the word. Even a sixth-century *Iliad* has no "author,"
but many contributors, and so has even a reconstituted text, as
near as we can hope to come to "Homer" (whatever is meant by
that word); what went before it is beyond our horizon and likely
to stay there.

What I wrote in 1948 (*AJPh* 52, 45–50) remains true. But
it has been given new support by the interpretation of the My-
cenean Linear B script (Ventris and Chadwick, *JHS* 73, 1953,
84–105). It has often been maintained in the past that we had
no Greek inscriptions older than the eighth century; but now
we have many of them, as far back as ca. 1400 B.C., representing
speakers of a form of Greek speech whose ancestors had been
in southern Greece as far back perhaps as ca. 1900 B.C.; and now
we do know something of the character of the mainland "Old
Achaean" dialect (no longer specifically Aeolic) of the second
millennium B.C., such as Homer's heroes may have spoken, not
very different perhaps from that of poets like Demodokos
(*Odyssey*, 8.472) and his contemporaries who sang the "Achaean"
lays from which our "Homer" grew, and from which they were
turned into Ionic when literary supremacy was established in
Ionia, and still later established according to an Athenian canon.
It had -οιο gen. sg. of ŏ-stems, the "instrumental-sociative" in
-φι, a dative singular termination -ει, labio-velar consonants, the
consonant group νϝ (cf. Homer's ὁποπρῖνῷ *Il.* 5.5), a preposition
ὁπί, a generalizing particle conjunction ("anyway," i.e., "besides,
and") κʷε (cf. the later τε), and above all a 3d pl. pres. of the
verb *to be* ἔενσι, in which ἑ- is the old laryngeal (cf. Hittite
ašanzi, Indo-European *ḫ₁s-e/onti : Latin s-unt), and for "father" and "mother" it has *pater- and *mater-, unlike the Anatolian languages (except Phrygian). Some examples: qe-to-ro-po-
pi i.e. κʷετροποδφι or τετράποδ(ο)φι, qo-u-ko-ro i.e. γʷουκολος or
βουκόλος, po-ti-ni-ịa-ṃe-ịo i.e. ποτνιαῖος, and above all the successfully deciphered continuous texts, e.g. (in an expanded system of transcription) *hiereia echei-que euchetoi-que etonion echeen
(theon ktoinoochons-de ktoinaon kekeimenaon onata echeen [tos-*

sonde spermo:] WHEAT 3-9-3, that is, "The priestess holds and solemnly declares that the god has the true ownership, but the plotholders the enjoyment of the plots in which it is laid out [so much seed:] $3\frac{57}{60}$ units."[13] Another text, this time transcribed into the Greek alphabet (Furumark):

$$\text{ἱέσθω}(ν)κ^υ\epsilon \text{ Ποσιδαίῳ ἅγεκ}^υ\epsilon \text{ ϝάστυδε}$$

Πύλος	δώρακ^{υ}ε	φερεφόρενά(?)κ^{υ}ε
	διϝία	δοέλᾱ	κομαϝεντείᾱ

$$\text{ἱέσθω}(ν)κ^υ\epsilon \quad \text{Ἰφι(?)μηδείᾳκ}^υ\epsilon \quad \text{Διϝιαίῳκ}^υ\epsilon$$

5   Πύλος   δώρακ^{υ}ε   φερεφόρενά(?)κ^{υ}ε   ἅγε

Ἰφιμηδείᾳ   Διϝίᾳ

Ἑρμάᾳ   Ἀλείᾱς (?)

ἱέσθω(ν)κ^{υ}ε   Διϝίῳ δώρακ^{υ}ε φερεφόρενάκ^{υ}ε ἅγε

Δίϝει   Ἥρᾳ

Πύλος

10   Δρυμίῳ (?)   Δίϝει   ἴει

—a requisition for offerings to certain deities (Poseidon, Hermes [?], Zeus and Hera, Potnia) and heroes. All this is compatible with our Homer, and compatible with the belief of an oral tradition of the text.

The literate "Homer" of a later date did not use a syllabary, but he was not the composer of our *Iliad*, but the compiler. If, as Wade-Gery has ably argued,[14] this "Homer" could and did write, then he used an alphabet composed of what I should call *graphemes*, i.e. στοιχεῖα or *elementa*, the strictly limited number of which, with their limited permutations and combinations,

---

[13] See now, in addition to the references given in note 5 above, Chadwick and Ventris, *Antiquity* 27, 1953, 196–206, Arne Furumark ("Ägäische Texte in griechischer Sprache"), *Eranos* 51, 1953, 103–120 and 52, 1954, 18–60. There is a popular account in the *Scientific American*, May 1954, 70–75. Ventris distributed a paper giving a key to the script and a list of more than five hundred names and other words on 12 July 1952; and Wace had a preliminary announcement of Ventris' achievement in the *Illustrated London News* of 25 October 1952. See also J. L. Myres, *Antiquity* 25, 1951, 70–71. The paper of T. B. L. Webster, *Antiquity* 29, 1955, 10–14, appeared too late for me to use it in this lecture: "Homer has a poetic ancestry which stretches back into the Mycenaean age."

[14] *The Poet of the Iliad*, Cambridge 1952. On στοιχεῖα "series" cf. Diels, *Elementum*, Leipzig 1899, pp. 57–58.

are statistically determined.[15] But it is hard to believe that literacy and the *Iliad* came at the same date; otherwise I do not find the differences of opinion so great.

In the first place I am no "separatist"—that is, I have no confidence in the attempts to analyze (on either literary or linguistic grounds) the Homeric poems into a number of distinct compositions. I have no interest whatever in any such undertaking, which I regard as unnecessary and bound to be unsuccessful. It is not useful to ask, or to know, who wrote what among the many contributors to the multiple tradition (for I am no "unitarian" either), "Homer" being the work not of one but of many, the creation of centuries, no longer presented solely in oral, but also in visual shape. In fact, the deciphering method (of Ventris) may be applied to any visually presented code. A frequency count of Etruscan phonemes would be a necessary first step toward interpretation of Etruscan documents that, so far as I know, has never been taken.

It will be seen that I consider Ventris' and Chadwick's work essentially correct. This I do chiefly because they proceeded on the basis of frequencies of occurrences of symbols and of their phonetic values and so, working with a syllabary, were able to reduce the eighty-four signs to a total approximately that of the Greek phonematic system. Their success in this procedure rules out mere chance agreements or coincidences or lucky guesses of translation. In fact, translation alone is not the proof; Carl Pauli once "translated" Etruscan as Lithuanian (!)—this was done to ridicule other "translators"—the proof comes when the frequency method breaks the code and produces intelligible results. Translation follows; it does not precede decipherment, which in this instance might have been achieved long ago if the archaeologists had not been so sure that Linear B could not be Greek. The present result is, in fact, close to some of Ridgeway's views, that won only scorn from his inferiors but really anticipated the decipherment that was virtually postponed for fifty years by the prevailing and persistent insistence that Ridgeway

---

[15] See my *Language*, 1955, chapters vii and xi.

could not be right. In the same way, the view that there must have been an Ionic redaction of an "Old Achaean" "Homer," comparable to a Modern English rendering of Chaucer by Dryden, Pope, and Wordsworth, is made many degrees more certain than a postulated original and single Ionic Homer as determined by the subjective and fluctuating canons of aesthetics. Current criticism on this basis, of both *Iliad* and *Odyssey*, is completely bewildering. It is not at all like criticism of a Byron, for there is no comparable Byronic "problem"; we may form our estimate of him without this complication. Nor is the case of "Homer" at all a case comparable to that of Spenser, who deliberately and consciously mingled contemporary dialects, with ludicrous results; but the survival of forms older by several centuries than any "Ionic" epic of Asia Minor, as well as geographically far remote.

Greek settlements in Anatolia impinged upon peoples who had used systems of writing that antedated any form of true alphabetic writing such as the Greeks developed from an old Canaanitish variety of Semitic writing, leaving behind once and for all anything in the nature of a syllabary (except in Cyprus). The Mycenaean Linear B is a syllabary, like some forms of Anatolian writing. But within the Anatolian triangle (based on a line drawn from Lesbos to Cos, with its apex at Mount Dindymus), alphabetic writing, related very closely to Greek, is found in Phrygian, Lydian, Lycian, and other groups of inscriptions, and especially within a smaller triangle (based on a line drawn from Smyrna to Ephesus, its apex at Buladan). This is a momentous matter.

There is no necessary connexion between language and "writing," although once the momentous step had been taken, the union proved immediately and continuously, to this day, fruitful. Pictographs are mere imitation (like onomatopoeia), not true writing (just as onomatopoeia is not true language); genuine writing avoids the cumbrous and uneconomical devices of pictographs, logograms, or syllabic signs, by reaching a stage of true symbolism in which there is a correspondence of grapheme and phoneme, and a conventional relation between the symbol and its value. The union of writing and language was in its way as remarkable an achievement as the union of electric waves in radio and television and language in the present century. There is in writing, as in speaking, a matching of the code—visual or vocal—with cerebral patterning; in both there is what we may call "inner form," that is, development from one internal structural stage to another. Now the phonematic and inflexional structure of Greek or of Indo-European is ill adapted to anything other than a true alphabet, and it was inevitable that a syllabary (of whatever origin) would in time be abandoned for alphabetic writing, which is a tremendous help to literary composition. It is hardly going too far to associate the final shaping of the epic (in Ionia or at Athens) with the use of φοινικήια γράμματα (instead of, as in Elean and Arcadian, γράφεα); prior to this it had been handed down orally, gradually being made to match the Ionic instead of the "Old Achaean" pattern in which it was first composed but not written. The older type of writing, Linear B, was not at all, or rarely used, so far as we know, for what may be called literary purposes—unless proverbs are "literary"; even the true alphabet was used at first for messages, votive or memorial inscriptions, and after a time for public documents of some length, and at last for literary texts, both prose and verse.

An event of almost equally great import as the decipherment of Linear B for the understanding of Homer against the Mediterranean background has been the publication, at the very same time, of Parry's *Serbocroatian Heroic Songs*, edited by A. B. Lord (Cambridge, Mass., 1953–1954), a work which throws even more light than had been promised. These songs certainly have a Homeric quality about them. But not one of the singers claims to have *composed* his songs. They all *learnt* them, that is, they inherited them from the original composers. I commend to the consideration of my readers in particular the songs of Salih Ugljanin, Sulejman Fortič, Ðemail Zagič, Sulejman Makič, and Alija Fjuljanin. Thus (p. 60, Vol. 1 of Parry and Lord) Salih

Ugljanin sang in *two* languages, Albanian and Bosnian, and had learnt his songs, each of which must be a *complete* performance. Similarly (p. 225) Sulejman Fortič had *learnt* many songs; and Sulejman Makič turned songs both from Bosnian into Albanian (p. 236) and from Albanian into Bosnian (p. 237), being at home in both languages. He reported (p. 239) that some singers add lines or leave out lines, that improvisation is common, and that if some singer omits a considerable part of a song, still he knows the rest; that a song can be mastered (p. 240) in a single hearing in a single night, but (p. 241) when two singers learn the same song in one night, their subsequent versions are different; he himself knows twenty-five or thirty songs (p. 243). Alija Fjuljanin learnt to sing (p. 292) when he was ten years old, and knows no Albanian.

A common introduction is found to more than one song, as "Let us make merry; God bring merriment" (Ugljanin, pp. 58, 90; and Fjuljanin, p. 293). Still more striking are certain formal characteristics of the Serbo-Croatian songs. I take the following details from Parry and Lord (Vol. 2, pp. 327–333): readings are often uncertain and conjectural, abnormalities of pronunciation frequent, and also metrical irregularities (despite a "formulaic" style), accompanied on occasion by errors and faltering. The dialect of a particular version is that of a particular city (Novi Pazar), like the Ionic-Attic version (quasi-Athenian?) of our Homer (not Corinthian or Spartan, as it might easily have been); but Turkish, Arabic, and Persian words appear, like the Anatolian words of Homer (and of Hipponax). Variations occur not only in the same song as sung by different singers, but even as sung by one and the same singer. Or there may occur considerable variants, amounting almost to different versions of a single song. If the singer halts for a rest or interlude, or because of forgetting or making a mistake, when he resumes a line or lines will be repeated. Sometimes words get out of place and two formulas may be confused, especially where there is internal rhyme or the grammatical construction is not clear, and as many as four alternatives arise in badly constructed lines or in mixed formulas. Hypermetric lines (with eleven instead of ten syllables) are not unknown; nor the first half or second half of a formula alone, without the other half. All these features remind us of Homer, though they are perhaps less pronounced in our vulgate, presumably as the result of editing such as the story of the Pisistratean recension suggests, or of subsequent criticism in ancient times; and in Homer relics of such features, which editors have removed, or tried to remove and would fain remove, do most unmistakably point to multiple composition. Other Serbo-Croatian features are "slips of the tongue," the premature anticipation of later lines, reversal of the order of action produced by adherence to formulas; faults and recovery and occasional linguistic irregularities (e.g. the dropping of final -š), or even "grammatical" blunders (e.g. an auxiliary hanging without its participle, or an unexpected shift to the aorist form). What could be more like "Homer"? Yet all these are features, some of them anomalous as judged by severe grammatical and literary criteria, but fully in accord with all that we know of linguistic events, untainted by scholarly interference, that clearly mark, indeed stamp, the product of an oral illiterate multiple tradition of many singers that we know it to be; and they cannot result from the studied and carefully polished literary effort of a talented literate poet, and certainly are not characteristic of a work of genius, or what we take a work of genius to be, or think it ought to be.

Now such studies as we have of Homer's usage, especially those that employ statistics, do indicate a certain residual amount of deviation, even when editors have done their best (or worst), deviation such as might be expected to occur with multiple authorship, and with a complex linguistic background such as the history of Greek indicates, from Minoan times on, and especially when transferred (and the epic with it) to a different milieu in western Asia Minor; far exceeding the standard deviation that is necessary to accommodate the writings of Hipponax, Catullus, or Vergil, and considerably higher than is necessary for other works of unique authorship like those of

Aristophanes or Sophocles, in whose writing (especially the latter's) anomaly falls to a minimum. The decipherment of Linear B has expanded greatly our view of the total anterior linguistic history of Greek, some gaps notwithstanding. No less significant, cumulatively, than the publication of the Serbo-Croatian heroic songs, is the total result of investigation of Homeric usage ever since the days of August Fick, if not of Richard Bentley. Among the more recent of these investigations Leumann's *Homerische Wörter*, Basel 1950, is easily, I think, the most outstanding.

Let me say at the outset that the matter, whether "Homer" is one or many, is not of earth-shaking importance; but that, if it were, it would have to be conducted with the same kind of scientific precision as that with which engineers conduct their affairs, not, for example, confusing inches with yards as Hellenists confuse distances of hundreds of miles and times centuries apart in their notions of what is and what is not possible in a Greek dialect; and as doctors conduct theirs, not confusing drugs like *morphine* and *strychnine* because they happen to end in the same syllable. (One of my Berkeley colleagues has heard, or read, of a druggist who did confuse *paraldehyde* and *formalde hyde*, with dire consequences.) And second, for the enlightenment of one of my critics, who (*AJPh* 71, 1950, 338) does me too great honor, that I wear no mantle but my own. There is some risk, as Lejeune has said, that the Homeric problem is becoming also a pathological problem, but at least Leumann seems not to be affected so far, and I trust that I am not, by this frailty.

Not that literary critics are all on the "unitarian" side. The recent works of Merkelbach and Jachmann, sustained by Wackernagel's earlier linguistic discussion, are able defenses of multiple authorship.[16] But there is often a deplorable misapprehension of the linguistic facts on the part of advocates of "uni-

---

[16] R. Merkelbach, *Untersuchungen zur Odyssee*, Munich 1951 (reviewed by Bolling, *CP* 47, 1952, 177–182); G. Jachmann, "Homerische Einzellieder" (pp. 1–70 in *Symbola Coloniensia Iosepho Kroll oblata*, Cologne 1949); J. Wackernagel, *Sprachliche Untersuchungen zu Homer*, Göttingen 1916.

tary authorship," who seem capable of any distortion in striving to gain a point. Thus we are told that ϝ was in a "transition stage" (that is, presumably, between currency and loss). But this facile label, if it is intended to mean that ϝ might or might not be used, as it were, as a matter of convenience, can prove only multiple authorship—with one author ϝ was current, with another it was not. For phonematic substitution always is, and must be, completely regular. If it were not so, then a language or dialect would accumulate so many phonemes, "transition stage" or not, as to exceed the permissible number upon which communication depends and above which unintelligibility supervenes. Either a phoneme exists or it does not; there *is* no "in between" or "transition" stage. Only the assumption of different dialects (with and without ϝ), different authors (with and without ϝ), and different ages can account for the observed facts, as every tyro in linguistics knows. An editor who does not know this is, in my judgment, and in the judgment of all who know the history of Greek, or of any language, simply incompetent to edit Homer, and a corrupter of youth whom he is educating in the misuse of evidence, evidence of the clearest and most convincing kind. Comparisons with varying pronunciations of English *wa(r)*, *idea(r)* reveal the incompetence of those who make them. These pronunciations appear inconsistently in the usage of *different* speakers, *and there only*; a *single* speaker (or author) is absolutely and always consistent, down even to the matter of allophones. Again, if an editor appeals to items of vocabulary common to Homer and to Arcado-Cyprian, unless he is prepared to identify Homer's "dialect" with Arcado-Cyprian, as of course he is not, then he confounds geographically, as he had already confused chronologically, clear and unequivocally discriminatory criteria, and his argument falls to the ground.

Some metrical phenomena, like ὄφις discussed above (p. 73), may be shown to be genuine, *but very old*, pronunciations, not licenses at all. In ἐπιχάρην for example, ē is from h₁e (compare Linear B ἔενσι), for no Indo-European root may begin with a vowel. Even in τὰ περὶ καλά the quantity of τὰ[17] is a legitimate variant (cf. Sanskrit tā́); Greek -ă (neuter plural), so far as it does not represent -ə (that is, ḫ, a reduced grade of eḫ₂ or ā), is secondary (τὰ ὀστέα from τὰ ὀ-), and κᾱλά represents καλϝά. But relics of ḫ in "Homer's" verse imply a very ancient pronunciation which, wherever it occurs, implies a date of "composition" that, all the other facts considered, cannot be conceived at all without the assumption of multiple authorship, extending over some centuries. A scholar so unwilling as G. P. Shipp (*Studies in the Language of Homer*, Cambridge 1953) to involve himself in questions of authorship admits the presence of Aeolisms; and his argument seeking to discredit the evidence of certain forms, on the ground that they were used also in Attic, is surely unconvincing, since they are mostly, if not entirely, forms which Attic owed to "Homer."

It has been held, by Meillet and others, that the Homeric hexameter arose from the union of two shorter verses, the second being a paroemiac (like παθὼν δέ τε νήπιος ἔγνω Hes. *Op.* 218). Such lines would tend to disfavor a break before the final $- \cup \cup - \underset{\smile}{}$ unless preceded by a short syllable; or, if by a long vowel, then long "by nature," and here may lurk the reason for the Homeric restriction that goes by the name of Wernicke's Law, not "that the fourth foot should not sound like the end of a line" (Leaf, *Iliad*, Vol. 2, p. 635), though the effect is much the same. In any event, the assumption of an older short (paroemiac) verse accords well with the common observation that peasants, who are much given to proverbial sentiments, do not sing private, but only communal, poetry, and so pave the way for oral, multiple composition.

The contributions of archaeology to the solution of any literary or linguistic problem are not primary except in the recovery of new written documents. Opinions of the archaeologists themselves on the question of authorship, for example, fluctuate too widely and too often to inspire confidence. Their criteria seem to me inapplicable to this particular question save in so far,

---

[17] See Sturtevant, *Hittite Grammar* ed. 2, New Haven 1951, p. 91.

which is not very far, as they may furnish support to linguistic criteria and judgments, which after all are, and must be, paramount when the evidence of any written document is summoned: "words not sherds." In may be noted, however, that a recent archaeological pronouncement, that of Miss Lorimer in her *Homer and the Monuments* (London 1951), is on the side of multiple authorship. It is a pleasure also to observe, here at Berkeley, that a competent literary critic, whose competence is all the more emphasized by his own achievements as a poet, Professor L. A. MacKay, has conceded in his *Wrath of Homer* (Toronto 1948) that those who will may speak not of "Homer" but of many—at least, several—"Homers." I have previously indicated (n. 6; cf. p. 82 above) my opinion that a unitary force played a leading part, about the eighth to the sixth century B.C., in shaping the Homeric poems as we now have them, whether a "great poet" (as Professor MacKay believes) or merely an "editor" of unusual talent, as I suggested. But we agree to this extent, that *one* man enters the picture at this stage, and my view is not really very different from that expressed by some other Homeric scholars on this point as well (p. 84 above) as on "separatism."

I return now to Leumann's *Homerische Wörter*, which seems to me to stand to some current twentieth-century Homeric criticism as a jet plane to a rowboat. His thesis, which is brilliantly argued, is that just as linguistic peculiarities in Alexandrian poetry often depend on Homeric precedent, so linguistic peculiarities in Homer that appear to be utterly inconsistent with all the development of all other Greek must depend on pre-Homeric models. Leumann also has identified a number of late—almost barbarous—inventions (such as οὐδ' ἀπὸ δόξης *Il.* 10.324, *Od.* 11.344, and nowhere else in Homer, the troublesome δόξα having been a sigmatic neuter participle, mistaken as an ἄ-stem); but over these we need not stay. More interesting, and more important, is Leumann's solution of a large number of such oddities as κελαινεφής in the sense of κελαινός, namely, that in κελαινεφὲς αἷμα, one of two types of phrase in which this adjective appears, the other being, for example, κελαινεφέι Κρονίωνι, κελαινεφές has been mistakenly paired with αἷμα, presumably in a line in which it was properly a vocative form applied to (say) Zeus. The argument is developed in some detail, and is likely, I think, to convince any unprejudiced reader. It assumes a model, no longer extant, in some pre-Homeric epos. But there are peculiar situations for which the model may be found in our Homer, and in which the chronological relationship was already clear before Leumann wrote. Although I think it possible that ἀγγελίης (. . . ἤλυθες) in *Il.* 13.252 might be defended as a genitive of the sphere (just as in the later τοῦ βίου εὖ ἥκειν, which must historically have been "to come to a point of well-being in the matter of"), Leumann, like Leaf and others, rejects this interpretation; instead he finds a masculine ἀγγελίης "messenger" that is the equivalent of ἄγγελος, not recognized by Liddell and Scott although it was the explanation of Aristarchus. But the thing is an utter impossibility on the evidence of normal Greek morphology. I cannot do better than quote Chantraine's enthusiastic approval (*Grammaire homérique*, Vol. 2, Paris 1953, p. 46) of Leumann's illuminating investigations (*Homerische Wörter*, pp. 168 sqq.): "Ce singulier ἀγγελίης 'messager' est issu d'une fausse interprétation de Γ 205 ἤλυθε δῖος 'Οδυσσεὺς σεῦ ἕνεκ' ἀγγελίης 'pour un message qui te concernait,' où le génitif féminin ἀγγελίης a été senti comme un nominatif masculin." These examples of Leumann's method and results must suffice. It is obvious that we have further proof of multiple authorship. The passages *Il.* 3.205–206, 11.139–141, and 24.234–235 were composed by three different singers. Not that it makes much immediate difference. But attention may be directed to Leumann's chapter vi on the appearance of "poetic" words not in poetry, but in prose, in inscriptions, or post-Homeric writers, and in non-Attic Greek, or in the grammarians, which should crack some ironclad illusions about the nature of poetic discourse in general, and of Homeric usage in particular.

The matter of Homer's dialect is not, I think, of first importance: nor is the question of single or plural authorship. I am convinced that the former is "Old Achaean," turned into Ionic; and that many minstrels, ἀοιδοί, not rhapsodes, contributed to the epic. But the problems of matching words, whether spoken or written, and meanings, and of the formation of a linguistic pattern, are of far greater moment. To this, with the examples of Catullus and Hipponax before us, and an illustration of method from Vergil and Homer, four separate specimens of Mediterranean "area and language," we shall now turn. The illustrations will come next; Catullus and Hipponax in a later chapter.

One feature of language that is little remarked is the way in which words follow one another in sequence without premeditation. This is conspicuously so for an oral "composer." For a "public" speaker there is normally no apparent hindrance to the flow of words, but it is a predetermined sequence in the sense that the pattern of a given language must be followed. Psychological disturbances are familiar and frequent; but a genuine mixture of language or dialect patterns is impossible; in writing English one does not lapse into a Lowland Scots or Frisian or into any other pattern. The curious thing about Homeric diction is its extraordinary catholicity, unparalleled in any other Greek —phonematic pattern, morphology, syntax, and vocabulary are all found in a bewildering variety. All writers show some anomaly; but in Homeric usage, as compared with any and every variety of Greek, anomaly is excessive. In the terminology of statistics, the "standard deviation" is abnormally high. Theoretically this freedom ought to be difficult to follow. What is it that redeems Homer from becoming unintelligible, or at least extremely difficult? It is the conjoint use of formulaic expression—often literal repetition—and metrical pattern; a complex but easily anticipated structural sequence that, in "Homer," combines in an unusual degree system and economy. In the first twenty-five lines of both *Iliad* and *Odyssey* there are but three lines out of fifty which do not find a counterpart or repetition somewhere else in the two poems, some of them more than once. We know what is coming—noun or adjective, nominative or genitive, as neatly as we know the form of the verse. Not only that, meaning too is not abandoned; we know, as "Homer" knew, what the meaning is in virtue of the degree of determinacy required by the sequence. An extreme example is βλήτροισι (*Il.* 15.678); the reader knows what it means, as he knows the meaning of a technical term which he meets for the first time and does not find in his dictionary, does not even stop to look up, say *feedback* or *network*.

But δῖος in πολύτλας δῖος 'Οδύσσευς is determined in a far higher measure, and no one stops even to ask *its* meaning either, or to interpret it in a literal way. As the determinacy increases, the meaning diminishes. In the same way, Aeneas is still *pius* no matter what he does. The expression was no offense to an ancient reader (e.g. Serv. ad *Aen.* 1.378); it is the modern reader who dares to criticize. But if an ancient author has some things which astonish us, our astonishment is as nothing compared with what the ancients would think of *it*, or the astonishment with which *they* would regard either our impudent criticisms of their writings or our attempts to write their languages and to rewrite their writings. One modification of this assertion that *pius Aeneas* was no occasion for objection to Vergil (obviously) or to his contemporaries may be admitted, namely, that the subsequent decline in the frequency of occurrence of *pius* is probably to be interpreted as indicating that it had been used to excess.

This adjective *pius*, like some of those used by Catullus, is Italic (Oscan *piíhiúí* dat. sg. "pio")[18] and Old Latin. In Ennius it has *ī* (as well as *ĭ*), and the Romance derivatives also imply *ī* (cf. the *piius* and *pĪus* of inscriptions). Like δῖος, with which it was at one time metrically equivalent, it comes to fill a definite place (∪ ⏑) in the verse, where its appearance is predetermined also by the phonematic, morphomatic, and semantic pattern.

---

[18] In Oscan there appears to have been some mistaken association with a borrowed πίστιος, whence the spelling *piístíá* (Tab. Agn. *a* 14); at least recent attempts to find other explanations are unconvincing, difficult as the reference to πίστιος (itself a translation of *Fidius*) may be.

It is believed to be cognate with *pūrus* and therefore perhaps with *pudīcus*.[19]

Statistics of the frequency of occurrence of *pius* are available for representative Latin authors from Plautus to Apuleius. To compare word distribution in different authors, the crude frequencies should be reduced or expanded so as to correspond with equivalent bulk of text, or be based on samples of equal length. But this would give a false picture of the actual distribution in genres. The comparisons which follow, then, based on crude statistics, are applicable to genres. In comedy, *pius*, common in Plautus, drops to one occurrence in Terence. There is a similar pattern in elegy; after a brief increase in Horace as compared with Catullus, there is an abrupt drop in Tibullus. History makes very little use of the word, but a slight and slow rise in frequency may be observed from Caesar to Tacitus, followed by a decline. Epic poetry uses *pius* far more frequently than any other kind of Latin writing. But the pattern is the same: a sharp increase from Vergil to Ovid,[20] then a correspondingly sharp decline in Lucan and Valerius Flaccus, but (in this genre) followed by a subsequent rise of frequency in Statius. Only philosophy and satire, with rising frequencies of about equal steepness, from Cicero to Seneca and from Petronius to Apuleius, violate the oscillatory pattern of the other styles.

A purely phonematic pattern is not, so far as I can see, to be found.[21] Graphs of twenty occurrences of *pius* in the *Aeneid*, showing the several patterns based on the relative frequency of occurrence of the phonemes in the entire verse, show no conformity of pattern either with one another or with random lines taken as indicating the permitted sequences within the metrical pattern. There is a more or less regular oscillation of peaks and dips as the line moves from one permitted sequence of bounded

---

[19] Ultimately *$p\bar{e}u$- W.-P. 2.12–14?

[20] An accommodation between the impossibility and the necessity of finding a single classification for a many-sided poet must be made; there is at least a quasi-epic quality in much of Ovid's subject matter, and the *Metamorphoses* is epic, notwithstanding its subject. The frequency of *pius* is indicative.

[21] Cf. H. A. Roe, Harvard honors thesis in Linguistics and Classics, 1954.

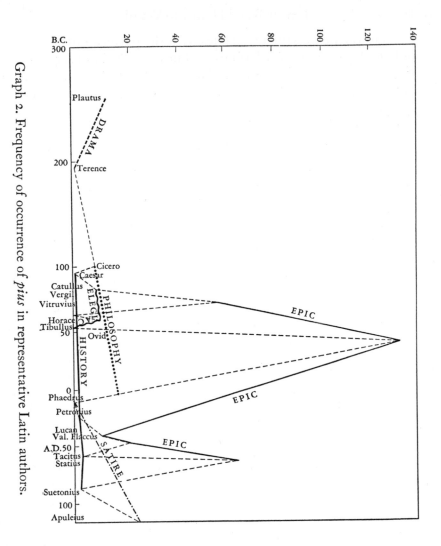

Graph 2. Frequency of occurrence of *pius* in representative Latin authors.

forms to the next, which coincides with the pattern of the verse and the location of word types within it (that is, observation of caesura and diaeresis, the regular – ◡ ◡ – ◡ ending, restrictions on spondaic lines, and so forth), and in other alternations of fre-

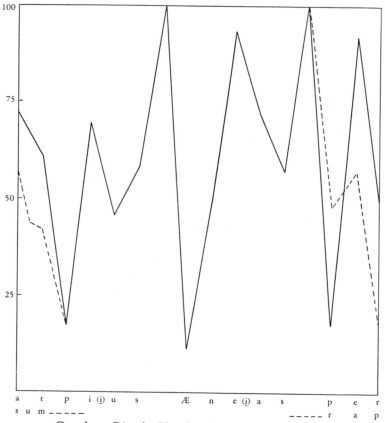

Graph 3. *Pius* in Vergil; phonematic pattern.

quent and rare phonemes which any linguistic structure imposes. But similarities of pattern even on the phonematic level appear once *pius*, or some other equivalent form (*pater Aeneas, bonus Aeneas*), is yoked with *Aeneas*, and in the total sequence there also emerges what may be called a semantic pattern governing the sequence, even in the extreme case of 4.393

At *X* Aeneas, quamquam lenire dolentem
solando cupit

in which *X* may be one of but a few items of vocabulary, however unsuited any one of them seems to modern sentiment: *iussa
tamen diuum exsequitur.* No wonder *pius* gains currency in
Christian Latinity, as it had in pagan philosophy (the rise in
satire must be satirical), until it becomes the name of popes.

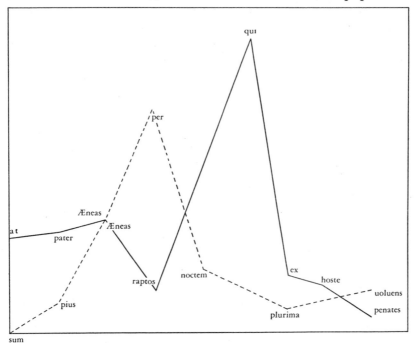

Graph 4. *Pius* in Vergil: word frequency.

In Vergil the problem is not in the "meaning" as that word is
commonly understood. We may fairly ask whether it has
"meaning" in the same sense as, say, *duo*; or whether its sense
is gathered, like that of Homer's βλήτροισι or ἔστωρ, as one
gathers the sense of an English word seen or heard for the first
(and perhaps last) time and not further explored; and also ask
whether it is not merely an adjunct of a heroic name. So far as
the statistical evidence goes, it appears to indicate a certain degree of determinacy by virtue of which one may assert that *pius*
makes a good fit, independently of nuances of connotation. But

when we push the investigation to strict semantic relationships, it becomes clear that the appearance of the word is determined by the permitted sequences of the language and that to quibble about Aeneas' desertion of Dido is to miss the poetic form and to substitute criticism for understanding. We shall reach the same conclusion on a larger scale and in a different setting when we come to deal in general terms with the peculiar vocabularies of Hipponax and Catullus (chapter vii), many features of which are similar to those of the vocabulary of Aristophanes, in which the occasional $\cup\ \cup\ \underset{\smile}{}$ (– –) ending must be admitted in the name of understanding. In νὴ Βελσοῦρδον there is at least as much "fit" as in αἰόλον ὄφιν or in *pius* (or *bonus, pater*) *Aeneas*, or in *gingiuas . . . ploxeni*, or κολλητὸν βλήτροισι, δυωκαιεικοσίπηχυ, or βασγικόρλαζε (Hipponax, 92 Kn.), and I am prepared to stick to it, if at all, on that ground.

To put the matter as broadly and simply as possible, semantic *relationships* primarily determine the selection of words. It is clear that once a writer has embarked upon a word group, less choice is possible than before he had done so. "Let slip . . ." Well, what? Tigers, lions, bears? No: the segment of *experientia* designated *dogs* overlaps that of *bark* more than of *seals* or *guns* or *hyenas* or *sergeants*; *cats purr* and *ducks quack* and *hyenas laugh*. So the segment *let slip* overlaps the segment *dog*. The percentage of overlap between *dog* and (*let*) *slip* may be measured by comparing the number of times (*let*) *slip* is used with *dog* against the number of times it is used with some other word, and then by treating *dog* in the same fashion. The *dogs of war* are not *dogs*, but still it is *Cry "Havoc!" and let slip the dogs of war*. Similarly *pius* and *Aeneas*, or *pius* and *Oeclides*. There are recurrent key words that predetermine *pius*, independently of the dictionary meaning which a critic finds inept. The linked word pairs appear not only in certain contexts but also in a variety of writers; in other words, in the linguistic pattern, and the pattern gives the content, thus:

pius : *deus*   Vergil *A*. 5.685, 9.255; 4.393; Horace *c*. 1.24.11; Ovid
   Tr. 1.9.32; 4.4.68; *F*. 1.528; Plautus *Rud*. 26; Statius *Th*. 6, 358;
   Ovid *Ex P*. 4.9.108; *Am*. 3.9.26

pius : sacer   Vergil *A.* 8.24; Ovid *Am.* 2.13.12; 3.9.37; *Ex P.* 4.9.106–
107; *Tr.* 4.68; *M.* 13.640; *F.* 1.527(2)

Among other words linked in these authors with *pius* are
*scelus, colo, sepulcrum, morior, funus, mater, pater, frater, patria,
genus, natus, comes.* In addition to the nineteen occurrences of
pius ∼ *Aeneas* in Vergil there are also thirty-seven occurrences
of one or other of the words listed above as linked with *pius.* But
in the thirty-one occurrences of *Aeneas* with other epithets
(*meus, pater, Troius, ille, ferus, bonus, magnus, ignarus, Anchisi-
ades*) there are only six occurrences of the linked words, roughly
one-tenth of the frequency of occurrence with *pius.* It is likely
also that *Aeneas* through its association with *pius* plays a part
in the determination of these words, as if *pius-Aeneas* were as
much a unit as "John Jones," the meaning of "John" being as
unimportant as the meaning of "Jones." The vocabulary surrounding *pius* in Vergil surrounds *pius* in Ovid, Statius, Horace,
and Seneca (among others). From these observations it is clear
that the occurrence of *pius* is in large part determined by linked
words in the context.

Gallons of ink have been spilt over *pius* Aeneas. It is not
amiss, therefore, to expend a drop more that will not be wasted.
In the *Aeneid* alone, 49 verses that begin with the formula *A*
(e.g. *praecipue, at, sum, quam, tum, hoc, quem, quid, et, iam,
actutum, sic, huc, quos, cum, hinc*) + *B* (e.g. *pius, pater, bonus*) +
C (e.g. *Aeneas, Arcitenens, Anchises, Euandrus*) occur in the proportions 20 (*pius*) : 27 (*pater*) : 2 (*bonus*). Why has not *pater*
(*Aeneas*) 16 times aroused the criticism that *pius* (*Aeneas*) 19
times has? Or why not *pius Arcitenens* (once), or *bonus Aeneas*
(twice)? How did Vergil come to use *pius Aeneas* with almost
the same frequency as *pater Aeneas*? Not for metrical convenience, since he could easily have found equivalents. The item
pius must be determined, wherever it occurs, by some other
factor or factors. The structure of the utterance in each place
in which *pius Aeneas* appears is, I believe, the determining
factor, thus: the speaker of a language possesses a statistical
knowledge of its structure in virtue of the very command which

he has of the language, by which he is able to predict, within limits, its sequence when the preceding text is known.[22] Each unit of utterance contributes to the structure but at the same time is subject to constraints imposed by the structure of the particular language, and the upper and lower bounds within which these factors operate may be calculated. Results are roughly comparable in scientific writing and in poetry, a fact that may be interpreted to mean the same degree, more or less, of variation as measured against other kinds of discourse.[23] In actual experiments, prediction improves rapidly with increasing knowledge of the immediately preceding utterance. The probability of being right in the first x predictions when the preceding n units are known is greater than or equal to that when only $(n - 1)$ are known, for all x. A contemporary of Vergil found nothing to criticize in his use of *pius* in any context in which Vergil used it; nor would a modern English-speaking reader whose Latin were that of Vergil and his contemporaries, any more than he does in a like situation in the poetry of Shakespeare or Milton. The same remarks apply to *castus, pudicus, lasciuus* in Catullus, or to *pius* in Catullus or δῖος in Homer; or to *sin* in Donne, or to *love* in Byron. The words communicate without being defined; they have associations, and groups of words in association have associations for the sender and receiver, at least the contemporary receiver, of a message, who does not stop to ask what they mean. Nor should we, if we really *knew* our Greek and Latin; but we "construe" precisely because we cannot use the reverse process of inferring the image, the essence of which is in the interrelationships of the linguistic symbols. To seek a precise referential relationship such as the pro-presenting elements give in the lexical scheme of *pius* and the rest is mischievous. The symbols have turned into the binary choices, the ciphers, of the code and thus, in a well-known phrase, establish "communion without communication." A new

[22] C. E. Shannon, "Prediction and Entropy of Printed English," *Bell Telephone System: Technical Publications*, Monograph 1819, New York January 1951.

[23] P. Guiraud, *Les Caractères statistiques du vocabulaire*, Paris 1954.

Poetics is likely to emerge in the framework of structural linguistics broad enough to comprehend phraseological and stylistic analysis. Units of "meaning" are inherent in the linguistic structure, but I have found no promising way of demonstrating this relation between form and content other than the statistical, and especially the concept of selective variation of which it has given the proof the first time, thereby bringing the old question of anomaly and analogy into true focus. Outside of structure there can be neither norm nor departure from it; at the same time "meaning" is structure (which is not to be limited to metrics and diction), and surprise—in a word, anomaly—is the amount of its "in-formation."

ADDENDUM (p. 86)

Since writing this chapter, I have come upon *Memoirs of the American Folklore Society*, Vol. 44, Philadelphia 1954, *Albanian and South Slav[on]ic Oral Epic Poetry*, by Stavro Skendi, from which I note the following evidence:

Not all the oral epic poems are new; there are reproductions and many variants—"the songs of Mujo are sung in tens of variants for every song," and the element of tradition is conspicuous, both in form and in content (p. 23).

There is a remarkable congruity, almost identity, between the Albanian *Halili merr gjakun e Mujit* ("Halili Avenges Mujo") and the Serbian song (of Salja Ugljanin) *Mujo ranjen* ("The Wounded Mujo"), not a matter of direct influence of the Serbian upon the Albanian, but through versions which arose in places where both Albanian and Serbian speakers (or speakers of both languages) lived together; and some of the Albanian songs, especially the Mujo-Halil cycle, are elaborations of the Bosnian "with a strong Albanian imprint," to the degree that they become quite novel songs (pp. 113–116).

Turkish influence also is found in the Albanian oral epic, or Arabic and Persian words (usually transmitted through a Turkish medium); in *Orët e Muji* ("The Fairies and Mujo"), from mountainous northern Albania, the Turkish words are part and

parcel of the Albanian vocabulary and even of the Balkan vocabulary in general (pp. 145–146). Grammatical irregularities
are often ascribed not so much to lack of schooling as to exigen-
cies of meter (p. 154). The evidence of dialect variants is clear
and abundant (pp. 154–157), but there is remarkable agreement
of Albanian and Serbian when the formulaic expression of
proper names and titles appears (p. 186). The subject matter
(as in Homer) may be concerned with events centuries older
than the accepted dating of the poems themselves (p. 198). Who
will speak for "single authorship" here?

IV

Scientific Discourse

ΓΛΩΤΤΑΙ

WHEN Professor MacKay wrote to me in June, 1952, about the subject matter of these lectures he said, among other things: "I have always regretted that Aristotle did not go into more detail and more depth in his linguistic asides in the *Poetics*. Chaotic as the study may have been in his time, a long chapter on γλῶτται, for example, would be a priceless addition to the work." Some ten months later I delivered to my London publisher the manuscript of a book called *Language*, and it had been part of the bargain to provide a glossary for that book. Dipping into treatises on Chemistry or Physics used by my own children, I find that as often as not these books also have glossaries at the end; and I sometimes notice that elementary texts in German or in Greek, and even a guidebook to Haiti published in 1952, are similarly embellished.

Now Aristotle in the *Poetics* (1459a10) declares that heroic poetry finds γλῶτται well adapted to its usage; he repeats this statement in his *Rhetoric* (1406b3), that γλῶτται are especially employed by epic poets. His definition of *gloss* (*Poetics* 1457b2-3) is, however, incomplete; he contrasts γλῶττα with a current word (κύριον), with metaphor, with ornament (κόσμος), with a newly coined word (πεποιημένον), lengthened (ἐπεκτεταμένον), contracted (ὑφῃρημένον), or altered (ἐξηλλαγμένον), and goes on to explain that by a current word he means one in general use in a given language or dialect, by γλῶττα a word in use elsewhere, adding that "plainly, therefore, the same word may be at once γλῶττα and current, but not in relation to the same speakers." In the *Rhetoric* (1404b5) we are admonished that γλῶτται, like compound and coined words, should be used sparingly, since they depart too much from "fitting" (τὸ πρέπον) usage (1406a2), are a cause of "frigidity" (τὸ ψυχρόν) of style, or (surely an unexpected conjunction) are "entirely poetical" (πάντως ποιητικόν, 1406a3), and (1410b2) not being known, as κύρια are, convey no information. I take the remark about excess (πολύ 1406b3) as applying to the διό clause, not to the οἷον clause merely: cf. 1406a3 init. ἂν ᾖ κατακορῆ, . . . ποιεῖ φανερὸν ὅτι ποίησις ἐστίν.

The reason why Aristotle's definition of γλῶττα is incomplete is that while the term as he defines it must imply obsolete words as well as "foreign" words, which he mentions explicitly, Aristotle seems to have excluded, or at least not to have mentioned, the category of words that have become obsolete in all dialects of a language, which obviously need explanation as much as obsolete (in some dialect or dialects, but not in all), archaic, foreign, or dialectal words. The essential characteristic of a *gloss* is often not its meaning (for this may be expressed by some other word or words, as in the very explanation of the gloss), but in its *form*, whether foreign or not; it is an item of vocabulary that is related not at all, or at best only remotely, to any other item in the current usage of the author's public. Γλῶτται are words of more pronounced dignity (σεμνόν) and singularity, independent of ordinary usage (αὔθαδες, *Rhetoric*, 1406b3). This last quality, of self-assertion, willful utterance, reaches an extreme in the γλώσσαις λαλεῖν of New Testament Greek (e.g. Acts 10.46, 19.6; cf. 1 Cor. 12.10, 28, 30; 14.21–22; Mark 16.17; and λαλεῖν ἑτέραις γλώσσαις Acts 2.4, cf. LXX Is.28.11) if, as seems most likely, it means "talk in strange words" rather than "in strange languages," though this interpretation also is held (e.g. by T. E. Page in his commentary on The Acts, London 1886).

A modern instance of willfulness in the use of *glosses* is *Finnegan's Wake*: they are unknown words, and require explanations. Certain *hapax legomena* would surely fall in with the definition, such as Catullus' *ploxenum*, and many of the words of Hipponax, to whom the glossographers, notably Hesychius, pay a good deal of attention; and, in general, words of low frequency

of occurrence and therefore of correspondingly high conspicuousness (see pp. 36, 37 above).

But the quality which Aristotle stresses most in *glosses* is described by the terms ξένος, ξενικός (or τὸ ξενικόν), a term applied
also to style, which thus ceases to be ordinary (e.g. *Rhetoric*
1404b3); but this term is apt to be misunderstood by editors and
translators of Aristotle. It is a quality to be sought (ib.) as excit-
ing admiration; "if a speaker manages well, there will be something ξενικόν about his speech" (1404b6), and τὰ ξένα are appropriate to an emotional speaker (1408b11)—the emotive use of
language, as well as emotional language, being a feature much
stressed by modern students (see my *Language*, chap. vi; *New
World Writing* No. 6, October 1954, pp. 292–293); they also
arouse surprise (1404b3, cf. 1415b7). There is even a hint of the
wonder and pleasure of learning, in particular of linguistic learning, "the worst voluptuousness, which is an hydroptic, immoderate desire of human learning and languages," as of Donne,
the scholar "soul-hydroptic with a sacred thirst" of Browning's
"Grammarian's Funeral" (line 95), something to which we shall
return in chapter viii, and Aristotle's definition well describes
this adjective (*hydroptic*), which we shall consider later in this.

The usual rendering of ξένος, ξενικός, τὸ ξενικόν in the contexts
in which I have cited them is "foreign." But this is not it; "unusual," as if from abroad, out-of-the-way, the opposite of commonplace, of ordinary, plain, or homely, would be better. The
term almost verges upon "anomalous," but "distinctive," which
I have seen ascribed (without reference) to Jebb, is not bad.
Not, indeed, quite in the linguist's sense. This rendering, however, does imply a sound linguistic insight, if not the actual
modern technique; a phoneme is distinctive (not significant),
and similarly morphomes and words are distinctive and are in
fact distinguished by means of distributional operations performed upon crude linguistic data, i.e., by operations which deal
with the *occurrence of parts of the entire flow of speech relative to
one another*. Among these are operations which depend on criteria of differences in meaning as well as on statistical criteria.

Hence came Γλῶσσαι as the title of a work (such as the Ἀττικαὶ
Γλῶσσαι of Philemon of Aixone), collections of *glossae* (with explanations), or γλωσσάριον (a diminutive of γλῶσσα), and eventually *Glossarium* in the sense of "glossary," a meaning ex-
tracted from a misunderstanding of a passage in Aulus Gellius
(18.7.3; see *TLL* 6.2, 2108.66–67).

One of the earliest pieces of work that I undertook on leaving
Cambridge was, at the same time that I was writing the *Prae-
Italic Dialects*, collaboration, under the late W. M. Lindsay's
direction, in the British Academy's edition, the first complete
edition, of the *Glossarium Ansileubi* or *Liber Glossarum* (Paris
1926), being Vol. I of the *Glossaria Latina*). It was the very
driest kind of dust, with only now and again a grain of gold to
encourage us to continue. Six men worked on this task for five
years; it would have been all but one man's lifework, more than
one's, except the most hardy. I also undertook to edit the glossary of Placidus, but fortunately I was able to shelve this after
coming to Harvard, and Lindsay had to find someone else. I had,
however, learnt a good deal about glossaries, and about the way
in which they had grown in antiquity, and during the Middle
Ages.

Homeric γλῶσσαι were not generally understood by the time
the *Iliad* had been formed (another testimony to its long and
complex growth). Appeal was made less to living dialects than
to etymology, which meant largely guesswork. Later the Peri-
patetics fostered study of the vocabulary of natural history (the
sciences); and the Alexandrians, characteristically enough, became preoccupied with all sorts of linguistic oddities—lists of
names of winds, fishes, months of the year in different localities,
or of hard words in certain authors. By the first century B.C.,
independent research had given way to mere compilation. In its
turn, the study of Latin literature led to marginal and inter-
linear interpretations; in some Latin glossaries it is easy to detect batches of words from Terence or Vergil, arranged only in a
crude alphabetical order. The elephantine *Liber Glossarum* (believed to be of the ninth century) is a huge encyclopedia and

dictionary combined, with long extracts from Isidore, Gregory, Ambrose, Jerome, and others. It, like other Latin glossaries, gives (in the lemmata) a large number of rare and many Old Latin words; some textual evidence and occasionally quotations from lost books; a few scraps of genuinely ancient lore; and (in the glosses proper) Late Latin or Early Romance forms.

Finally we should notice bilingual glossaries (Greek into Latin, Latin into Greek); and glossaries with Old English, Old High German, and Keltic lemmata or interpretations. Specialized vocational glossaries, intended to serve the same purpose as modern botanical, medical, and other such dictionaries, or alphabetically arranged handbooks of Engineering or Chemistry or Music and the rest, also make their appearance, and we shall see presently that works of similar scope by modern scholars are by no means rare; or, instead of treatises on (say) the Greek or Latin names of fishes, we find modern specialized works on the vocabulary of some particular author or authors, quite in the ancient style, no matter how changed in detail, accuracy, theory, and procedure. But it was only in fairly recent times that the method of reading and "slipping" authors, as for the *New English Dictionary* or the *Thesaurus Linguae Latinae*, with the purpose of achieving completeness, was evolved and generally practiced. At this point, however, let me quote (with a few trifling changes) from a review of two works on Greek and Latin fish names that I wrote for *Classical Philology* 44, 1949, 209–211:

Scholarship goes round in circles. The compilers of medieval glossaries, misguided enough to be born before the technique of punched cards for retrieving information, were no more widely read than their modern brethren who produce the Brobdingnagian monsters of our day. However, they had their special lexicons of hard words in authors; and they had their modest files of classified names, strung together on a common topic, for example the "index nominum animalium" of Polemius Silvius. Items from suchlike *spicilegia*, once they have been entombed in this or that *thesaurus* are buried forever in the arbitrary arrangement that loses semasiologically as much as it gains alphabetically—except for the well-read, who knew what to look for. The rest are not likely ever to find research made easy by any *thesaurus*. Brains are better than *fiches*, and the Cains who till the horistic ground, foreknowing the curses that will be theirs, would do well to praise the Abels that keep the sheep. The editors of the new Liddell and Scott, at least, deplored the "want of a glossary of the Animal Kingdom"; and the fullest of commentaries, those deserts of footnotes around an oasis of text, smother their fauna and flora as effectively as the dictionaries. The wheel has come the full circle; dictionary and commentary still have occasion for concordance and glossary. Names of plants and animals are among the most defeating, both in definition and etymology. Sir D'Arcy W. Thompson, I need not say, is a natural historian of renown as well as a classical scholar; M. de Saint-Denis goes fishing with his two sons. So both know whereof they speak.

In the present lecture I propose, after this brief, and somewhat dull, historical introduction, to consider first the nature of scientific discourse on a broader and, I hope, more philosophical basis; and then to take up some matters of technical and scientific vocabulary; and, finally, to set forth in a paragraph or two, a theory of *glossai*. First and foremost we need to consider the criteria of what normally constitutes a good symbol (as distinguished from a *gloss*); language, and especially scientific language, being a systematic symbolism. Here I must express my gratitude for a stimulating paper which Professor Chao contributed to the Thirteenth Conference on Science, Philosophy, and Religion, 1952, a copy of which its author was good enough to send to me; as for the Conference itself I add only, first, that it did not publish the paper, and second, that it merits a smart rebuke for its conceit that it can pursue successfully its studies with no, or only the most casual and amateurish, attention to linguistics. Language obviously is fundamental to all its goings-on, and in its meetings of 1954 many contributors talked freely about smoke or the national flag, or the physical universe and the like, as symbols, without producing any specimen of these for study (except perhaps tobacco smoke), but only *words*, of the behavior of which, being largely or totally unaware, they assume they know everything.

Professor Chao begins by observing, and I agree, that symbols are for us "anything that one can produce ['utter'] . . . to
represent [I prefer 'pro-present'] objects for the user, and which
form part of a system," since we "have to do with symbols in
their systematic aspects." Here the first step is identity or differentiation (a recurring symbol is or is not the same) and indi-
viduation, that is, segmentation (an important linguistic technique). The symbols may be extended in space "such as two-
dimensional marks on a surface," or in time "such as spoken
words," the former (e.g. = as a symbol of equality) being the
more convenient, especially for the purpose of making records.
As for Carnap's comment, quoted apparently with approval,
apropos of the complexity of symbols, that to any postulated
longest utterance there may always be added "and the moon is
round," this seems to me a mere quibble, falsified by all experience. Normally there is little difficulty in finding the written
boundaries of a symbol, but some difficulty does arise, for example, in the Homeric δάκρυ χέων (so Leumann, not δακρυχέων),
which was ambiguous enough to give rise to δακρυχέειν "bewail"
in Nonnus; or the better-known κάρη κομόωντες, first systemati-
cally separated into two words in Byzantine times, or αὐλὴ τρὶς
(αὐλητρὶς) πεσοῦσα. But the small blank space of our printed
texts, and the phonemes of transition junctures (like French *un
invalide* : *un nain valide* or English *it swings* : *its wings*) or the
limit of permitted sequences, usually make the matter clear, no
less than the speaker's "Sprachgefühl."

An important observation made by Professor Chao concerns
the substitution of symbols and the necessity of distinguishing
between such substitution and symbolization proper, a confusion into which scientists are not likely to fall, though others
constantly do: for example, in the formula $R = Df^{V/I}$ the symbol R is not the symbol for the symbol V/I, but another symbol
for that which is symbolized by V/I. Now language, as a natural
symbolic system, is pervaded by vagueness, ambiguity, and
generalization, insomuch as the "many-to-many relation is typical." A most striking situation in modern abstract thought is

not to fit symbols to objects, but, the symbolic system having been constructed, as in theoretical physics, to look for a concrete case.

As criteria for "the making of good symbols" I cannot do better than reproduce Professor Chao's list:

1) *Simplicity*, subject to the reservation that there must be a certain degree of complexity for the purposes of discrimination and also some "redundancy." In scientific discourse redundancy is, as would be expected, less than in other forms of discourse, since discrimination is provided in other ways.

2) *Elegance*. This aesthetic quality of symbols is prominent in the dynamic and emotive use of language, as well as in aesthetic discourse as such, manifested chiefly but not solely in poetry and other deliberately cultivated styles; but it is a desirable quality also in informative discourse. Often, however, it is a question of association, whether or not a symbol is "elegant"; *red* of the poet's "red, red rose" has more of aesthetic value than *red* of the "red light district"; again (to quote Professor Chao's own example), *onion* and *rose* differ considerably in associations of elegance, though I cannot follow him in his assertion that the word (or symbol) "onion" is more elegant than "rose," and least of all on the ground that he gives—"as one can tell by pronouncing the words backwards, *zwor* and *naina*." Nearer the mark is his declaration that elegance of symbols counts more structurally—indeed this factor is fundamental.

3) *Ease of utterance and transmission*. This is the principle of economy emphasized by Zipf and Mandelbrot, who maintain that the principle is, as it were, "built into" any linguistic system, which indeed produces its own economy and could hardly function at all otherwise. But again scientific discourse is at least not inferior to other kinds of discourse in satisfying this requirement: in fact it satisfies the requirement constantly by means of the two-dimensional figures of its symbolism, whether in words or in graphs of two variables such as I gave above (at pp. 16, 97-99). Linguistic constructs, whether of morphomes (i.e. morphological) or of words (i.e. syntactic), are usually rep-

resented in serial order; scientific discourse is under the same necessity, not least for purposes of transmission, as when Mathematics (like Music) is taught, or expressed, through the medium of some natural language, that is, in words.

4) *Limitation of size*: a symbol should be neither too brief nor too lengthy. Again we have Zipf's empiric law on the size of linguistic symbols and the relation between size, frequency, and conspicuousness or perspicuity (also a good criterion). A single symbol that is too long is difficult to take in together with the rest of the complex of symbols of which it is merely part. *Antidisestablishmentarianisms* (if the word exists except as an illustrative invention) some people comprehend only with difficulty, or not at all. Aristophanic (and Sanskrit) compounds present the same problem; most of those of Aristophanes are so-called *hapax legomena*, and serve (like Sanskrit compounds) as syntactic constructs, notwithstanding the fact that in form they are morphological. Modern languages have for the most part got rid of this kind of symbol; and those which have not, again for the most part, are out of step with modern life—for example, some American Indian languages, or Eskimo, or the paleo-Siberian languages, in all of which the so-called polysynthetic structure prevails, so that utterances are commonly single units in which adjective, noun, appositional units, and direct object are soldered together along with the main verb and are not analyzable into words in the same way as the English equivalent—elements of expression which to us would be free-standing words never begin an utterance. The clear distinction which standard English, or Greek, or Latin gives of a transition or bridge intervening between the end of one word and the beginning of the next is wanting. A person not trained in Chemistry may get the same impression from the chemical terminology and resort to a glossary. Scientific discourse abounds in γλῶσσαι such as *cryopedology* (not yet in the dictionary, I think); but it is true that such items of scientific vocabulary do not usually disturb the pattern of "standard average western European"; even if they are not ideally good symbols, however, tested by all

possible criteria—what symbol is?—they are good as tested by the criteria of scientific discourse itself, since a new simple symbol such as *cryopedology* may be defined in terms of a series or complex of older simple symbols. As Professor Chao points out, "great discursive systems . . . have been built up" just this way, despite the objection that "too many steps of substitution and [the] possible danger of hypostasis" may become obstacles to intuition and insight into mutual relationship, if the initial simple symbols are too complex or if they offend the criterion of suitable size.

5) The relation between the total number of simple symbols in a system and the size of symbol complexes is, if I mistake not, kept in *balance* automatically in natural languages (Zipf's and Mandelbrot's formulas). But again scientific discourse makes use of languages that are not natural, and it needs, therefore, to keep this relation in balance in its own choices and inventions of symbols.

6) *Clarity of relation* between symbol and referend is an obvious requirement. Scientific discourse, just as obviously, is superior to many other forms of discourse in satisfying this requirement, notably more so than is some modern poetry, not to mention advertising or propaganda. In fact, if there is any risk of failure to satisfy it, the scientist usually takes special pains to show just where the risk lies and to what extent it goes. Similarly, the glossary to a scientific treatise will define its symbols in other, traditional symbols (words); or ostensive definition is provided by experiment and observation. In Professor Chao's words, "a museum of natural history may be regarded as a dictionary" that gives "ostensive definitions."

7) The more closely the *structure of a complex of symbols* agrees with the structure of its referend or referends, the better the symbol. This seems a hard saying. Pushed to an extreme it would seem to mean that the counters or tokens used by human consciousness in arranging the symbol situations the features of which are taken to be those of the universe are words, or symbols derived from words, together with the functions of these,

structurally and semantically; cosmic regularity is pictured in the regularity of the discourse of symbolic logic (or *vice versa*); or, in Bertrand Russell's argument (*Meaning and Truth*, New York 1940, chap. xxv) concerning what, if anything, can be inferred about the structure of the universe from the structure of language—not so simple as it sounds.

Scientific discourse, the more it transcends national languages, comes the nearer to satisfying what is perhaps the most important of all criteria of good symbols, namely, universality, and this without any attempt to concoct an "interlingua" of scientific or other conundrums. Symbols such as *polymer, chromosome, thermal conductivity* are understood by scientists everywhere. A universalized symbolism is, and always has been, a necessary component of even a partly universalized human outlook, as when Greek after the time of Alexander, Latin under the Roman Empire, Arabic since its expansion in the sixth century, the "classical" Chinese of scholars, have bound many millions of minds together. It is not going too far to say that much of the universality of scientific discourse is owed to the fact that its symbols have been drawn so extensively from Greek especially, and from Latin in less degree, not from some modern national language.

In what follows I hope to avoid as much as possible any discussion of phenomenalism or behaviorism or like problems, which are largely irrelevant to a linguistic account of the nature of scientific discourse. Language has to be explained from and through itself, or not at all. This is the reason why modern structural analysis has been so successful. But it is also the reason why an important school of structuralists deny all interest in symbolism; their method breaks down completely when this problem is broached. The method of symbolic logic seems more promising, and its metalanguage to be genuine, not fanciful. But its logistic is still symbolic, not mathematical, and therefore open to some of the objections brought against ordinary discourse.

The mathematical theory of information, well known from

Shannon's now classical theorem, has opened an entirely new approach. This is being carried forward by Mandelbrot and others who show that words, i.e., linguistic symbols, constitute *natural quanta of information*. Phonemes are not symbols, but classes of equivalence of speech sounds; phonematic oppositions are simply coding dichotomies. Morphomes also (except when a morphome is identical with a word) are below the level of effective linguistic symbolism, which presumably matches certain neural or cerebral activities (e.g. discrimination of homonyms, as *rank* adj. and *rank* subst., or *write, wright, rite,* and *right*). Phonemes (or better, allophones), and in some measure letters of the alphabet, and morphomes (except when they are identical with words) are differentiae, i.e., *distinctive*; not symbolic, i.e., significant. As for words, there are some languages in which, it is said, "word" is not a suitable entity for analysis. If this is so, I suggest the term *epilegma* (P. Grenf. 1.37.15, second century B.C., cf. ἐπιλέγω, first recorded in Herodotus, but doubtless older). A word has been defined by Shannon as "a cohesive group of letters with strong internal statistical influences." But this, good as it is in communication theory, will hardly do for our purpose. Words are symbolic entities, vocal or written.

By a *symbol*, as distinguished from a *sign*, I understand (i) a surrogate; (ii) an interpretrand. (i) We speak of mathematical symbols, for example x for any number, x^y for any number multiplied by itself any other number of times, Σ for any sum, and so on; or logical symbols, as "a" or "b" as propositional variables and then "$\bar{a}$" to mean "not a" "$a \vee b$" for "a or b," the symbol ⊃ for implication, as "$a \supset b$" to mean "a implies b." But all these surrogates have one feature in common. There is nothing in the nature of things that gives them the meanings stated; that is something we have given them, by agreement or convention, so that the symbol acquires a certain arbitrary character. This is something quite different from a sign. A sign has a direct relation to its object, like water dripping from the trees as a sign of rain; but the word *rain* (which is not rain, nor a sign of rain) is a symbol of "rain" or "raining." (ii) Qua surrogate, a symbol can be reproduced by the interpreter. Both to the producer and to the interpreter it is something that has an interpretation of its own; but this is a matter of convention between them, usually convention that is learnt by them from others, not invented by them.

Moreover, the order of the symbols is systematic. Take as examples of symbols the English words *table*, or *beer*, or *embryo*, or *drunk*, or *have*, each interpretable by itself. But we do not normally utter the sequence "table and embryo have drunk beer." It is of the essence of symbolism to be systematic; to speak of unsystematic symbolism is to verge upon a contradiction in terms. The sequence just produced is so unsystematic as to symbolize nothing unless incoherence on the producer's part. The same is true at each step; *table* is a symbol, *letab* is not. It is not even necessary to add that *elbat* or *letab* is not a symbol in English, implying that it is, or may be, in some other language. What we have said so far is true of languages, or of a language, as well as of language at large: for every case is a given case when you come to it. To raise the question of system or no-system of a symbol outside its own systematic symbolism is idle. How deep-seated the principle is may be seen by taking the following pairs or groups of Latin words:

saxum "stone," but *sexum* (acc. sg.) "sex," and *sex* "six";
lacus "lake," but *locus* "place";
līquens "clear" but *lĭquens* "fluid," *lŏquens* "speaking," and *lĭquans* "liquifying."

Lucretius, like the ancient atomists, was aware of all this, and fond of it as an illustration of his theories: *ignis* is "fire," which may be had from *lignum* "firewood" by disturbing, or subtracting from, the constituent particles. The principle may be illustrated from the system of any language whatever. It is astonishing how few of the primary units will serve, and how little strain is put upon them by efficient use. Even a child, or even a very dull adult, can easily make this powerful instrument serve all his needs.

Now the theory of selective variation in language, as I had the pleasure of pointing out here in 1951 (the first public announcement), views language as a sequence of symbols purposively produced in such a way that encoding and decoding proceed word by word with economy of effort; and in such a manner that the verbal symbol can be effective both in a given status of language and also historically. Since language is not reproduced biologically, but learnt by imitation, variation is inevitable, which, left to itself, would lead to an excess of variables beyond normal requirements; or, at the other extreme of leveling, would lead to a lack of variables adequate to the symbolic needs of man, i.e., for intelligibility. Selection preserves the equilibrium from excessive variation.

As the incoming message is segmented and recoded, it attains the "conceptual" level by successful matching, or goodness of fit. And this depends in turn upon the equilibrium of statistical structure, as well as upon the principle of least effort. The correspondence of symbol and referent (*significans* and *significatum*) was historically invented in this way, and is maintained among contemporaries in this way. But all linguistic data belong to history, whether a cuneiform tablet baked four millennia ago or a phonographic recording of yesterday afternoon. De Saussure's distinction between synchronic and diachronic grammar is a fiction, albeit a useful and in some contexts a convenient fiction. Any linguistic status, orderly relationships in the data of which we pretend to be able to describe, is *ex hypothesi* a closed system. We say that anything may happen to it; but until an innovation has been accepted into the system, and has modified the system (or not, as the case may be), it cannot be said to be part of the system.

All discourse may be said to feed on its environment, but in scientific discourse the environment includes other languages to an extent that no nonscientific form of discourse ever enjoys, by becoming a parasite on another language or other languages. In its semantic rules or operational definitions, its logical rules, and its analysis of relations between symbols or equations between physical quantities, scientific discourse approaches an optimum of communication in its highly formalized and standardized languages: a *color*, for example, is now presented ultimately as a symbolic construct, a mathematical function of periodic character depending on variables that as coördinates represent the medium of space-time. We may say that scientific discourse is concerned with particular provinces of meaning within which it uses and operates its symbols regardless of commonsense notions of everyday life.

But although scientific discourse is thus a kind of parasite language, still in science language itself is not a part of the content expressed to the degree to which it may be in literature, in which the utterance is involved in itself, and in extreme cases the form is everything and the content very little. In both kinds of discourse, however, the subject matter must be brought into a certain kind of form and order, and these, so long as they remain linguistic, must obey linguistic rules, the chief difference being the predominance of logical order in scientific, and what (for want of a better name) has been called rhetorical order in literary, discourse. What I just called linguistic rules, it must be emphasized, are not rules of grammar imposed from without: they are rules of the language itself, inherent in a language, and governing all its features of arrangements from phonemes to constructs and corresponding meanings, all the units of which (both of form and of meaning) as they appear in the stream of discourse collectively run the entire gamut from complete identity to partial similarity and ultimately to total difference (contrast, opposition).

In both kinds of discourse, scientific and poetic, there is a goodness of "fit." This necessity has long been recognized, and repeated attempts have been made to discover its nature. The rhetoricians speak of relevancy, propriety, affinity, decorum, ornament, and what not? But this is only to define one word by another and leaves unanswered the fundamental question of what constitutes "fitness" or goodness of fit. We shall see that the only concrete measure of fitness is statistical, concerned with

the status and therefore variable from one status of discourse
to another; and that *glossae* (in the technical senses of the term)
arise in direct proportion that there is departure from an ideal
or arbitrary standard of equilibrium. That is to say, the formal
dimension of fitness (contrast, recurrence, variation, equilibrium,
and selection) is in itself both significant and functional.

Oh my offense is X, it smells to heaven.

What is X? Here is an answer from Guy de Maupassant: "Whatever one wishes to say, there is one noun only by which to express it, one verb only to give it life, one adjective only which
will describe it. One must search until one has discovered them,
this noun, this verb, this adjective, and never rest content with
approximations, never resort to trickery, however happy, or to
vulgarisms, in order to dodge the difficulty . . . one must discriminate, and with the utmost lucidity, all the modifications in
the value of a word which are established by the position it occu-
pies in the sentence" (preface to *Pierre et Jean*). It is *le mot juste*
in its proper order. The choice of words in sequence, their functional and significant fit, is a statistical property. It has been
held that in the *Ancient Mariner* of 1798

> Sometimes a-dropping from the sky
>   I heard the Lavrock sing;
> Sometimes all little birds that are,
> How they seem'd to fill the sea and air
>   With their sweet jargoning!

jargoning is less a recollection (*thei songin in their jargoning*)
from the *Romaunt of the Rose* (*lavrock* notwithstanding) than the
one inevitable word in the world. I agree: but how "the one
inevitable word in the world"? The statement is meaningless
except statistically—all other words in this sequence have a
zero probability save this one word, the probability of which
approaches unity, that is, its occurrence is certain. It is also an
exaggeration; the probability (in Coleridge) in that context,
after *Lavrock* ("alauda," not "jest"), is high (·85), higher than

that of other words of the same rhythmical pattern, but it is not unity.

It is a question of linguistic efficiency in the systematization and use of the means available, for formulating patterns of discourse, and, in scientific discourse, for formulating deductions. In ordinary discourse and even in literary form the efficiency is low at the phonematic and morphomatic level, as low as that of internal-combustion engines. But at the syntactic and semantic levels it rises, and the more that scientific discourse is driven toward the formulations of symbolic logic and of mathematics, the more "efficient," in the physical or mechanical sense (of the proportion of output to input), it becomes. Both poetic and scientific discourse, then, are precise, each in its own way, the one in its probabilities of choices (*le mot juste*), the other in logical and mathematical forms. The former has to do chiefly with qualitative, the latter chiefly with quantitative values. Instead of the *red* of the poet's "red, red rose, "or of politics, we have the physicist's wave lengths, frequencies, or Ångstrom units. Even when language chooses to be vague, that is still a formal-semantic characteristic; logical-semantic features appear in the recurrence, at more or less regular intervals, in the manner of the lecture room or textbook, of elements such as "however," "hence," "accordingly," "for example," or "therefore," and these too are formal as well as logical and semantic. Not that the referend of a symbol of scientific discourse must be accessible to sensible demonstration: modern physics has put an end to any such requirement. It is also commonly asserted that scientific discourse is impersonal. But as Bertrand Russell points out (*Human Knowledge*, 1948, pp. 85–86):

One of the aims of both science and common sense is to replace the shifting subjectivity of egocentric particulars by neutral public terms. "I" is replaced by my name, "here" by latitude and longitude, and "now" by date. Suppose I am walking with a friend on a dark night, and we lose touch with each other. He calls out, "Where are you?" and I reply, "Here I am." Science will not accept such language; it will substitute "At 11.32 P.M. on January 30th, 1948, B. R. was at longi-

tude 4° 3′ 29″ W and at latitude 53° 16′ 14″ N." This information is
impersonal: it gives a prescription by which a qualified person who
possesses a sextant and a chronometer, and has the patience to wait
for a sunny day, can determine where I was, which he may proclaim
in the words "Here is where he was." If the matter is of sufficient
importance, say in a trial for murder, this elaborate procedure may be
worth the trouble it involves. But its appearance of complete imper-
sonality is in part deceptive. Four items are involved: my name, the
date, latitude, and longitude. In regard to each of these there is an
element of egocentricity which is concealed by the fact that for most
purposes it has no *practical* importance.

Similarly (p. 258):

The words required in an empirical science are of three sorts. There
are, first, proper names, which usually denote some continuous portion
of space-time; such are "Socrates," "Wales," "the sun." Then there
are words denoting qualities or relations; instances of qualities are
"red," "hot," "loud," and instances of relations are "above," "before," "between." Then there are logical words, such as "or," "not,"
"some," "all."

Analysis of extended discourse in scientific treatises by the
techniques of commutation and substitution, by which many
or all of the linguistic elements of a particular text may be gathered into a restricted number of classes of equivalence, shows
that certain units recur in orders which are by no means disorderly or haphazard. In general, scientific discourse is simpler
to analyze than literary discourse; its orders of arrangements
are less complicated, they recur with greater regularity; on the
other hand, it turns out more frequently in literary discourse
that different morphomes are merely homonyms. Moreover, the
logical characteristics of sentences (for example, analytic, syn-
thetic, contradictory; existential or not) and the logical relations
between them (for example, compatible, deducible, contradictory) are solely dependent upon the syntactical structure (that
is, form) of the sentences.

It is sometimes maintained that two morphomes having different meanings may be presumed to differ at some point in dis-

tribution; and, hence, that any two morphomes having the same distribution have the same meaning. But, however plausible, these contentions are false, because of the equivocations they involve. Thus (cf. D. F. Pears in [*Essays on*] *Logic and Language*, second series, edited by A. G. N. Flew, New York 1953, pp. 113–122) *green* and *red* are different morphomes (and different Ångstrom units), but their distribution is almost entirely identical, that is, as far as a subset of special environments. The subset, however, is of measure zero (such rarities as *green-horn, red-skin*); otherwise there may be found pairs of significant sentences containing *green* and *red* respectively, if we are concerned only with sentence types. The difficulties arise in sentence tokens: then no two morphomes show identical distribution. Hence, with all respect to structural or descriptive linguists, difference of meaning, although not sufficient in itself, is by no means a dispensable condition for difference of distribution. Nevertheless, the differences between the procedures of structural linguistics and of formal logic are matters of emphasis and extent, since both aim at the construction of linguistic systems that correspond, in some measure, with "natural" languages. The linguist judges such a construct by the measure with which it mirrors the "natural" language; the logician judges the "natural" language by the measure with which it approaches an efficient, well-constructed language system. Here we reach scientific discourse—the efficient, well-constructed language system that also satisfies the requirements of formal and logical syntax; and hence, in their turn, of semantic considerations, that is, both of meaning and of reference, which rapidly becomes a matter of taking "all knowledge" for one's province, from astronomy (*morning star* and *evening star* are the same physical entity) to zoölogy (*For death, he taketh all away* is a true statement). But neither the linguist's, nor the poet's, dependence upon others for his facts frees either of them from the duty and responsibility of concerning each himself with both meaning and reference.

Science, then, from astronomy to zoölogy, has its own languages, with their own properties and limitations, and they form only part of the totality of discourse. In each of these varieties of scientific discourse there are exact equivalents to every unit of utterance, on the meaning of which there is general agreement; and the agreement may be verified. Or there are units of utterance in direct opposition (contrast). Moreover, the meaning is independent of features of rhythm, assonance, alliteration, symmetry, rhyme, and the like, which are features of poetic discourse.

In fact, the broadest twofold division is that between scientific and poetic discourse, which leads naturally to a broad classification of choices;[1] namely, in science (S), for example, males over 6 feet in height, or in poetry (P), for example, men to whom the epithet *pius* is applied. A true random choice results in a normal (Gaussian) distribution; that is, when terms are commutable, say *orient* is *east, occident* is *west* in a treatise on geography, but Wordsworth has only

> Once did she hold the gorgeous East in fee,
> And was the safeguard of the West. . . .

We find random choices, or rather the usage of words so chosen, in everyday discourse, but far less in scientific discourse and still less in poetic. A choice S the criterion of which is formulated by scientific discourse is not a random choice, and a choice P does not appear (for example) in the language of mathematics. What

---

[1] See Pius Servien [Coculescu], *Le Choix au Hasard*, Paris 1941; *Principes d'Esthétique*, Paris 1935; *Lyrisme et Structures sonores*, Paris 1930; *Les Rhythmes*, Paris 1930; and, most recently, *Esthétique*, Paris 1953. Coculescu has developed an analysis of Greek lyrics intended to reveal symmetry in their structure, not only of strophe and antistrophe, but also of *cola* and periods. I recall, however, that when I was reading Pindar in my second year at Manchester, an undertaking for which I was not at all prepared, the schemes of J. H. Heinrich Schmidt were still in favor, and baffled me almost as much as Pindar's logaoedic verse. To compare Turyn's *Pindar* (1952) would lead a reader to conclude that colometry has not changed much. But if a scheme commended by Gildersleeve and (in his *Sophocles*) by Jebb, less than a century ago, is now so little regarded, what will become of Coculescu's when less than another century has gone by? In any case, it is generally agreed that symmetry is, or may be, a mark of poetic diction.

astronomer would call the moon "weary" or "joyless" as Shelley did:

> Art thou pale for weariness
> Of climbing heaven, and gazing on the earth,
> Wandering companionless
> Among the stars that have a different birth,
> And ever-changing, like a joyless eye
> That finds no object worth its constancy?

Scientific discourse has some commutables without change of meaning, and thus is in part independent of the phonetic features which carry it; poetic discourse the very opposite, in which choice, an essential human operation, is reflected in the fundamental structure of the utterances and their sequences. Accordingly, what are designated faults in poetic discourse are of two kinds: (1) There are pseudo-faults, which are a violation not of some profound fundamental principle (such as choice itself), but of a rule of meter or of grammar—these vary in frequency from one author and age to another, as Homer and Hipponax or Aristophanes. And (2) there is the true fault of a work which begins, say, as Lucretius' does, with the appropriate choices (sequence of utterance) of an epic—an appeal for the assistance of the gods,—but continues with a dedication (to Memmius) that has a poor fit, and then is given over, for the rest of six books, to an exposition of atomic theory and Epicurean philosophy, with the ludicrous consequence that the proemium itself (of Book 1) is now incomplete, and passes in a line from the invocation of Venus to address Memmius; the initial appeal for the assistance of the gods is doubly inappropriate, that is, both in substance and in form. No apology will ever fit vv. 1–49 (or even 1–43) of Book 1 to the rest of the poem.

   Instead of apology it would be better to discover, if possible, the route, expressed in terms of calculus or rank, by which this result has come about. What operations or mechanisms produced this choice? This question is more searching than considerations of sources, influences, and the like. And if some term such as "sublime" or "beautiful" is applied to a work of literature, to ask in the same way what are the mechanisms, again expressed in terms of experimental method, by which this judgment is reached. As things are, criteria inherited from generations of literary historians, philologists, and grammarians, notably in the matter of metrics, are applied as if they were juridical laws laid down by some body of lawgivers from Parnassus. The problem is not to slice discourse into "feet," but to discover the scientific laws governing the observed phenomena of rhythm, which is not likely to be accomplished by conducting archaeological excavations devoted to unearthing the shears of a second-century metrician, or reducing poetic diction to rules, by which the poet is required to abide if he is to compose correctly in the judgment of modern critics—but on a model already antique to him. We do not imagine that poets began with an abstract theory of rhythm, to which they fitted words; but that they began by practicing rhythms and that, quite late in the practice of them, they discovered their structure, precisely as they had been constrained all along by the structure of the language itself, what it could and what not permit.

I do not believe that there can be a trenchant, all-exclusive, division between scientific and other, in particular poetic, discourse. Even for Aristotle γλῶτται are found in epic (p. 105 above), and on his definition of γλῶτται scientific discourse has such words still more abundantly. But some distinctions, as well as some agreements, may be noted. Scientific discourse starts from observation (protocol or verifiable statements), poetic from choice or selection; the logic of scientific discourse continues with tautologies, that is, secondary statements (cf. von Mises, *Positivism* 1951, p. 114), poetic with involvement. By this I mean that, like mathematics, poetry may continue its structure without ever leaving language, relying upon oppositions as well as equivalents. So does scientific discourse to some extent—definitions, for example, are linguistic equivalents. There is a universality, even a "quasi-translatability," about scientific discourse, which poetry lacks, and if poetic discourse often shows what for want of a better word I may call transcendence, this is matched by the intuitions of science—both are "creative." The features of sonority, rhyme, meter, and the rest, often remarked in poetry, are cultivated, more or less deliberately and consciously; they are almost entirely wanting, or, if present, present more by accident than by design in scientific discourse. Symmetry in physics, a topic about which Curie wrote in 1894 (*Sur la symétrie dans les phénomènes physiques,* reprinted in his collected works, Paris 1908, p. 127), inheres in its subject matter and only by derivation in its language; whereas in poetry it is often the very essence of design, as in Greek lyrics (cf. note 1), the Hebrew psalms, or Welsh *cywyddau.* Coculescu has devised a numerical notation of the sequence of accents according to which he counts the number of syllables as far as the first accented one and then subsequent accented syllables, which appears to indicate more than accidental symmetry, for example in Chateaubriand:

> La *lu*ne bril*lait* au mi*lieu* d'un a*zur* sans *ta*che
> Et sa lu*miè*re gris de *per*le descen*dait*
> Sur la *ci*me indétermi*née* des fo*rêts*

which would go 23332 444 353, a principle of analysis which he applies also to Pindar.

The most recent treatise on structural linguistics, that of Z. S. Harris (Chicago 1951), essentially seeks to set up linguistic elements as logical symbols, upon which the various operations of mathematical logic may be performed. This is a recognized type of scientific discourse, in which the operations are described that must be performed in order to arrive at the significance of this or that item of technical or scientific vocabulary. Poetic diction is concerned more with appraisal than mere designation, and judgment enters the area of assertion; it deals with ensembles, totalities—"the beautiful," for example—of a kind that are not accessible to scientific diction.

But forms of discourse overlap and merge into one another like the colors of the spectrum. There is hardly any type of literature which does not appear both in verse and in prose—

Cato, Varro, Columella, or Palladius treat the same subject as
Hesiod (in the *Works and Days*), and as Vergil (in the *Georgics*);
Parmenides and Xenophanes put their philosophy, and Horace
his poetics, into verse. Prose epics are no novelty. Form and
structure, therefore, not content or subject matter, are the decisive features; the line of cleavage is not between prose and
verse, but between scientific discourse and poetic discourse. As
for subject matter, nothing comes amiss to either kind of discourse; the frame of reference is coextensive with the universe,
and for a given author is never less than that author's entire
environment (which includes *his* language as one of its parts).
Inevitably there is inconsistency of response in the two great
distinctive varieties of discourse, poetic and scientific. The poet
and the scientist may treat of one and the same natural phenomenon, but their treatments differ, and these differences are
inherent in and necessary to all linguistic symbolism. Neither
philosopher, nor poet, nor scientist can dispense with verbal
constructs. Nature is seen and recorded by all three as the structure of events in mutual relations; poet, philosopher, and scientist offer each his own view of the universe, expressed in his own
symbolism. But it is the *linguistic* act that gives literature reality
as part of *our* environment, of the world outside us; and it is
from this point of view that literature is characterized by peculiarities of structure and form. Both a Shakespearean tragedy
and a treatise on relativity have to do with man's realization of
himself in the world in which he lives. The finest achievements
of genius of the very highest order appear in both kinds of expression, aesthetic and intuitive, theoretic and axiomatic-logis-
tic. The creative imagination of a Shakespeare or a Milton, of an
Einstein or a Newton, both demand the total resources of form
and meaning of a language.

   In Coculescu's words, language is the one current that bathes
both scientific and poetic discourse, albeit in different ways. As
a classificatory medium, S gives classifications which proceed
from operations conducted entirely in S-terms (verifiable, logical, and communicable); P gives the rest (e.g. "beautiful" or

"eloquent"), its appeal is aesthetic and it must be felt (by somebody) as a work of art, even if the answer that the percipient gives, when challenged to say why he so feels it, goes no further than the response (otherwise limited, according to the wits, to females) "Because."

Can there be a "science" of aesthetics? There are those who answer "No": for example, Herbert Dingle.[2] He maintains (p. 31) that there are "no commonly accepted premises" for a science of literary criticism, but he cannot have read Coculescu, who has been writing on this and related matters since 1925. Take, he says (pp. 37–38), all the words in the *New English Dictionary*, each twenty times, in combinations of all possible sequences of 250 words more or less (each punctuation counting as one word). The number of passages would be finite, and the task would be performed in a finite period of time. The result would contain all the sonnets that ever have been written in Modern English, together with many others that have not, and "even if we exclude the unintelligible" would be a fit matter for criticism. This, he adds, is beyond all question: the thing could be done, by a machine; "all possible literature could be produced this way."

It is not clear whether by "all possible sequences of 250 words more or less" Dingle really means "all possible" or whether he means those which would be *possible in accordance with permitted English sequences*. From his reservation "even if we exclude the unintelligible," it appears that he means the former. If so, those sequences which do not accord with the pattern of English would certainly have to be excluded as totally irrelevant to the rest of his argument: for intelligibility is precisely this, (1) real English words (nothing like Homer's unintelligible words, the γλῶτται), (2) in patterned sequences, and in such

---

2 *Science and Literary Criticism*, London 1949, not a good book. Nor can I make very much of William Empson's *The Structure of Complex Words*, London 1951, or of his *Seven Types of Ambiguity*, ed. 2, London 1947, which take the opposite side. I should expect the volume of essays, *Aesthetics and Language*, Oxford 1954, under William Elton's editorship (Bousma, Isenberg, Passmore, and Pyle are among the contributors), to be better.

sequences only. The restrictions upon breaking these two rules, as Gerard Manley Hopkins or Lewis Carroll broke them, are severe, and Dingle's machine would, if given absolute freedom of combination, produce more nonsense than sense. The machine would require instruction in permitted, if not favorite, sequences. Dingle holds that since the "literature" could be made by machinery, it has nothing to do with psychology; that therefore "criticism" must be independent of the psychology of authorship. Literary criticism, which is always in danger as now practiced (being impure) of degenerating into mere exchanges of opinion, would, if pure, ignore the author and personal considerations (which on this view are not relevant), and proceed as if its materials actually *were* produced by machinery.

The argument is, I think, partly valid—in its distrust of psychology. But it fails to see that criticism should concern itself with the sequences, the orders of arrangement of the elements, and their mutual relationships, exactly what we did in dealing with Vergil's *pius* and with the *castus* of Catullus; and especially those words and arrangements which, while "legal" or legitimate so to speak—that is to say, do accord with the pattern of the language,—nevertheless show features of selection and variation that distinguish them as characteristic of different kinds and types of writing and even of different writers. A new fragment, for example, of Hipponax, if anonymous, is recognized in just this way. In poetic discourse not information, opinion, or action, but perception and appraisal are foremost. The "beauty of holiness" in the Psalmist (and in Cicero) is not an informative but an aesthetic utterance; it is not a discussion, but a presentation, of a significant intangible—but still an intangible.

One or more than one sequence normally calls for further, but finite, sequences. In the structure of the whole piece, the texture of its fabric, this continuation gives a measure of the degree to which the requirements of pattern—expectancy, satisfaction, failure, surprisal—are met; the mechanisms or linguistic procedures by which they are met; and the features of selection and variation. These are the factors upon which canons of criticism are to be founded, the criteria with which the critics are to operate. Then criticism, being redeemed from hopeless subjectivity, may reach hypotheses and results that will be universally accepted, as are such media of expression in S. It will hardly do to say that in Keats *beauty* is that which Keats loved (i.e., a name for certain units of his *experientia*), for then it becomes necessary to define *love* (according to Descartes, "aimer, c'est trouver son plaisir dans la félicité d'autrui"), and now it is necessary to define *plaisir, félicité*, and so forth. The meaning and validity of P are "inseparably tied up with the literary quality of [the poet's] writing; it needs no less than a poet to express fully and faithfully such fragile [qualities]. How you say it matters even more than what you say," a dictum that recalls Housman's words: "poetry indeed seems to me more physical than intellectual," which is what I mean by saying that it moves the feelings not the fingers, the heart not the head. So we come back to aesthetics, and the problem of finding a scientific, or at least a logical, aesthetics, just as mathematics is the science concerned with logical deduction from the general premises of reasoning, independently of particular subject matter. But both S and P are under the same sort of restriction, imposed by the necessity of using words (so far as S uses words—to some extent at least, combined with other symbols[3] in abstract thought as well as in written or spoken exposition); both have to struggle with words, and both are a form of human creative activity. "And so you morrowed on," wrote Walter de la Mare of a fiftieth birthday—"such a pretty phrase" it has been called, analogy coming to the rescue (like *love : love*, in Old English *lufu : lufian*, whence *stomach : to stomach*, or, in reverse, *write up : a write-up*).

No wonder γλῶσσαι present a problem. I find that I have re-

---

[3] See my *Language*, London and New York 1956, pp. 251–255. The quotation on p. 255 is from Flew, [*Essays on*] *Logic and Language*, second series, New York 1953, pp. 23–24.

viewed, in the last twenty years,[4] a round two score of books, books like Sir D'Arcy Wentworth Thompson's *Glossary of Greek Fishes*, Oxford 1947, mentioned on pp. 109, 110 above, that are preoccupied with the problem in one way or another, and I have on my shelves many others (for example, V. Basanoff, *Evocatio*, Paris 1947). The editors of the revised edition of Liddell and Scott, 1925–1940, recorded in their Preface (pp. vii sq.) special glossaries and dictionaries, in existence, projected, or needed, as indispensable to them if they were to cope with the vocabulary of alchemy, astrology, astronomy, botany, engineering, mathematics, medicine, natural history, tactics, and other technical subjects—all this within one single language; and also the help of specialists which they received in these and other fields, and, in default of such works, from a number of scholars, contributions to the vocabulary of politics, law, administration, philosophy, magic, religion, erotica, and the like. Actually, the treatment of items of vocabulary drawn from these areas—no small

---

[4] For example, Marouzeau, *Traité de Stylistique* (*AJPh* 57, 1936, 207–210); Svennung, *Palladius* (*CP* 33, 1938, 109–112); Löfstedt, *Vermischte Studien* (*CP* 33, 1938, 322–324); Hofmann, *Lateinische Umgangssprache* (*CP* 33, 1938, 320–322); Blomgren, *de serm. Am. Marc.* (*CP* 34, 1939, 74–75); Friedmann, *Ionische und attische Wörter in Altlatein* (*CW* 32, no. 15, 1939, 172–173); Elg, *in Faustum Reiens. studia* (*CP* 34, 1939, 398–399); Kent, *Varro de L. L.* I (*CP* 34, 1939, 379–383), II (*CP* 35, 1940, 82–86, *CJ* 35, no. 6, 1940, 368–369); Erikson, *Sancti Epiphanii interpr.* (*CP* 35, 1940, 318–321); Lejeune, *La Langue des actes d'affranchissement delphiques* (*CP* 36, 1941, 311–312); Norden, *Aus altrömischen Priesterbüchern* (*AJPh* 63, 1941, 225–230); Powers, *Commercial Vocabulary of Early Latin* (*CP* 41, 1946, 125–126); Bonfante, *Elementos populares en la lengua de Horacio* (*CP* 42, 1947, 67–68); Strömberg, *Fischnamen* (*CP* 42, 1947, 134–135); St-Denis, *Vocabulaire des animaux marins en latin classique* (*CP* 44, 1949, 209–211); D'Arcy W. Thompson, *Glossary of Greek Fishes* (*CP* 44, 1949, 209–211); Fournier, *Verbes "dire" en Grecque ancien* (*CP* 44, 1949, 271–272); auot, ieurus, tuθθos (*J. Kelt. Stud.* 1, 1949, 7–10); uimpi (*Language* 25, 1949, 388–391); Gries, *Constancy in Livy's Latinity* (*CP* 45, 1950, 125–126); Hubschmid, *Praeromanica* (*Language* 26, 1950, 298–299); Buck, *Synonyms* (*CP* 46, 1951, 42–45); *Beiträge zur Namenforschung* (*Word* 6, 1951, 239–242); Odelstierna, *Inuidia* (*CW* 45, 1952, 188); Herbig, *fler* (*AJA* 56, 1952, 99); Ernout, *-osus* (*CP* 47, 1952, 126–127); Hubschmid, *Alpenwörter* (*Language* 28, 1952, 268–269); Laroche, *racine* νεμ- (*CP* 47, 1952, 183–184); Löfstedt, *Coniectanea* (*CP* 48, 1953, 127); *Genius Cucullatus* (*Ogam* 5, 1953, 65–66), Newark, *Foreign Words and Phrases in English* (*CP* 49, 1954, 63); Gonda, *ōjas* (*CP* 49, 1954, 204–205); Erkell, *augustus* (*CP* 49, 1954, 207–209); Ronnet, *Demosthenes* (*Erasmus* 8, 1955, 298–299); Ernout, *Aspects du vocabulaire latin* (*CP* 50, 1955, 152). This list includes a few articles; and stops short early in 1955.

part of Greek in their total bulk—are the weakest part of Jones
and McKenzie's revision of Liddell and Scott (I forbear to criticize its etymologies, about which something is said in my reviews of Parts VIII–X, which I undertook for *Classical Philology*
after the death of Paul Shorey: *CP* 32, 1937, 168–170; 33, 1938,
233–236; 37, 1942, 96–98). I await the new Lewis and Short with
considerable interest.

What, for example, were the ἐφέσια γράμματα of antiquity—or
at least since the second century of this era? Liddell and Scott
do not enter the six words recorded by Hesychius and Clement
of Alexandria (see P.-W. 5, 2771–73): αἴσιον, ἄσκιον, δαμναμένευς, κα-
τάσκιον, λίξ, τέτραξ, and there is no agreement about their "meanings" (which we might be able to see in a long enough sequence),
despite the superficial resemblance of these words to Greek. But,
granted that, like the words used in curses, and some of the
words in the formulas of Marcellus of Bordeaux (*DAG* note xxv
Remark), they came to have a magical value, in association especially with the cult of Artemis, the great Diana of the Ephe-
sians (Acts 19.24, 28), any one of them might have come from
Hipponax of Ephesus, who had a fondness for words in -*x*
(μῶλαξ, κόλλιξ, καύηξ: see pp. 76–78 above, βέβροξ [?] cf. ἔβρυζε,
Βέβρυκες, βρύσσος pp. 76–77), and who actually used θρίδαξ and
λίς (p. 78) if not λίξ (for -s : -ξ cf. βέβρος : βέβροξ p. 76,
and μῶλυξ : μῶλυς L.Sc. s.vv.). Are they not γλῶσσαι "strange
words" of an Ephesian brand (γλώσσαις λαλεῖν Acts 19.6, p. 106
above), if not of the Jerusalem variety (ib. 2.4)?

But to return to the aesthetic problem. It is often helpful to
begin with a concrete case. Instead of the poet's rose, let us take
actual roses, a bouquet of Paul's Scarlet, American Beauty, or
Rose of Freedom. The critic calls them "beautiful," not on account of botanical or horticultural reasons S, dealing with the
structure of roses, of which he may have no knowledge; but he
will extol their color or perfume, if asked to tell you why he calls
them beautiful. But the qualities which he extols might equally
well be put in terms of S, instead of the quasi-P words upon
which this admirer of your roses falls back. The color and the

perfume may be perceived as qualities; but what, for example, underlies that intuition of diagnosis which a physician may have and yet be unable to put into the scientific terminology of a textbook of Materia Medica? Is this also a matter of qualitative knowledge, somehow outside "number, the language of science"?

Without conceding that "perfume" is a fit term of literary criticism (p. 26 above), I will admit, with Coculescu, that there is a certain force and fitness in seeking to apply to literary judgment tests comparable, up to a point, to those that are employed to meet the tastes of those who use or purchase perfumes. The precise nature of the sense of smell is, I find, not understood, is in fact the subject of much speculation. It would appear that several characteristic traits exhibited by this sense may be accounted for, without violating basic physical principles, if it is attributed to the inhibition of certain enzymes contained in the olfactory organs: a system of reactions may be supposed to be causally related to the system of olfactory nerve signals, different signals in the nerve fibers being activated as the concentration of a compound is altered; that is, some mechanism is required by which changes in concentration of several active enzymes are converted into distinguishable nerve signals. The effect of some object possessing the quality of odor is then inhibition (of one or more of the enzymes), thus leading, through variation in relative concentrations, to signals in the nerves that respond to the corresponding compounds.

Now so far as scientific discourse is of a restricted kind, of limited range, beyond which S-utterances do not go, a scientific aesthetics must submit itself to similar procedures and limitations. Some substances are odorless, or practically so, others have marked odors, and the perfume industry has to discriminate and evaluate these latter. How? By a succession of choices, or a succession of tests which involve choice. At this point analysis gives the structure of the particular chemical compound concerned in terms S, say, molecular weights. So in literary criticism: first choice and evaluation, then observation of the regularity of structure, order of arrangement, symmetry of the total expression P in terms S (for example, sonority). Spectrographic analysis[5] of poetry, spoken not written, seems likely to reveal, clearly enough, qualitative (and quantitative) features of linguistic structure or form (not content) hitherto inaccessible, even in quantitative terms, terms at least as precise as those of what I find is called "odorimetry" and "olfactometry."

Certainly poetic diction may not be entirely indifferent to features such as meter, rhythm, or rhyme, even if it undertake to deal with some scientific question, say the "light" of the moon, as prosaically as Lucretius (5.575–576)

> lunaque siue notho fertur loca lumine lustrans,
> siue suam proprio iactat de corpore lucem

where the structure is easily analyzed. But there are utterances P in which the smallest variation of the particular feature at issue imports also a change in the total effect, whereas utterances S are indifferent to such changes. Nothing could be simpler than the diction of Donne's *Hymne to Christ:*

> Wilt thou forgive that sinn, where I begunn,
>   W[ch] is my sinn, though it were done before?
> Wilt thou forgive those sinns through w[ch] I runn
>   And doe them still, though still I doe deplore?
>   When thou hast done, thou hast not done,
>   for I have more.
>
> Wilt thou forgive that sinn, by w[ch] I'have wonne
>   Others to sinn, & made my sinn their dore?
> Wilt thou forgive that sinn w[ch] I did shunne
>   A yeare or twoe, but wallowed in a score?
>   When thou hast done, thou hast not done,
>   for I have more.
>
> I have a sinn of feare y[t] when I have spunn
>   My last thred, I shall perish on the shore;
> Sweare by thy self that at my Death, thy Sunn
>   Shall shine as it shines nowe, & heretofore;
>   And having done that, thou hast done,
>   I have noe more.

---

[5] Cf. *Language,* London and New York 1956, pp. 123, 217. As for the analogy from smell compare ἀνθεμώδης, *herbosus, fumosus, citrosa (uestis).* Those who doubt the view of *-osus* here implied should reflect on *uinosus : uinolentus* and *odi* "sense a disgust for, dislike" (not "hate") : *odor.* Cf. *CP* 47, 1952, 126–127.

Its effect depends almost entirely on its poetic form, and especially on the use made of two and only two rhymes.

Now, given criteria by which to classify aesthetic qualities
(beauty and the rest), and the subdivision of, say, n objects
into two groups (those which show a specified quality and those
which do not) by the choice of the critic, we expect to be able to
predict, by the means S thus determined, into which class any
further objects $n + 1, n + 2, \cdots n + x$ will fall. The aim of
aesthetic "research" will thus be to establish its criteria in terms
S, not in terms P as now, a procedure which ends only in an
endless *petitio principii*. The results of choices based upon material or substance P will be studied in accordance with form,
order, or arrangement S. As we shall see (in chapter vii), the
methods best adapted to research of this kind are statistical.

If it is a question of rhythm in Pindar, for example, its aesthetic quality is to be sought not through the arbitrary division
(feet) of traditional metrics, but in the features imposed by the
text itself, in which the actual divisions are made by the *syllaba
anceps*, as it were a punctuation between rhythms but itself outside the rhythm, dividing the ode into strophes, antistrophes,
and epodes, and each of these into cola and verses; in this way
the text exhibits its musical quality. As Gildersleeve puts it
(*Pindar*, New York 1885, p. xlvi), quoting with approval Offen-
bach's remark that music is an algebra, "poetry, like music, is
made up of equations"; and Coculescu claims to find (e.g. in
Ol. 8) a single theme and its inversion. The very physical nature
of rhythm, common to music, instrumental or vocal, to the
dance, and to verse, lends itself the more readily to scientific
treatment; and if initial choices P are subject to occasional
error, as investigation proceeds such error may be eliminated by
the test of correct prediction already indicated above, and
ultimately a scale or graph may be constructed showing the
constant relationship of structure and conspicuousness or any
other chosen quality, in the light of which aesthetic judgment
assumes the role of a systematic relationship between the dimension S and the dimension P. Aesthetics in literary criticism

may thus be defined as observation and deduction S of choice and form P, the study (in discourse S) of orders and arrangement (in discourse P). On a physical basis, spectrography, using the visible speech recorder as a register, is at present the most promising line of attack; structurally and analytically, statistical investigation, which with modern scanning and computing devices is greatly simplified, promises equally well. Both point to the conclusion that in reality the significant units of analysis, in the stream of speech, are neither syllables, nor words, nor phrases, but a sequence of similar, but varying, orders of arrangement in mutual relationships, which as a complex unity convey differentially the import of entire sentences. Descriptive linguistics is likewise concerned with orders of arrangements, and even goes so far as to regard language as a form of activity, independently of meaning. The convergence of these different attacks upon language, which includes poetic as well as scientific and other forms of discourse, is the best possible evidence of their correctness.

The affectivity of features P, as in the sensation of color or of odor, is perhaps—notwithstanding a previous reservation (p. 130 above)—likely to be made more intelligible with the help of a psychological study of aesthetics; but this has nothing to do with the psychology of the author, with whose product—not the man himself—we are primarily concerned. Finally, the old division into prose and verse loses nearly all of its importance, which was never great: a more valid division is into poetic, scientific, and other forms of discourse, with prose or verse as two merely outward types, which any of these forms may assume without let or hindrance.

It must not be supposed, however, that statements of the type S, even those of the most positivistic character, are altogether devoid of implications of the type P. The work of the late Edler Richard von Mises called *Positivism* (Cambridge, Mass. 1951) which I have quoted or referred to more than once, and which I greatly admire—its subtitle is "A Study in Human Understanding,"—has several chapters on subjects which would not usually be considered scientific, such as ethics, religion, art, and poetry.

It is my own conviction that language, pervaded by good order and capable of restoring its own orderliness, as it is, is a very model for a good human society. I am not prepared to go so far as Dr Philipp G. Frank, who maintains that hypotheses of great generality, say of the origin of planetary and galactic systems, are "always made according to the fitness of the hypothesis to be a support of moral or religious creeds that seem desirable to the holder of the hypothesis." But it is not to be denied that any widely accepted picture of the physical universe is usually interpreted as having a symbolic as well as a literal meaning, and that this symbolic meaning is one from which religious or political, ethical and educational, aspirations or doctrines are, or may be, derived by the society which accepts the particular physical theory. Books such as Sir Arthur Eddington's *Philosophy of Physical Science* (New York 1939), *Nature of the Physical World* (London 1928 etc.), *Science and the Unseen World* (London 1929), or Sir James Jeans's *Physics and Philosophy* (New York 1943), have had a strong appeal for intelligent readers during the last decade or so. These works lend support, at least by implication, to the view that the universe is not a dead machine, but a system somehow comparable to human systems, to which it is an ideal, but otherwise meaningless—a view that would have appealed to Plato, and is explicit in Dante's *Divine Comedy*, where the linguistic form is of course P, not S, and where a moral interpretation of physical law is obvious. Or modern theories of the atom are distorted to sustain an argument that, by reducing the amount of matter in the world, physics has purged the world of evil. Or that physical laws are symbols that reveal moral law to men. Copernicus saw in his heliocentric system an analogy with human and divine government. Parallels are drawn, from all over the world, of conceptions of the universe as a well-ordered economy, with rules of nature corresponding to rules of human society, which thus in its turn is pictured as having an "ideal" or "natural" structure like that of the physical universe, the *cosmos* ("order [of things]"). Today moralists are apt to appeal to the prevalent "nondeterministic" theory; or, in dialectical materialism, social doctrine is said to be based on physical analogies, and an accumulated economic drive to change society all at one burst is defended (as a natural law) by comparison with the sudden change of water to vapor when rising temperature reaches the boiling point—this as a "symbol" for rules of human behavior. Logically the argument is poor. Even on the most favorable interpretation we can only say (with Topitsch)[6] that such "procedures generally lead into purely analytical propositions which are either eternal truths" because they are tautological (i.e., disguised definitions), or "eternal problems" because they are self-contradictory.

English poetry for more than a century concerned itself repeatedly with expositions (*P*) of Newton's theories, notably of light and color (that is, the *Opticks*).[7] It is not so well known, however, since his work on quite different subjects is almost entirely still unpublished, that Sir Isaac Newton wrote extensively on chronology, theological doctrine, church ritual, prophetic language, even alchemy. A profound reassessment of Newton's thought may well follow complete publication and full study of these other writings. One of them is said to show that Newton saw a connexion between a prophetic God and the God described in the final Query of the *Opticks*. It is at least certain, however, that Newton himself considered this and related aspects of his thought of equal importance with his scientific thought.

De Quincey distinguished between "literature of power" and "literature of knowledge," in modern terminology more or less the same as the "emotive" and "informative" uses of language. But scientific and poetic discourse may both of them manifest these uses of language. The true distinction is in form and order.

---

[6] "Society, Technology, and Philosophical Reasoning," *Philosophy of Science* 21, 1954, see pp. 295–296.

[7] See Marjorie Hope Nicolson, *Newton Demands the Muse*, Princeton 1946, which, like J. N. D. Bush, *Science and English Poetry*, Cambridge Mass. 1950, is concerned with the poetic treatment of science, not the scientific treatment of poetry.

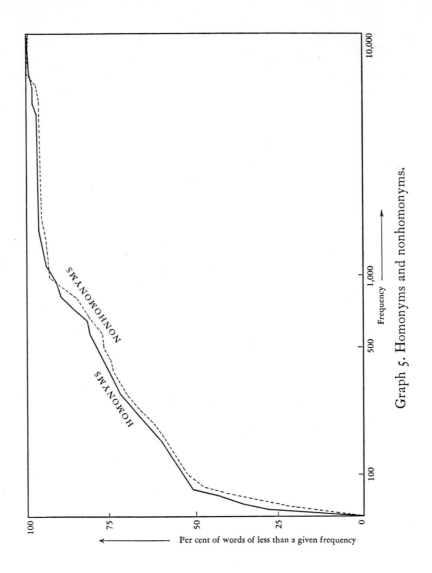

Graph 5. Homonyms and nonhomonyms.

Scientific statements are part of scientific procedure itself, and therefore fall normally into appropriate form and arrangements. Thus, scientific discourse disfavors homonyms, in contrast with poetic discourse; everyday usage has no objection, either. In fact, when punning (which may be good, bad, or indifferent) was considered a legitimate form of wit, homonyms were deliberately cultivated. Nevertheless, in certain examples the conflict of homonyms in everyday English has been held to operate to such a degree as to lead to the displacement of a word by a synonym, or at least to limit the use of homonyms, or to differentiations by means of change in form, great as the actual degree of tolerance is. Thus *let* "to hinder" is believed, even by linguists, to be comparatively infrequent; and words that are homonymous with taboo words, it is said, tend to be avoided, or the taboo word itself to fade and disappear. The best principle, however, on which to proceed is the well-established generalization that the measure of conspicuousness of any word is inversely proportional to its frequency of occurrence. Now homonyms have arisen in part from changes in form or pronunciation, especially where monosyllables result; English has, in fact, about four times as many monosyllabic as polysyllabic homonyms. The total number of homonyms is high; but random samples (based on the words in Webster's *Collegiate Dictionary*), reducing the total bulk to one-tenth, afford representative evidence. For example, *sash* has the meaning "scarf" in 66.7 per cent of its occurrences, "window frame," 33.3 per cent. The question is not considered here of separating words (*a*) in which divergent meaning has produced what are regarded (say by the makers of dictionaries) as homonyms from an etymologically unique source; and (*b*) words originally distinct in form or etymology or both, which have become homonymous through phonematic substitution or morphomatic development. Current usage is the criterion. General figures—the average and the median—show no distinction in frequency of occurrence between homonyms and other words. But more discriminating distribution, in a graph, does reveal significant differences; yet these are less than purely objective observations and opinions had maintained.[8] The conclusion is that in English no serious discrimination is made against homonyms as such: the total environment of a homonym in the stream of speech, and the mutual relations of the constituent items in the environment,

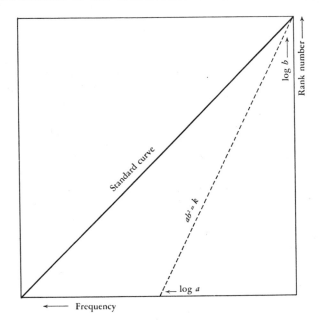

Graph 6. Monosyllabic negative particles in Old French (p. 144).

protect the homonym. There seems to be little awareness of homonyms except in such sequences as those in which equivocalness creates a pun.

A different problem arises in connexion with the development of an auxiliary monosyllabic negative particle where previously there was no negative meaning at all, such as French *pas* (and its synonym *point*). This is a phenomenon of some semantic

[8] Marjorie J. Hill, "The Tolerance of Homonyms in English" (Radcliffe honors thesis in Linguistics, 1953). As for English poetic diction, see Robert Bridges, S. P. E. Tract no. 11, Oxford 1919.

interest; we all recall Agnes Rogers' classic "Lines to a Daughter —Any Daughter":

> One of the things that you really should know
> Is when to say "yes" and when to say "no."
> There aren't any textbooks, there aren't many rules,
> The subject's neglected in orthodox schools.
> You can't be consistent; there's often a reason
> For changing your mind with a change in the season.
> You may be quite right in accepting at seven
> Suggestions you'd better refuse at eleven.
> Perhaps you'll consider these tentative hints:
> "No" to a dirndl of highly glazed chintz,
> "Yes" to the bashful young man at the dance,
> "No" to the man who's been living in France,
> "Yes" to a walk in the park in the rain,
> "Yes" if he asks for a chance to explain,
> "No" to all slacks unless you're too thin,
> "No" to that impulse to telephone him,
> "Yes" to a baby and "no" to a bore,
> "No" if you're asked if you've heard it before,
> "Yes" to a Saturday, "no" to a Monday,
> "Yes" to a salad and "no" to a sundae,
> "Yes" to a stranger (but use some discretion),
> "No" to three cocktails in rapid succession,
> "No" if he's misunderstood by his wife,
> "Yes" if you want it the rest of your life.
> Remember, my darling, careers and caresses
> Depend on your choices of "noes" and of "yesses"

or the ribald jokes about the distinction between a diplomat and a lady in *their* use of "noes" and "yesses." In any event, usually the contrast between Yes (1) and No (0) is considered to be trenchant.

But statistical method again is enlightening. The numbers given below are based upon an examination of the negatives in the poetic diction of the *Chanson de Roland*.[9] Here it is the law

---

[9] Robert G. Funke, "Determinacy in the Development of a Monosyllabic Negative Auxiliary Particle in French" (Harvard honors thesis in Linguistics, 1954).

of abbreviation which prevails: this says that the length of a word bears an inverse relationship (not necessarily proportionate) to its relative frequency of occurrence; for example, laboratory workers having frequent occasion to use the concept designated *laboratory* habitually shorten the word to *lab*. A corollary to the law is that where a choice is possible between two synonymous locutions, the choice is found likely to have been made, *ceteris paribus*, automatically in a way that accords with a correlative scale of word frequencies and word lengths prevalent at the time in the language. In other words, it was not mere chance that established *pas* and *point* as negatives in preference to *goutte* and *mie* (both of which were dissyllabic in Old French); or, if we stay within the text of the *Chanson de Roland*, which has neither *pont* nor *goutte*, *pas* in preference to *mie*. If *a* is the number of words of a given frequency, and *b* the given frequency of occurrence, then $ab^2 = k$, where k is constant (excepting only the few most frequently used words).

When we examine the status of *ne* in regard to the ab^2 distribution, we find k out of equilibrium (in Old French) if context be disregarded; but taken in those contexts in which in modern French *ne* would be followed by *pas*, k is in equilibrium. In other words, a differentiating context, in the shape of an auxiliary particle, was an inevitable development; *ne* has become a "fractional" or "subunitary" word, the status of which, imaginary or even absurd as it seems on superficial examination, is best appreciated in the light of an important concept of modern "information theory," viz., redundancy. A unit of information is said to be redundant if it is more complex than is necessary to convey the message (i.e., contains superfluous features); "information" is the ratio of the probability of making the "right" choice from a repertory (after the transmission of the message) to the probability of making the "right" choice without any such message (i.e., it has to do with unexpectedness, what was called "surprisal" above, pp. 103, 130). A completely economical system, from which all redundancy has been removed, is undesirable and not even possible (except theoretically); in fact, all

languages are redundant (the redundancy of English is estimated at about 50 per cent). In a system entirely devoid of
redundancy, the slightest amount of "noise" or interference
would cause so serious a loss in the transmission as to destroy
or at least seriously to impair the message. Only a limited number of discriminations (out of all that are furnished) is actually
called for, except to overcome "noise"; the listener's choice
among these is assisted by the redundancy, and thus communication becomes a reasonably satisfactory undertaking.

Consider, for example, a noun used infrequently outside
scientific discourse, *laboratory* (cf. p. 144 above). In scientific
discourse its frequency increases, its unexpectedness ("information") decreases. It might have been predicted that its length
would decrease also, that is, that the word would be abbreviated
(*lab*). The redundancy of the morphomatic pattern is greater
than the "information" conveyed, as is clear from the fact that
communication is not interrupted by this innovation. In the
reverse case that we are considering, too brief or ambiguous a
form (*ne*), being subunitary, is expanded or increased in size.

The relative frequencies of the segments of a discontinuous
sequence *ne . . . pas* (*point*) have a direct relation to their respective redundancy, and an inverse relation to the amount of information which each element or segment conveys. Hence for Latin
non we now have not *ne* alone, but *ne . . . pas* (*point*). In the
diction of the *Chanson de Roland* (which has *ne . . . mie*, as well
as *nen* and *ne, n'*) the practice of adding an element of context
(*pas* or *mie*) to *ne(n)* had not progressed far enough to be uni-
form or universal. The high frequency of occurrence of *ne* (without . . . *pas, mie, guant*) gives k a value that indicates the reduction of *ne* to subunitary status. This is intolerable in view of the
high economy of the form as compared with the low redundancy
of the concept. (It is of some interest that Latin *non* arose in
exactly the same way from **ne oinom* "not one.") Still later, the
use of *pas* spread at the expense of the dissyllabic *mie*.

The particular variety of γλῶσσα known as the *hapax legomenon* I shall illustrate, briefly, and without discussion, from

Old English poetic diction. Of the 1,886 separate words, which have 168,500 (more or less) occurrences as they appear in the 30,000 (more or less) verse pairs of the Old English poetical corpus, 238 words occur once only; and of these actually one-tenth are distinctively "foreign" (ξενικά, to use Aristotle's term), e.g. *culpe* "fault," *mynster* "monastery," *port* "market town," and *wermód* "vermouth" (cf. *DAG* 158 *briginus* or *bricumus*, 178 *aloxinum*, 246 *exacum*, as well as note xxvii *gontaurion*).

Already this chapter has become too long. It was my intention to deal in some detail with the discourse *S* of representative Greek and Latin writers (Dioscorides, Theophrastus, Galen, Hippocrates, Archimedes; Cato, Varro, Columella, Vitruvius, Palladius, Celsus, and others in the Corpus Medicorum Latin-orum, the Mulomedicina Chironis, Anthimus). As it is, I must be content to offer three examples only of ancient scientific dis-course, one mathematical and physical, one medical, and one zoölogical.

A) In Archimedes there are several allusions to problems known as νεύσεις, which is also the title of a lost work by Apol-lonius of Perga. The term νεῦσις (: νεύω) must be distinguished from its homonym νεῦσις (: νέω). As a mathematical term[10] it refers to problems of which the two following are particular cases of the general form of the problem:

1) "Two lines being given in position, to place between them a straight line given in length and verging (νεύειν) towards a given point."

2) "If there be given in position (*a*) a semicircle and a straight line at right angles to the base, or (*b*) two semicircles with their bases in a straight line, to place between the two lines a straight line given in length and verging towards a corner [γωνία, also 'angle'] of the semicircle."

Thus there are two requirements: that the straight line re-quired to be laid across two lines or curves must pass through a given point, and that the intercept on the line must be of a given length. Neither the Greek νεῦσις nor its Latin translation

---

[10] See Sir Thomas L. Heath, ed., *The Works of Archimedes*, Cambridge 1897, chap. v.

inclinatio states the second requirement; this is stated only in the particular problems, for example:

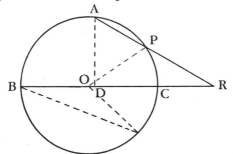

If A be any point on a circle and BC any diameter, to draw through A a straight line meeting the circle again in P and BC produced in R, such that the intercept PR is equal to any given length.

The νεῦσις, which evidently has to do with the angle ARB, though solved mechanically at a later date by means of the conchoid of Nicomedes, is not capable of solution by means of the straight line and circle alone. Let x represent the length OR, where O is the middle point of BC; let k be the given length to which PR is to be equal; and let $OD = a$, $AD = b$, $BC = 2c$. Then

$$AR \cdot RP = BR \cdot RC,$$

therefore $k \sqrt{b^2 + (x - a)^2} = x^2 - c^2$. Now denote AR by y, and we have

$$y^2 = (x - a)^2 + b^2$$
$$ky = x^2 - c^2$$

and the values of x and y satisfying the conditions of the problem can be determined. In the special case in which the intercept PR is equal to the radius OP, the arc AB is three times the arc PC; thus the trisection of an angle is reduced to a νεῦσις, and in fact the intercept of given length may, generally stated, be between two lines *or curves*, or between a curve and a straight line.

Νεῦσις is, therefore, an appropriate, though inadequate, term to describe the mathematical problems concerned, from its more literal meanings of "inclination" or "tendency" of physical forces to or from a center (as in the work ascribed to Timaeus of Locri), and "gravitation" (as in Plutarch). For, in his work *On Spirals*, Archimedes deals with problems of "solid" distinguished from "plane" or "linear" νεύσεις, and νεύειν ἐπί ("verge to") is the verb which he regularly uses (e.g. Proposition 8).

It is impossible to show that the philosophical doctrine of κίνησις κατὰ παρέγκλισιν had any basis in an analogy drawn from physics or mechanics. But it is striking that the Latin *inclinatio* is the equivalent not only of the mathematical term νεῦσις, but also (with *declinatio*, and in Lucretius *clinamen* and *momen*) of the παρέγκλισις of Epicurus; and it has been held that if Epicurus had had but part of the geometrical knowledge of his contemporaries, such as Euclid, and conceptions of cosmography current in his own day, he might have framed a mechanical theory of universal gravitation. We should remember also that Epicurus, in devising his theory of κίνησις κατὰ παρέγκλισιν, was seeking an explanation and justification of his doctrine of free-will. This alone made νεῦσις almost as little suitable a term for his purpose in Greek as *numen* ("divine nod," i.e., assent) would have been in Latin.

B) To the argument that motion is a mere exchange of place between two objects, Lucretius retorts (1.372–374) that, for example, neither a fish nor water (*liquidas uias*, Homer's ὑγρὰ κέλευθα) could begin to move if there were no void. The phenomenon of "dead water," in which the headway of a small ship is unaccountably arrested, was explained scientifically for the first time in 1906; the ancients believed that the vessel was held by a fish, called ἐχενηΐς, a name applied also to the lamprey,[11] in Anthimus *naupreda*. This is one of the γλῶσσαι explained by Polemius Silvius in his list of names of fishes. It is surely mere accident that the Gaulish word for nine (*nau-* in *nau-metos*) and the German name for the lamprey, viz. *Neunauge*, seem to confirm each other, so that *naupreda* has mistakenly (see *DAG* 178)

---

[11] Sir D'Arcy W. Thompson, *Glossary of Greek Fishes*, Oxford 1947, pp. 67–70, 162–165.

been considered a Gaulish word. If I mistake not, it is simply a translation of ἐχενηΐs, a compound of the same type as *nau-fragus, homi-cida*. The *n-* (for *l-*) of Anthimus is due to a popular etymology, influenced perhaps by ναυκράτηs (cf. G. M. Messing, *CP* 37, 1942, 155).

C) I come now, and last, to the medical term. In his edition of the poems of John Donne (Oxford 1933, p. xxix) Grierson quotes (without reference) from a letter of Donne ("after 1601") in which the poet speaks of "the worst voluptuousness, which is an hydroptic, immoderate desire of human learning and languages; beautiful ornaments to great fortunes; but mine needed an occupation and a course, which I thought I had entered well into when I submitted myself to such a service as I thought might have employed these poor advantages which I had." The *New English Dictionary* (s.v. *hydroptic*) refers this apparently to a letter of 1631, viz. no. 51 in the edition of 1651, but the reference is incorrect. Moreover, in Izaak Walton's Life of Donne (1640) there appears (p. 22, in a reprint of 1903, New York) a different text: "the worst voluptuousness, an hydroptic immoderate desire of humane learning and languages: beautiful ornaments indeed to men of great fortunes, but mine was grown so low as to need an occupation; which I thought I entered well into, when I submitted myself to such a service as I thought might exercise my poor abilities." Perhaps the letter was to Walton himself; and Donne may have written in much the same words to two different friends. Unless an original or originals can be found, the text must remain in doubt. The interest lies in the word *hydroptic* "swollen" (not, I think, "insatiate"), which was picked up by Browning, who must have had Donne's letter in mind when in the "Grammarian's Funeral" he wrote the lines (95–96):

> He (soul-hydroptic with a sacred thirst)
> Sucked at the flagon.

We are reminded of Aristotle's pronouncement (*Rhetoric* 3.2.3, 1404b) that a distinctive (ξένη) air must be given to discourse (διάλεκτος), since people wonder at what is remote, and all that is wonderful is agreeable (cf. *Rhetoric* 1.11.21, 1371a on the wonder and pleasure of learning). The reverse is Horace's (*Epist.* 1.6.1–2)

> Nil admirari prope res est una, Numici,
> Solaque quae possit facere et seruare beatum,

the μὴ θαυμάζειν of the philosophers (Horace can hardly have had in mind, like Lucilius, some Tappo who took *omnia* for *monstra*, Catullus 104.4), more cynically echoed by Pope (ed. Ward 1924, p. 300):

> Not to admire, is all the Art I know,
> "To make men happy, and to keep them so."
> (Plain truth, dear Murray, needs no flow'rs of speech,
> So take it in the very words of Creech.)

The form ὕδρωψ "dropsy" and ὑδρώψ "dropsical person" is of obscure formation. That it contains ὕδωρ "water" is not to be doubted; but so does ὕδρος (p. 74 above), and the derivative local name *Hydrea*, the island which Byron calls *Hydra* in "The Curse of Minerva," and *Idra* in *The Corsair*; but ὑγρός (in Homer's ὑγρὰ κέλευθα, p. 148 above, for example) is commonly supposed not to be related, though I see no reason why u̯ed- and u̯egu̯, both of the pattern Cu̯C, should not have d : gu̯ in alternation much as ὕδωρ (-ατος) itself has r : n—and both u̯egu̯ and u̯ed- are attested independently outside of Greek, no less than u̯es- and u̯er-, all with the same range of meaning ("wet, water"). The simplest account of -ωψ is to suppose that it is ὤψ (ὠπός) "face, appearance," but this is by no means certain (Schwyzer 1, p. 426). It was not Attic, which had ὕδερος, the form preferred by Galen, but a *koine* form,[12] and there are other variants in the sense of "dropsical" (ὑδεριώδης, ὑδερώδης, ὑδερικός, ὑδρωπικός, ὑδατώδης), while ὕδρωψ εἰς ἀμίδα (Galen) means "diabetes." Other terms are ὑποσαρκίδιον (v.l. ἐπι-) or ὑπόσαρκα (glossed *hydropicus*) ἀνὰ, σάρκα, and κατὰ σάρκα for varieties (not a cause) of dropsy. In

---

[12] Wilhelm Herbst, *Galeni Pergameni de Atticissantium studiis testimonia*, Leipzig 1911.

English *hydrop(t)ic* is a learned form, *dropsy* and *dropsical* come through Old French.

All three of these items νεῦσις, *naupreda*, and ὕδρωψ, like some of the words in Hipponax and Catullus, satisfy our definition of *glossa*. The first is inadequate and a homonym, the second deformed by popular etymology, the third a dialect form with a variety of synonyms; some other words considered in this chapter are *hapax legomena*, or newly invented, or words of higher importance (αὐθαδές) and dignity (σεμνόν). But in many of these respects we are confronted with an excess of variables, which constitute "noise" in the system just as much as anomalous features. Nevertheless all "natural" languages have a measure of "noise"; scientific discourse, the more it departs from "natural" language and resorts to its own special kinds of symbolism, especially the more mathematical it becomes, the less "noise" it exhibits. Its inhibitions, as compared with literary discourse, reduce the amount of "noise," and at the same time lower the amount of compensating redundancy.

"Noise," in the sense in which we have been using the term, covers any phenomenon which transforms the message in an unpredictable manner (like γλῶσσαι) and therefore produces a change of probability. The fraction of "information" that is modified (per unit equivocation) must fall within a measurable degree of tolerance; there is a compromise effected between perfect transmission and total unintelligibility. It is redundancy which is the effective agent in achieving this end. The units of utterance are not independent of one another; hence the alternatives among which the receiver of a message ultimately must choose are fewer than those actually presented to his attention, if he attended to all of them. By this means the message is able to resist distortion, and there is far more effective communication than otherwise would be possible.

Redundancy may be either too high, as in Basic English; or too low, as in James Joyce's *Finnegan's Wake*. These are extreme cases; but even the most casual observer would find Basic English unsatisfactory as a vehicle of English literature. The deficiencies of *Finnegan's Wake* are equally obvious, even to a learned reader. Poetic and scientific discourse stand nearer the golden middle way. These observations, as well as some of the theory of γλῶσσαι already set forth, are inspired by recent statistical study of language, which recognizes two processes, both statistical, at work: the source and the "noise." Equivocation is regarded as a conditional entropy and measures the ambiguity of any part of the message. Scientific discourse reduces uncertainty to a minimum; poetic discourse actually gains from a certain amount of uncertainty—it is as if payment were taken for the other features of its discourse by the exaction of just that much uncertainty. But the message is reconstructed from the mutual relationships of the units in the message, from the context. It might even be maintained that the sequences of poetic discourse are not too far removed from "random" selection (the term "random" being used in the statistical sense)— that is, not haphazard, but a selection that accurately reflects the character of the parent population). But the presence of "noise," the unexpected and unpredictable features of poetic discourse, increases the "information" or freedom of choice. The received signals in the message are selected from a more varied set, and "uncertainty which arises by virtue of freedom of choice on the part of the sender of a message is desirable uncertainty." That is why we prefer Shakespeare to Cibber.

V

A Byron Legend

Style and Authenticity

LIKE SOME of the stories of wide circulation told by Albanian and South Slavonic singers, that of the legendary character Don Juan has found currency, in Europe alone, from Iceland to the Azores and from Spain to Russia. Pushkin, as well as Byron, has a poem *Don Juan*. But Byron's shows more originality, and has little kinship, other than its title, with the tradition of a profligate who invites a dead man to dine with him and finds his invitation accepted—a theme said to have been current before 1630, the year in which it first appears in literature in a play printed at Barcelona. The *Don Juan* of Byron, during its author's lifetime, had a career as turbulent as Byron's own, and the merits and demerits (depending on the critic) of both poet and poem have been as hotly debated, of the one as of the other. Byron, among other grounds of interest to me, at his best satisfies most of my criteria, both of good symbolism and of form and structure: this including what the critics call being "slipshod." His *Don Juan*, as every schoolboy knows, has embedded in the third canto the famous lyric

I.

The Isles of Greece, the Isles of Greece!
  Where burning Sappho loved and sung,
Where grew the arts of War and Peace,
  Where Delos rose, and Phoebus sprung.
Eternal summer gilds them yet,
But all, except their Sun, is set.

10.

You have the Pyrrhic dance as yet,
    Where is the Pyrrhic phalanx gone?
Of two such lessons, why forget
    The nobler and the manlier one?
You have the letters Cadmus gave—
Think ye he meant them for a slave?

14.

Trust not for freedom to the Franks—
    They have a king who buys and sells:
In native swords, and native ranks,
    The only hope of courage dwells:
But Turkish force, and Latin fraud,
Would break your shield, however broad.

As every schoolboy knows; for Henley included it in his "Book of Verse for Boys" (London 1891 etc.), *Lyra Heroica*, which I read in the fourth form, when I was made to learn the entire poem by heart.

It is by no means the only one of Byron's writings that is instinct with his love of Greece, the Greece of old and the Greece chafing to throw off the Turkish yoke, or that endears him, or should endear him, to every student of Classical literature, Greek in particular. "Byron and Greece" is the title of a sizable volume by Harold Spender (London 1924) in which were collected, in the centenary year of Byron's death, "the passages both of prose and verse—poems and letters—in which Lord Byron gave form and expression to that passion for Greece which he sealed with his death on 19 April 1824." Another large volume might well have exhibited the passages in which Byron shows how deeply, with all his brilliant originality, he had absorbed and remembered Greek and Latin literature, if not from his Harrow and Cambridge days, then from his own wide reading, which included also modern literatures. The fact is so apparent to any reader of Byron that it need not be labored.

George Gordon Noel, Lord Byron, with his four names (one

of them given, two inherited, and one acquired from his wife's family), would not be distinguished on that ground nowadays, unless possibly in the United States, where three is the rule, or in those societies (e.g. American Indian) in which individual names are somewhat like our nicknames and draw attention to individual peculiarities or achievements. But the matter of proper names, and especially personal names, deserves some consideration apropos of the Byron legend that I am about to relate. "I would rather make my name than inherit it," Thackeray makes one of his characters say in *The Virginians*, appropriately enough at the beginning of a new nation in a new world, and Thackeray was thinking more of titles than of names as such. Still, it is a fact that most of us, at least nowadays, and often enough in times past, do in effect inherit our names, whatever we may add to them by way of making the name a name to be remembered. And people who go in for investigating the past of the families from which they come, hoping to find some very distinguished ancestor, like people who go in for acquiring heraldic arms, are apt at times to discover things not altogether to their liking.

Names are rather like integuments. To lose your name is as bad as to lose your clothing. We all remember the example of the French President (Deschanel) in the early 'twenties who opened the wrong door of his Pullman car in the nighttime and stepped out of the train instead of stepping into his bedroom. The train fortunately was going very slowly, but still, there he was; it had got past him, and there was no other open door by which he might reënter it. He walked, not unnaturally, to the nearest farmhouse and announced himself as the President. "Nonsense, impossible," said the farmer, "the President of France wears a tailcoat and striped trousers. You cannot possibly be the President of France."

At any rate, names do serve to identify. And for the most part a single name may be enough. But for many purposes, even of daily life, it is by no means enough. What would the mailman do if letters were addressed by a single given name? Nevertheless, it is true that in small and compact societies a single name is often enough, even when rather lengthy. And the compound name of which the North American is so fond is fundamentally and essentially a single name. In the Old Testament, single names are usual: Abraham, Moses, Cain, Abel, and so back to Adam and Eve as well as downwards to Job and other outstanding figures, David and Saul for example. But in the New Testament already things are beginning to look a little different. James is not enough—it is James the son of Zebedee, to distinguish him from the other Jameses; and so with the rest of them. In the New Testament the taxgatherer plays a somewhat conspicuous role. "Render unto Caesar the things that are Caesar's." There was also the census taker.

In the Ancient Mediterranean the situation is not unlike that of the Old Testament until such times as larger communities were organized, and conspicuously under the Roman Empire, when the census taker and the taxgatherer are prominent. Greek names are very frequently single names—Aristophanes, Plato, Socrates, Aeschylus—but not always so. It is Demosthenes the son of Demosthenes. In addition to his father's name, the name of the deme is frequently added, and sometimes also the name of his city. This is true also of the Roman name. Cicero is not merely Cicero, he is Marcus Cicero, he is even Marcus Tullius Cicero. Marcus is his name, qua name, the given name; Tullius is his family name, and the first Tullius was actually the son of Tullus; Cicero is an added name, a cognomen—indeed a nickname in the first instance. Additional cognomina may appear, and a tribal name.

But with the Middle Ages the elaborate system of nomenclature, as it had persisted under the Empire, broke down. The disorganization that followed the time of migrations, and all the confusion that came with it, put officials like the taxgatherer and the census taker into the background, and people were content with single names. They needed no more. However, with the rise of the great mercantile states of the late Middle Ages and the early Renaissance, and with feudal establishments, it became necessary once more to distinguish individuals precisely. Yet there have been some curious survivals, even into modern times, of something which is not a real family name. In Scandinavian countries, until quite recently, it was the habit to call a man by his own name, then adding his father's name with some appendage meaning "son" added, with the consequence that after three or four generations the patronymic would differ in each case, and it becomes quite impossible to trace descent without explicit and full details. This procedure has had to be abandoned in favor of an arrangement quite similar to that of other European countries.

Or, again, it may be that there is a real lack of distinctive family names. I remember from my Bangor days how, in Caernarvonshire, where the Williams clan, not the Jones, is the more numerous, the number of John Williamses we had at the University College of North Wales was so large that the Registrar's office developed the practice of distinguishing them by inserting a middle name, usually the name of the village from which the man came—for example John Garmon Williams, or John Llanfair Williams. Unless there is a very considerable variety, not only of family names, but also of given names on which to draw, there is a tendency to use a third or a fourth name, and even more than four names, especially in aristocratic or would-be aristocratic circles.[1]

Very different from the sixth Lord Byron was a contemporary, a woman called Ailse o' Fussers (a quasi-patronymic nickname),

---

[1] A writer in *The New Yorker*, 28 March 1942, makes sport of the practice:

"Whenever," he writes, "I read an English work of fiction containing American characters, I am saddened and embarrassed by the sort of names the authors choose to give them. . . . Well, after a recent trip through [an English onomasticon], I can prove that the English are in no position to talk about funny names. . . .

"Such names as John Frederick Drughorn, Edward W. Billyard-Leake, Wilfrid C. Dumble, Thomas Blatherwick, and Christopher Bromhead Birdwood will serve as introductory examples, but they are really very mild.

"There are some names which I am convinced are not even real; they must have been lifted out of Dickens. Take, for instance, Coventry Dick Peddie, Ernest Tom Neathercoat, Rita Francis Mosscockle, and Richard Deare Furley Oldman. . . .

"Quite a few British names have to do with legs and feet. I came across Percy Joseph Sillitoe and Percy Joseph Shrubsole, and was beginning to wonder whether all such who used to haul coal in sacks from Lord Byron's coal mines on his Manor of Rochdale in Lancashire, the moneys from the sale of which Byron devoted to the cause of Greek Independence in 1823. The municipal borough of Rochdale, my birthplace, was incorporated in 1856, but there is still a Lord of the Manor of Rochdale, whose claim is based on land tenure. This estate was held from 1462 to 1823, at first by lease from the Crown and eventually through purchase, by the Byrons, an old Lancashire family of Norman origin, one member of which became the first Baron Byron in 1643. The poet Byron sold it shortly before his death, and there are many references to the Rochdale property in his published letters. Neither they nor his biographers hint that he ever visited Rochdale more than once, but tradition declared he did. Moreover there are, or were, unpublished letters, concerned with litigation about, and the eventual sale of, the Manor, still in the hands of Byron's local agent, of the Dearden family who bought the Manor from him, and of their solicitors. The stories of Byron's two visits to Rochdale were told there as

---

people had to be called Percy Joseph when I found Frederick George Shinn, Dingle Mackintosh Foot, and William John Townsend Shorthose. . . .

"Then there are what might be called Wodehouse names. These fall into two classes—ordinary and super-Wodehouse. Ordinaries are Sir Ernest Wingate Wingate-Saul and the Reverend Maxwell Homfray Maxwell-Gumbleton. The supers are those that Wodehouse might have considered but would probably have discarded as a little extreme. I give you Sir Alex Logie Elphinstone of Glack, Hyde Charnock Whalley-Tooker, Lieutenant Colonel Gordon Dalyell of the Binns, Geoffrey Rupert Cecil Twisleton-Wykeham-Fiennes, Baron of Saye and Seele.

"Other names are playfully evocative. The Honourable F. W. Coneybeer [sic] suggests summer and the boardwalk. Then there's Joshua Whatmough (what mo' could you ask?) and Charles Urie Peat (will you repeat that, please?) Let our allies call us Goosenpfeffer and Jazzbo until we have jointly won the war, but let us remember, in addition to those listed above, that the following are real British names: Saxon Snell, Ion Richard Stavely Shinkwin, C. H. Falloon, Charles Talbut Onions, Burnett Napier Henderson Orphoot, Colonel Robert Jebb Few, and George Muff." I have omitted a few words and several sentences.

My own name is often enough a source of enquiry, so I give here the following extract from Bardsley's *Dictionary of English and Welsh Names* (Oxford 1901):

"*Whatmore, -mough;* v. Watmough.

"*Watmough, Watmuff, Whatmore, Whatmough.*—Nick. 'Wat's brother-in-law,' i.e. the brother-in-law of Walter, familiarly Wat. A very interesting North-English sur-

gospel and gossip mixed. It would never have occurred to me in
my Rochdale days to discredit them. What sets me wondering
now is the lack of independent confirmation. Minuteness of detail in the telling is of course no guarantee of authenticity.

Lancashire people pride themselves on their independence;
"what Manchester thinks today, London will think tomorrow."
But independence sometimes lags behind, and then it takes on
the garb of conservatism. Old mansions in remote Lancashire
hamlets kept hideaways ready with water and provisions for
fugitive Catholic priests long after the need for refuge had
passed. As a young boy I knew a schoolfellow whose family professed themselves Jacobites, though Bonnie Prince Charlie
made his all but last stand in Lancashire as long ago as 1745.
Nonconformity passed through the same cycle. The passion for
independence surely could go no further than the schisms which
split even the Wesleyan movement into the United Methodist
Church, to the Sunday School of which I was made to go twice
every Sunday until in the critical agnosticism of youth I rebelled

---

name, and one of a small but distinct class (v. Muff and Hitchmough) compounded of
the Christian name and *maghe* or *mauf*, probably in general a brother-in-law, though
other relationships are included. 'Maug, a brother-in-law. North E.' (Halliwell).
'Mauf, Maugh, or Meaugh, a brother-in-law' (Brockett). 'Mow, husbondys syster, or
wyfys systyr, or syster-in-lawe' (Prompt. Parv.). 'Mauf denotes a brother-in-law. N. of
E.' (Grose). 'A.S. *mæg* or *mag*, the guttural sound being changed into that of *f*, as in
laugh' (Jamieson). Only a few of these compounds have come down to us in the form
of surnames, Watmough and its variants being the prominent instance. The Yorkshire
Poll Tax, however, has several others, which although now obsolete are uncontrovertible
evidence of the former familiarity of such titles.

"William Barnmawe, the child's brother-in-law, co. York, 1273. A.

"With the above we must cf. the Yorkshire Barnfather (the child's father).

"Cf. also Robert Susannemagh, Fines Roll, 10 Edw. I.
"Johannes Elysmagh (Ellis's brother-in-law): P. T. Yorks. p. 272.
"Willelmus Hudmagh (Richard's brother-in-law): ibid. p. 251.
"Ricardus Gepmouth (Geoffrey's brother-in-law): ibid. p. 114.
"Johannes Tailliourmoghe (the tailor's brother-in-law), ibid. p. 283.

"Coming to Watmough we find:
"Robertus Watmaghe (Walter's brother-in-law): ibid. p. 287.

"Later we find it as Watmough (now Watmuff):
"Myles Watmough, vicar of Medomsley, 1582: DDD. ii. 287.
"Hugo Watmouth, rector of Thornton-in-Craven, 1599: Whitaker's Craven, p. 120.

in my early teens; the Free Methodists; the Primitive Methodists; the Wesleyan Methodists; and who knows how many other varieties of Methodist, leaving the Wesleyans simon-pure as a sort of Rump? The Primitive Methodists were familiarly known as Ranters, to such excesses of noisy singing and noisier interruptions of prayer or preaching did their religious enthusiasm carry them every Sabbath. Owd Betty would exclaim "Bless the Lord!" in season and out, until at last a few more restrained members of the congregation intervened, gathering respectability along with profits from their cotton spinning, and wrapping both around them as manifest evidence to the outer world of the fineness of the "count" of the Sea Island or Egyptian calicos of which they were so proud. Betty was promised a pair of blankets and a load of coals at the coming of winter, if only she would agree to hold her peace in Chapel. Promise she did, but keep the promise she could not. Once she had blankets and coals, a few Sundays went by, and, moved by the preacher's oratory, up she stood exclaiming, "Blankets or no blankets, praise the Lord!" How could such people so "dearly love" an earthly lord, a mere and minor peer of the realm, and an absentee at that? Yet they did; of course Byron must have visited his manor of Rochdale more than once.

"The modern variant Whatmough is imitative. With this class of surname cf.

"William Gamelstepsone (the stepson of Gamel), 25 Edw. I: BBB. p. 544.
"Henricus Parson-cosyn, 1379: P. T. Yorks, p. 91.
"Thomas Viker-cosyn, 1379: P. T. Yorks, p. 226.
"1581. Hugh Watmoughe, co. York: Reg. Univ. Oxf. vol. ii. pt. ii p. 114.

"I am glad to find that this most interesting North-country name has reached America.

"West Riding Court Dir.; commercial directories of Huddersfield; Manchester; and Philadelphia."

References:
"A. Hundred Rolls, 1273.
"BBB. Calendarium Genealogicum: Henry III–Edw. I. Ed. by Chas. Roberts.
"DDD. Hist. and Antiquities of the County Palatine of Durham (Robert Surtees)."
Walter was my father's name; my given name I have from *his* father, and from an uncle of my grandfather. In the northern dialects it is commonly pronounced *Water*, as in Shakespeare's Water (Whitmore), 2 Henry VI, 5.1.3. As for pronunciation -*muf* : -*mōu̯* is a matter of dialect (cf. *laughter* but *daughter* : *dafter*).
The local name Rochdale also has migrated to Massachusetts (a township west of Worcester), and, for all I know, to other states.

Nonconformity and radicalism notwithstanding, lords temporal by no means lost their hold entirely upon popular feeling.
Tradition was far too strong for that. Besides, these lords were
none of them so easily shocked as the puritanical Nonconform-
ists at some of the rather earthy goings-on of north-country
folk with more than a hint of the pagan about them. The Chapel-
goers among them would have heard with astonished disbelief
that the Rushbearings of their fathers' and grandfathers' days
were more pagan than Christian. As for the frankly scatological
character of one of their wedding customs, that perhaps was not
so much pagan as a universal manifestation of childish copro-
philia that had lingered on among grown-ups, as it clearly does
in many an Aristophanic joke.

Rushbearing and the rushcart I did once see, but only once,
and that as a revival, in 1906 at the jubilee celebrations of the
incorporation of the municipal borough. It had in older days
coincided with the August holiday. The custom was to cut loads
of rushes on the local moorlands and cart them, when dried, into
the churches to be strewn on the floor to keep, after a fashion,
the feet of worshipers warm through the winter months. Shakespeare transplanted this simple use to northern Italy when he
made Grumio ask, "Is supper ready, the house trimmed, rushes
strewed?" and Romeo speak of "wantons light of heart" who
"tickle the senseless rushes with their heels." But some ten years
later I had to learn the names of the months in the ancient
Athenian calendar; and there was *Skirophorion* "Brushwood-
bearing," but in June, a difference of season and emblem that
the difference of climate would account for.[2] It is likely enough

---

[2] The meaning "brushwood" is clear in *Tab. Heracl.* (*IG* 14.645) 1.19 σκίρω δὲ καὶ
ἀρρήκτω καὶ δρύμω "of brushwood, barren, and wooded land." So L.Sc. "hard (perh.
chalk) land overgrown with bushes, scrub." Cf. *Tab. Heracl.* 1.144. Hesychius has σκῖρα·
χωρία ὕλην ἔχοντα εὐθετοῦσαν εἰς φρύγανα and σκῖρος·ἄλσος καὶ δρυμός. In the writing of *Il.*
23.322–323 as one line by Aristarchus (ἠὲ σκῖρος ἔην νῦν αὖ θέτο τέρματ' Ἀχιλλεύς), the
meaning must be the same, despite the impossible σκιρον δὲ τὴν ῥίζαν διὰ τὸ ἐσκιάσθαι of
Sch. T. (a confusion with σκίρον "sunshade")!

The quantitative alternation between σκῖρος and Σκῖρα, the festival of Athena on
the 12th of Σκιροφοριών, may be simply a matter of ablaut (cf. ἰτέα : ἴτυς), but the
variant spelling -ρρ-, whatever its explanation, should not be overlooked. A festival of

that Rushbearing stems from some pagan festival, perhaps ultimately Keltic, concerned with harvesting, in which the rushes
were substituted for crops of more intrinsic worth as in harvest-
home and thanksgiving. Be that as it may, the celebration had
been turned into one of jollity, accompanied by a good deal of
alcohol. The symbolic rushcart was stacked high with well-
packed rushes, securely tied and pegged, then trimmed with a
pruning hook until it resembled the sharply pitched roof of a
thatched cottage. A copper kettle, a timepiece, a barrel of ale,
and various other insignia were strung on the front, and perched
astride the top ridge sat a celebrant who from time to time let
down on a string a mug to be replenished with ale from the
barrel. His fellows, eighty of them, drew the cart. They wore
bright blue knee breeches, white shirts and white stockings, blue
caps bedecked with red ribbons. In twenty ranks of four abreast
they held in front of them horizontal poles fastened at intervals
of about six feet by ropes, the far ends of which were attached
to the rushcart. On their feet they wore clogs, and as they drew
the cart they danced from side to side of the street. The costume
was rather like that of Morris dancers, but the clog dancing was
peculiar to Lancashire.

Until near the turn of the century the rushcart was a regular
feature of the Rushbearing holidays. But legislation in the second half of the 1800's, the purpose of which was to make conditions of work in factory, foundry, and mine less inhuman, had
extended the August holiday, from a single Saturday, first to
three days, and then to one whole week. More and more work
people went off to the coastal towns for a few days' sea breezes,
shrimps, bathing, roller coasting, and crowded lodginghouse

Athena Σκιράς on the 6th day of Pyanepsion was called ὡσχοφόρια (also, ὡσκο- and ὁσχο-)'
ὡσχός or ὁσχός being a vine branch with grapes. The etymology of this last word (: ἔσχον,
σχεδόν) is parallel to that of ὄζος "branch" (*o-zdo-, *sed-), but the etymology of σκιρο-
is entirely unknown. Keltic words meaning "brambles, briers, brush, underwood"
seem to imply a root *squoi- : *squi- (W-P 2.602), and others (also Keltic) meaning
"reed, rush" are referred to a root *seq- "cut" (ib. 475); conflation of these with one
another, and with *sqer- and *sqēi-, is conjectured. Latin scirpus "reed" is also without
etymology. It is possible that neither it nor σκιρο- is Indo-European at all. Pfister in
P.-W. I find unconvincing.

life. The rushcart no longer drew crowds of spectators or even the hundred or so clog dancers needed to make it a success. So it was given up.

Other factory legislation had included a provision requiring a medical inspection before mere children of thirteen were permitted to start work in the factories. But the factory doctor often performed his duty in the most perfunctory manner. One had a favorite, almost invariable, treatment for any ailment or deficiency whatsoever, namely, tonsillectomy. One fine day his bicycle had a punctured tire, and a bunch of youngsters, just going through the factory yard as the 12:30 P.M. whistle blew for the midday meal, gathered round to see the doctor in distress cope with his bicycle: "Take its tonsils out," was the ready comment of one of them, who had had other troubles with this very medico. Up for medical examination, the lad had been asked in routine fashion his name: Bob Sheep, came the answer. Your father's name? Charley o' Lory's. And your mother's? Betty o' Bobbie's. An imputation of illegitimacy brought a profane denial. Then the fledgling M.D. from another county was made aware of the names of a large family of brothers and sisters, nearly all of them different from one another and from all the rest, Sam Sloper, Ben Pippin, and the like among them.

Nicknames were well-nigh universal in a community in which most people seldom wrote or received letters, paid no income taxes, and had only recently been enfranchised by a succession of Reform Acts, the latest of which actually was later even than the act that established voting by ballot. The custom by which everybody is at once distinguished from all others and is confirmed in his own identity by a distinctive appellation, that is, by one or more given names as well as a family name, usually implies a highly organized form of society not only for the purposes of census and taxation, but also for compiling lists of voters. In our private dealings with one another we are apt to regard the use of anything more than a given name as somewhat formal, if not unfriendly. Nicknames are less formal still. But the supply of genuine given names, especially Christian names, is limited and the nickname is a useful supplement, which may in time take on the function of a family name. This accounts for the large number of nicknames which tie together a child's given name with the given name of its father, and occasionally of its mother.

But some of them were only imitative of genuine patronymics. Betty o' Bobbie's is Betty daughter of Robert—or, as we should say, Betty Robertson; but what is Ailse o' Fussers? Ailse is Alice, no doubt; but there is no family name Fusser. It may be just what it seems, the "fussy" chap's daughter. Yet that is somehow out of character. The simple moorland people, such as Ailse was, had nothing to fuss about; they took everything in stride, and Ailse manifestly did. She lived alone in a cottage sheltered by the hills running north of Rochdale to merge in the Pennines that form the county boundary between Lancashire and Yorkshire. Not quite alone, however. She had a donkey which, the story goes, when the day's work of hauling coal was done, slept indoors tethered to the bedpost. Ailse made a show of cultivating her bit of farm, hardly more than an oversized garden. She had had at one time a string of Galloway ponies, "lime-gals" they were called, and these carried bags of coal from the local coalpits driven horizontally into the hillside, or lime from neighboring quarries, over pack-horse roads between the two counties or down into Rochdale. Her comings and goings, with her ponies or the donkey, were a familiar sight, and there is no hint that any suspicion of wrongdoing ever fell upon her.

The pack-horse trail she regularly followed ran past a few secluded cottages and farms higher up the moors, one of which did acquire an evil reputation, for it was occupied at the beginning of the last century by a "farmer" who took to counterfeiting specie. He and four others were concerned also in passing forged banknotes, and all five of them were tried at the Lancaster Assizes in 1809, one of them sentenced to transportation for life and the other four to death by hanging. A sixth member of the gang had evaded arrest and for several weeks hid in the thick beds of rushes adjoining the "Long Causeway" over which Ailse o' Fusser's lime-gals traveled. His family took him blankets and food after sunset and finally he made his escape. The Long Causeway was a path that traversed soft ground and had been constructed by laying flagstones in line, a stride apart.

The constables could never have made their arrests of these five criminals without the help of decoys, one of whom invested his blood money in a block of three stone houses in Rochdale that came to be known as Hangman's Row. But they never succeeded in discovering a go-between who had planted the false notes and base coin in half-a-dozen or more different Lancashire and Yorkshire towns within a radius of twenty miles or so. Could it have been Ailse o' Fussers, whose donkey slept indoors? Whose lime-gals gave color to what would otherwise have been mysterious comings and goings? Whose farming gave opportunity of hiding dangerous evidence under the sod and removing it again when needed? Whose sacks of coal or lime were good concealment too, and whose journeys took her regularly over the Long Causeway past the forgers' rendezvous? But all this is conjecture, and if the Lancashire dialect turns "false" into "fause" (as it does), then Ailse was known to everybody around as kin of the counterfeiter (Fausser or Fusser), entirely innocent herself. Her true name was Mary Alice Hartley and her mother was a Cudworth. One of the four hanged at Lancaster in 1809 was a James Cudworth, a farmer's son, of Meadowhead Farm, Lobden, and Lobden adjoins Brown Wardle Hill and the Long Causeway. At the Lancaster Assizes he was charged on 14 August 1809 with uttering six forged Bank of England notes, an appeal from the sentence of death was denied, and he was hanged, in public view, at Lancaster Castle on 25 November of the same year.

The moorlands that saw Ailse's wanderings were part of the extensive Manor of Rochdale, 8,000 acres and more, that George Gordon, Lord Byron, owned from 1798 to 1823. If he was there in 1803, as legend had it, as well as in 1811, he saw at least twice the Rochdale of rushcarts, lime-gals, and counterfeiters.

Byron left England in 1809, but he was back two years later and evidently it had become necessary for him to visit his Lancashire property. He was ten years old when he succeeded in 1798 to the title and landed estates on the death of his granduncle, Lord William Byron, the fifth Baron, who was more than a little mad. One of his wild acts had been what purported to be a sale of the Rochdale manor. But the buyer had no valid title, and suit was entered in Chancery for recovery of the property, a process which dragged on for many years and cost well over ten thousand pounds sterling. Between June and September 1811 there is repeated mention of a projected and, at last, an accomplished visit to Rochdale in Byron's letters, of which there is now a good edition (by Peter Quennell, published by John Murray, London 1950). On 19 June 1811 he writes of having to visit Rochdale on the 25th, and again, on the 28th, he declares that he will shortly be on his way to Rochdale, which he must (17 July) visit "in person." But as late as the 2d and 30th of August and again for the greater part of September (letters dated 2d, 5th, 7th, 20th, and 25th September 1811) he is "going to Lancashire on business," where his "stay will be prolonged," or he is "going to Rochdale on business," or "about to visit Lancashire." The actual date of this visit, which the death of Byron's mother on 1 August had delayed, is fixed approximately by two letters of 11 and 14 October 1811, when he writes, "I have been down to Rochdale with Hanson" (this was Byron's London man of business) and "I have returned from Lancashire." Accordingly, the "prolonged" visit fell between 25 September and 11 October of that year. Quennell gives no letters at all between these dates, on both of which Byron wrote from Newstead Abbey. It would seem that he was away from Newstead the greater part of the intervening time, about two weeks. Prothero (*Letters and Journals*, Vol. 2, 1898, reprinted 1903, pp. 49–51) narrows the dating further, for Byron was writing from Newstead on 26 September and on 10 October (to R. C. Dallas, with a postscript, "Yesterday I returned from Lancs.").

The stories current in Rochdale in my boyhood speak of a visit to the Manor by Byron in the late summer of 1803. This is the year of the affair with Mary Chaworth, who is represented as having accompanied him. We have Byron's own word for it that he and Mary Chaworth were two of a party of eight that was gathered at Matlock in Derbyshire: he is describing events that took place when he "was fifteen years of age. . . . We were a party—a Mr W., two Miss W.'s, Mr and Mrs Cl——ke, Miss M., and my M. A. C.," runs an entry in the "Detached Thoughts," a sort of notebook of recollections and obiter dicta put together in 1821 (Quennell, p. 632). Mrs Cl——ke is M[ary] A[nn] C[haworth's] mother, Mr Clarke her stepfather; who the others are I do not know. Byron went to Harrow in 1801, and stayed there until he went up to Cambridge four years later. But he certainly missed the whole autumn term in 1803, and he seems to have gone his own way not only during the summer holidays of that year, but all the rest of it, and did not return to Harrow until January 1804. His mother complains in answer (30 October 1803) to a letter of Dr Drury, Headmaster of Harrow, that she could "not get him to return to school, though I have done all in my power for six weeks past." His own testimony is that a good deal of the time was spent "among the Malvern Hills" and again it appears that Mary Chaworth was on the scene. According to Medwin's account in the *Conversations*, the holidays of 1804 also were passed near or with Miss Chaworth, and he adds that their meetings were "stolen ones"; Moore's *Life* gives a different account, that the love affair was all over by the end of 1803, and Jeaffreson in *The Real Lord Byron* sought to reconcile the discrepancy by supposing that the news of the marriage of Mary Duff, Byron's child-love, which came to Byron in 1804, led to gossip that confused the two Marys. This is hardly likely. And Byron's actual visit to Rochdale in 1811 could no more likely have led to a tale of an imaginary one, accompanied by Mary Chaworth, in 1803.

Rochdale is three times as far from Matlock as Matlock from Newstead. But Cheltenham and the Malvern Hills are further, and if Byron and Mary Chaworth were so far from Newstead, with a party of relatives or friends no doubt, a visit to Rochdale can hardly be considered improbable merely on account of the distance from Matlock, from which they are supposed to have started. The story rests upon the testimony of a Rochdale lawyer, a Thomas Fferrand, steward of the Byron manorial estate, as related to a Rochdale newspaperman many years later. It represents Byron's party as leaving Matlock early in the day and reaching Rochdale in the course of the afternoon, which is reasonable enough for a journey of fifty miles, though some of it was over hilly roads. Byron was Fferrand's guest (nothing is said about the others) at his house just across the river Roach, opposite the old and unoccupied Manor House. The site is easily identified as that on which the Town Hall now stands; as for a later Manor House, the one built by the Dearden family who purchased the Manor from Byron in 1823, and known as "The Orchard," it was still standing as late as 1914, when it was used as a recruiting station for volunteers after the outbreak of war in August of that year.

A detailed itinerary of Byron's tour of his manorial estate is given: up the river Spodden, a tributary of the Roach, and through Healy Dell which the Spodden waters, in my boyhood still a favorite picnic spot with its Fairy Chapel, up to the Vale of Whitworth where it was necessary to leave horses and carriage at the Hare and Hounds Inn, the rest of the road being both too narrow and too steep, and then over the moors at the foot of Lobden and Brown Wardle in the direction of Long Causeway. The circumstantial account continues with a description of the next day, given over to inspecting the town itself, Fferrand still in attendance on the Lord of the Manor, and then, the morning after, departure for Matlock.

In a letter dated at Ravenna, 3 May 1820, and addressed to Kinnaird (Quennell, p. 512), Byron once more recommends "Rochdale to your notice, the more so, that you will perceive that Hanson particularly alludes to it and to the proposal of accommodation made by the other party." The other party was

James Dearden. It was he who was lessee of the coalpits, and with whom Byron had been in litigation for years. A letter written early in January 1823, which I give below, suggests, improbably enough, that Byron was thinking of making a journey to England in order to get the troublesome business settled, but the Rochdale legend that he and Dearden met cannot be true. The sale was indeed completed and the moneys realized were devoted entirely, as everybody knows, to the cause of Greek independence. Here is the text of two letters (not in Quennell or Prothero), both addressed to James Dearden.

Genoa, September 18, 1822

Sir,

You and I have now been 18 years at law, with various successes. I succeeded in two decisions, you in one. The appeal is now before the House of Lords. Of the original occasion of this suit, I have no great knowledge, since I inherited it, and was a child when it began, and for aught I know may arrive at second childhood before it terminates, but I write to you to enquire whether an accommodation might not at last be attempted. I have not consulted my lawyers, because they of course would advise the contrary, as your own very probably—but I despatched my letter through the medium of the Honourable Douglas Kinnaird, my present friend as well as trustee, a man of name and of business, who will either meet yours or any friend to discuss the subject. I have no particular proposal to make, but I am willing to adjust the business on what may be deemed an equitable basis, either by arbitration or a mutual agreement. My motives for this are, simply that I think it would spare anxiety to both suitors, and I am neither instigated by avidity nor necessity. I will be willing to part also with the indisputable part of Rochdale manor, because I wish to invest the part of that as well as other monies abroad, since I do not reside in England, and have thought of permanently settling in Italy or elsewhere.

Yours etc.
Noel Byron

Genoa, Jan. 22nd, 1823.

Sir,

We have the honour to acknowledge your letter of the 7th instant. You frequently express a desire for an interview, although it would not be convenient at the present moment to take a journey to England, but in the spring (if we can come now to any previous adjustment) I would make my way to England and meet you there in any place you may please to appoint for the purpose. This need not prevent the negotiations from going on in the interim—and I could wish something to be arranged now speedily, that I may give orders for the suspension of the appeal.

Yours etc.

Noel Byron

It is strange that Byron should have become willing to compromise the long-drawn-out litigation. It would seem, however, from letters to Kinnaird of 10 October and 23 October 1823 (Quennell, pp. 751–753) that his determination to "expend monies on the Greek cause" had brought him "to sanction or approve your acceptance of the Rochdale proposition" (almost the same words in the letter of later date: "I have written through various channels to approve of your Rochdale proposition which I hope has gone on well").

The newspaperman writing in 1889 must have been wrong in asserting that Byron and Dearden met and negotiated for a week at Hopwood Hall (a mile or so west of Rochdale), unless he was in England in disguise, a suggestion not consonant with Byron's own character. It surely was Kinnaird around whom this legend grew, even though Byron is presented in his well-known habit of a vegetarian. But the letters in Quennell show beyond question that Byron himself never came to England in 1823, the year in which he parted with the Rochdale estate for £34,000. Since the letter of 18 September 1822 was sent through Kinnaird (it is not necessary to read "despatch" for "despatched," p. 169), so also the one of 22 January 1823 may have been. It is certain that Dearden would not have paid over the purchase price without some authority signed by Byron himself. Byron was eager to get his hands on it, and may well have sent the letter by Kinnaird in preference to dealing through the Hansons, who disapproved of the deal except under more formal procedure at law and at a much higher figure. The Deardens took advantage of the pretended sale made by Byron's great-uncle (p. 166).

Now are these two letters authentic? They are said to have been copied, in the Rochdale office of Dearden's solicitors, by the same journalist (p. 168) to whom Fferrand had communicated his story of Byron's alleged visit of 1803. But the improbability of the other story, of a visit twenty years later, is no ground for doubting the authenticity of the letters themselves, which are more likely to have been the source of the legend. The best test of authenticity, if the original letters could be found, would be handwriting. Failing that, the next best test is comparison with the rest of Byron's correspondence, and here I find no obvious inconsistency. The letters themselves are too brief to warrant a statistical investigation, which could furnish neither proof nor disproof; moreover, there is no concordance to Byron's prose, and none to his poetical works that is available.[3] When Macaulay reviewed Moore's *Letters and Journals of Lord Byron* in the *Edinburgh Review* of June 1831, he declared: "The Letters, at least those which were sent from Italy, are among the best in our language [a judgment echoed in 1924 by the captious Herbert Hensley Henson in his Rede lecture]. The style is agreeable, clear . . ." But Moore gave only a selection from Byron's correspondence, and naturally omitted the merely business correspondence. Six supplementary letters printed by Borst in Appendix B (pp. 158–160) to his account of *Lord Byron's First Pilgrimage* (New Haven 1948), though more interesting, hardly

---

[3] There is no complete concordance to Byron's works; and attempts made on my behalf to obtain access to an unpublished concordance to his poetical works (no date), believed to be at the Public Library of Tulsa, Oklahoma (see *Bibliographie critique de la statistique linguistique*, 1954, p. 32, no. 4.*18), have been unsuccessful. It remains, therefore, still to be seen whether, for example, Chew was right (*Childe Harold's Pilgrimage and Other Romantic Poems*, New York 1936), p. xvi, in asserting that a concordance to Byron's writings will "reveal the great number of times that the words 'clay' and 'clod' and 'dust' occur, often in conjunction with the verb 'to clog' and in antithesis to 'mind' or 'spirit' or their synonyms."

rise above the same level, and it is not to be expected, one hundred and thirty years after Byron's death, that any new letters which should now turn up will deserve Macaulay's words of praise. Macaulay's own essay, in fact, does not read so well today. Its spirit toward Byron is so unfair, even hostile, that one wonders just how closely Macaulay had read his Byron. There is no mention of those rhythmical faults, the ungrammatical writing, "loose slipshod lines," lame passages, jarring rhyme, and careless meter, which critics more generous to Byron concede, yet without denying the power of his poetic diction. This is all the more remarkable since Macaulay in the very same essay perceived that "correctness" in poetry means more than mere conformation to purely arbitrary rules. Yet it is Quiller-Couch who warmly defends Byron's poetry notwithstanding its technical faults, and Professor H. J. C. Grierson, more discriminating than "Q," who, while admitting the deficiency of the earlier poems, written before 1816, the year of the violent rupture of Byron's marriage, in the "finer qualities of poetry, beauty of phrase and rhythm," lays no emphasis whatever on the supposed linguistic and metrical shortcomings.[4] Grierson speaks of this man of "many moods and sparkling wit" pouring "himself forth in the most brilliant and buoyant conversation [today it would be 'communication'] in verse." Here is the key: "in verse," that is, in *form*. The matter itself *is* "conversation," and rarely more. Grierson alluded specifically to *Beppo*, but the words apply equally well to practically all of Byron's verse. We need not take too seriously his own confession:

> Oh! that I had the art of easy writing
>   What should be easy reading! could I scale
> Parnassus, where the Muses sit inditing
>   Those pretty poems never known to fail,
> How quickly would I print (the world delighting)
>   A Grecian, Syrian, or *Ass*yrian tale;
> And sell you, mixed with western Sentimentalism,
>   Some samples of the *finest Orientalism*.

[4] Both in the very uneven centenary volume edited by W. A. Briscoe, *Byron, the Poet*, London 1924.

But I am but a nameless sort of person,
  (A broken Dandy lately on my travels)
And take for rhyme, to hook my rambling verse on,
  The first that Walker's Lexicon unravels,
And when I can't find that, I put a worse on,
  Not caring as I ought for critics' cavils;
I've half a mind to tumble down to prose,
But verse is more in fashion—so here goes!

                    (*Beppo* 401–416)

No wonder some have asked, Is it poetry at all?

The total bulk of Byron's work, prose and verse, is enormous for a man who died a few months after his thirty-sixth birthday. Verse alone, to be precise, fills a thousand octavo pages of small print, in double columns, of More's edition of 1905, Byron's own notes excluded; the prose I have not counted. It would be astonishing if, in all this, there were not some lapses in that perception (and perfection) of form which (as More rightly observes) predominates over perception of color; " 'the most highly vaunted passages of the poets,' " More adds (quoting Gautier on Villon), " 'are ordinarily commonplaces,' " but "nothing is more difficult than the art of giving to these commonplaces an individual stamp." There could be no greater praise of Byron's achievement as poetic form, restricted as the range of variety in that form was; in fact the achievement is all the greater, the narrower the range and the bulk so vast.

Two collections of evidence, grammar and rhyme, one German, the other Swedish,[5] amount to very little when you come to it. But anomaly and analogy (false or not) *are* there, now the one, now the other, breaking the "rules" of "correct" usage, thus:

A) thou *wert* (over 60 times): thou *wast* (12)
     beat for *beaten*
     brast (dialect; possibly a recollection of Middle English ?)
     for *burst*

---

[5] A. Herrmann, *A Grammatical Inquiry into the Language of Lord Byron* (Wissenschaftliche Beilage zum Jahresbericht der Zwölften Realschule zu Berlin, Ostern 1902), Berlin 1902; A. Gabrielson, *Rime as a Criterion of the Pronunciation of Byron* [and others], Uppsala 1909.

> She found . . .
> Don Juan almost famished and half drowned;
> *But being naked*, she was shocked . . .
> <div align="right">(<i>Don Juan</i> 2.1026–29)</div>

—but, of course, it was Juan who was naked.

> . . . my name, and many an early friend's,
> Along the wall in lengthen'd line *extends*.
> ("Childish Recollections" 163–164)

> Let *He* who made thee answer that.
> <div align="right">(<i>Cain</i> 2.2.88)</div>

B) Some of the rhymes that are stigmatized as faulty may conceivably have been due to Scottish or dialect influence, such as Byron's early residence in Aberdeen and Nottingham would lead one to expect. Even his years at Harrow, in Cambridge, and in London would not eradicate these entirely. It is not necessary to be a phonetician, or even to listen carefully to me, to detect my Lancashire upbringing in my pronunciation. I cannot believe, however, that on the written page Byron would, except in the haste of composition, and perhaps with the expectation of later revision, admit these. Thus the rhyme *lady : heady, ready, already, steady*, or possibly *water* with *ă* eight times (like Spenser's *water : flatter, matter*); but Byron also rhymes *water* (six times) with his written *-aught-, -ought-* (e.g. *daughter*), and it is more probable that he pronounced *water* with *au*, barely possible that he used the northern *ă*. But the number of individual licenses is very large, and Byron is said to have resented, and denied vigorously, the imputation that even as late as about 1810 he retained a trace of Scottish "accent."[6] Here then are

---

[6] See John Nichol, *Byron* (London 1926, originally 1880), p. 17: "when, about the time of its production [sc. of *English Bards and Scotch Reviewers*, published in 1809], a young lady remarked that he had a little of the northern manner of speech, he burst out 'Good God! I hope not. I would rather the whole d——d country was sunk in the sea. I the Scotch accent!'" Professor A. E. Gordon has brought to my attention the interesting story of Byron's shoes that appeared in *The New Yorker* of 16 October 1954.

some of Byron's peculiar rhymes: *paternosters* : *cloisters, reach'd* : *stretch'd, beseeching* : *retching* (but the variant *retch* rhymed with *reach* was still current in Byron's day), *shadow* : *meadow, gather* : *together, thrashing* : *refreshing* (but there is a variant *thresh*), *answer* : *can, Sir, grant-O* : *portmanteau, water* : *clatter, scatter* (see above), *Aragon* : *war again, doctrine* : *yoked her in, dome* : *bomb*—these in vowels only (from Gabrielson).

Byron's poetry rarely deals with profound themes. It is readily intelligible, its subject matter simple and obvious—nature, history, social life, the tragedy and comedy of daily life, its paradoxes and absurdities, its commonplaces and platitudes. The man in the street finds himself mirrored, but in the grand manner. Of Byron's two great compositions, the mainstays of his reputation as a poet, *Childe Harold's Pilgrimage* Byron called "a romaunt," *Don Juan* More has called "the epic of modern life"; it is also a satire. Both would lend themselves to a statistical study—length and frequency distribution of words, range of meanings, length of sentences (number of words per sentence), range of vocabulary. It was impossible, as we saw (p. 178), to apply the method as a test of authenticity to the two letters formerly at Rochdale, partly because they are too brief for the test to be decisive, partly because we have no concordance to Byron's prose. But frequency distribution of sentences of different length even in those two brief letters, instead of having a much longer "tail" at the long end than at the short, which is the normal "skew" distribution, is almost symmetrical. It would, therefore, be of interest to discover the distribution in the published letters. An example of the method may be found in the *Hibbert Journal* (1948), where distinct evidence of dual authorship of the Pauline epistles of the Greek New Testament is established, not only from the varying length of sentences (a mean of 11 + words in sentences statistically indistinguishable on the criterion of proportionate length in 1 Corinthians, 2 Corinthians chapters 10–13, Galatians, and Romans; a mean of 17 − words, and a much higher proportion of long sentences, in 1 and perhaps 2 Thessalonians, Colossians, and Philippians), but also from characteristics of style and vocabulary. It is possible thus to discover the degree of determinacy in phrasing. Another way of looking at the framework of expectation of occurrence may be illustrated by these quotations from Marlowe:

a) Confusion X upon their heads
b) Revenge shall X upon thy head
c) Vengeance X upon you both
d) Arrows X upon thy horse
e) Confusion X on him
f) Victory X on me
g) Mischief X on Charles and thee

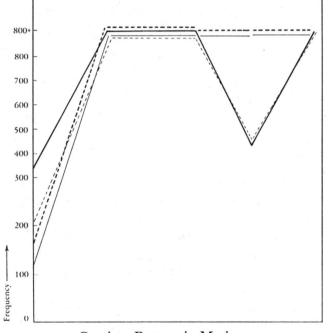

Graph 7. Pattern in Marlowe.

Heavy broken line = Confusion light upon their heads.
Light broken line = Revenge shall light upon thy head.
Light solid line = Vengeance light upon you both.
Heavy solid line = Arrows light upon thy horse.

in which X is determined by the rest of the sequence. In the first four the frequency pattern is identical; and again in the last three, except where the proper name (followed by *and*) produces a rapid drop succeeded by a rise back again to the same level as in the other two. The sequence is a matter of transition probabilities in the structure of the language. The statistical average is the result of a process in which an individual utterance is averaged into all the utterances of a single speaker and these into all the utterances of all speakers—in short, the language, which thus is seen to be a sequence of entities, an estimation of the probabilities of which is identical with the probabilities of morphomes and words. The formula is given as $p_n = 0.1/n$, where p_n is the probability of the nth most frequent word. The frequencies of the first word in each of the seven lines quoted from Marlowe vary within a very narrow range; for all the rest (since X is identical in all) hardly at all (except for the low-frequency proper name *Charles* and the high-frequency conjunction *and*). Different results are found for *light* a source of illumination, *light* the antonym of dark (or heavy), *light* to illuminate, *light* to shine, *light* mental or intellectual enlightenment, and all the rest.

Both *Childe Harold* and *Don Juan* are epics of travel, in which the author takes occasion to express his own reflexions on men and things together with his descriptions of the traveler's experiences. Between Byron and Classical epic, if closer (in date) to Byron, come the French epic chronicles known as *chansons de geste*, of which the earliest extant, and the most famous, is the *Chanson de Roland*, believed to have been composed between 1066 and 1095 or 1100. The author (or authors, if more than one) may not have been one of the Norman conquerors of England, but he surely belonged to the same Norman stock as Byron's ancestors. Thirty years ago, T. A. Jenkins published an edition of the *Chanson de Roland* (1924) in the introduction to which an attempt is made to discriminate with some precision between two distinct parts of the text. The possibility of at least two authors has been raised; and the fact that the legend is based on authenticated history of an older period than its actual composition, namely, the invasion of Spain by Charlemagne in 778, apparently confused with subsequent fighting in the same Basque territory, assigned in independent records of the Middle Ages to 813 and 824, and perhaps also confused with a still earlier tradition of 636–637 (the expedition sent by Dagobert against the Basques), indicates the existence of a continuous tradition from the original event of 778 to the date of the earliest extant version of the eleventh century. The identity of the poet, or poets, one or more than one, is not known. The theory of more than two contributors has nothing to commend it. But the circumstances that certain portions of the text of the Oxford manuscript of the *Chanson* are not found in other versions, and, above all, that there are in one and the same epic two entirely different stories, (*a*) that of the events which ended with the death of Roland, and (*b*) that of the defeat of Baligant and his Saracens by Charlemagne, at least lend countenance to the theory of dual authorship. The identification of the two alleged parts of the poem, on the basis of this theory, cannot, from the nature of the case, be certain; but for the purpose of a preliminary statistical investigation[7] the separation proposed by Jenkins has been accepted. Judged by purely linguistic criteria, it would be difficult, if not impossible, to distinguish the two parts. Instead, therefore, we may consider (1) lengths of sentences (i.e., maximum syntactic constructs) and their distribution; (2) the relative frequency of verb forms and of noun forms, and the relative frequency of words.[8]

It is known that authors do differ in the lengths of the sentences they write, and also in the number of words in each line of verse. Vergil, for example, has an average of 6.44 words to the verse; Thomas à Kempis a mean length of 17.9 words to the sentence, or, by a different method of computation designed to

[7] Mary Handy, "A Statistical Study of *La Chanson de Roland*" (Radcliffe honors thesis in Linguistics, 1954).

[8] Statistical evidence is readily available in the elaborate index by L. Foulet, contributed to Bédier's commentary (1927), see *Bibliographie critique de la statistique linguistique*, 1954, 4.73 (p. 35).

be more sensitive to the proportion of long sentences (the mean value of the *ninth decile*), 31.0.[9] In their sociological writings, the sentences of Shaw range from 3 to 142 words per sentence; of Wells, from 2 to 91; of Chesterton, from 5 to 91 (though he has only two sentences of more than 60 words)—all based on samples of 600 sentences.[10] No doubt much more should be known about the value of investigations of this kind, into the lengths of sentences of many more writers of different ages and, in different literatures and languages, and different kinds of literature, before complete confidence can be placed in the results. But, for what it is worth, I give the computations from the two parts of the *Chanson de Roland* as maintained (on quite other grounds) by Jenkins, taking no account of the exclamation (if such it be) *aoi*, which appears between many *laisses* (stanzas of varying length, fifteen verses each more or less), and is commonly regarded as a sort of refrain. It occurs 172 times in the Oxford manuscript, 158 at the end of the final verse of a stanza, 8 at the end of an initial verse, 6 indifferent (final or initial verse); some editors add it at the end of all stanzas (that is, 291 in all, of which 119 lack it in the manuscript!); Clédat omits it entirely from the text of his small edition. Jenkins' text is followed where the ends of sentences are concerned.

Number of words in sentence (ascending by 5)	Number of sentences Roland episode	Baligant episode
1– 5	14	8
6– 10	273	92
11– 15	169	72
16– 20	121	45
21– 25	142	47
26– 30	63	28
31– 35	47	27

[9] G. Udny Yule, *Biometrika* 30, 1938, 363–390; id., *Statistical Study of Literary Vocabulary*, Cambridge 1944, p. 278; see *Bibliographie* (note 8 above), 1.18b (p. 3), 5A.14 (p. 42). Cf. L. F. Hackemann, ib. 3B.70 (p. 25).

[10] C. B. Williams, *Science News* 24, 1952, 99. The accompanying graph (Marlowe) was made by my student W. J. W. Lewis.

Number of words in sentence (ascending by 5)	Number of sentences Roland episode	Baligant episode
36– 40	139	21
41– 45	24	15
46– 50	15	15
51– 55	9	6
56– 60	9	6
61– 65	7	6
66– 70	4	4
71– 75	3	1
76– 80	3	1
81– 85	2	2
86– 90	0	0
91– 95	2	1
96–100	0	0
101–105	1	0
106–110	0	0
111–115	2	0
116–120	0	2

In the first part of the *Chanson* the range of sentence length is 1 to 115 and the median 15.9 words; in the second part the range is 1 to 120 and the median 18.0 words, no very great difference. Greater accuracy may be had by using ascending intervals of one word instead of five words. Then the range is 3 to 112 and 5 to 118 words to a sentence, and the median 15.3 and 17.4 words respectively in the first and second parts, a still smaller difference. These figures are entirely consistent with the view that one and the same author composed the entire *Chanson de Roland*. Even if *aoi* be considered a sentence (of one word), the medians (14.0 and 14.9 respectively) are still closer, and the conclusion, namely, single authorship, is the same as before.

It is also the same when the relative frequency of verb forms and noun forms is considered. Of the former the *ratios* of verb forms, computed according to mood and tense and to person and number, and also according to total numbers of verb forms, reveal divergences between the two parts of the poem so slight as to be insignificant. This is equally true when the frequencies are stated in comparative percentages. It is still the same in the relative distribution of the forms of the nominative and accusative cases; and finally in the frequency of occurrence and distribution of vocabulary (see note 7).

Less weight should be attached to these latter statistics, concerned with the relative frequencies of different types of morphomes (grammatical categories), of different types and class of words (parts of speech), and of distribution of items of vocabulary; for this reason, that observation of such studies made hitherto tends to the conclusion that these variations are all inherent in the structure and pattern of a language, and not peculiar to the style of an individual author—provided always (and this is an important reservation) that differences of languages or dialects are not involved, as for example in the Greek epics. A trustworthy statistical investigation of the *Iliad* and the *Odyssey* along the lines indicated is a burdensome undertaking, occupying many years, which unfortunately it has proved impossible for me to carry very far before the writing of the present chapter. I hope (*si uita suppeditat*) to complete it; and I believe that it will demonstrate, once and for all, multiple authorship. But length of sentence is certainly a matter of individual style. It is a matter that can be imitated, no doubt; the presumption of an imitator, however, is rash in default of other correlations, or of independent, and preferably explicit, evidence.

What would Byron have thought of all this? The answer is easy; he takes the measure of the schools, and of scholars, more than once, and I cannot feel that he is altogether wrong:

> There, in apartments small and damp,
>   The candidate for college prizes,
> Sits poring by the midnight lamp;
>   Goes late to bed, yet early rises.

He surely well deserves to gain them,
　　With all the honours of his college,
Who, striving hardly to obtain them,
　　Thus seeks unprofitable knowledge:

Who sacrifices hours of rest,
　　To scan precisely metres Attic;
Or agitates his anxious breast,
　　In solving problems mathematic:

Who reads false quantities in Seale,
　　Or puzzles o'er the deep triangle;
Depriv'd of many a wholesome meal;
　　In *barbarous Latin* doom'd to wrangle:

Renouncing every pleasing page
　　From authors of historic use;
Preferring to the letter'd sage,
　　The square of the hypothenuse.
　　　　　　　　　("Granta" 29–48)

and

　　The Sons of *Science* these, who, thus repaid,
Linger in ease in Granta's sluggish shade;
Where on Cam's sedgy banks, supine, they lie,
Unknown, unhonour'd live—unwept for die:
Dull as the pictures, which adorn their halls,
They think all learning fix'd within their walls:
In manners rude, in foolish forms precise,
All modern arts affecting to despise;
Yet prizing *Bentley's, Brunck's,* or *Porson's* note,
More than the *verse on which the critic wrote:*
Vain as their honours, heavy as their Ale,
Sad as their wit, and tedious as their tale;
To friendship dead, though not untaught to feel,
When Self and Church demand a Bigot zeal.
　　　　　　　　("Thoughts Suggested by a
　　　　　　　　　College Examination," 49–62)

VI

Religio Grammatici

Understanding, Not Criticism

IN A PROSE comment to the passage in *Childe Harold* (4.665, 672) on Soracte and the "Latian echoes," Byron, conscious of his debt to Greek and Latin literature, but remembering his life at Harrow and Cambridge, was moved to express his opinion that "we become tired of the task before we can comprehend the beauty; that we learn by rote before we can get by heart; that the freshness is worn away, and the future pleasure and advantage deadened and destroyed, at an age when we can neither feel nor understand the power of compositions which it requires an acquaintance with life, as well as Latin and Greek, to relish, or to reason upon." Others have handled their schools and their teachers severely, as Nichol points out in his admirable, if perhaps partial, account of *Byron* (London 1880): "Bacon inveighs against the scholastic trifling of his day; Milton talks of the waste of time on litigious brawling; Locke mocks at the logic of the schools; Cowley complains of being taught words, not things; Gibbon rejoices over his escape from the port and prejudice of Magdalen; Wordsworth contemns the 'trade in classic niceties'" (pp. 36–37). This all long before the natural sciences even began to claim the attention that persuaded many observers, especially in the last century, into believing that only the sciences deserve attention, and others, more recently, that they are entirely mischievous. In the course of one of the discussions that took place in New York this very year (1954) on the topic "man's right to knowledge," the argument was once more renewed. Much might be said first of all about the assumption of

Part of the present chapter is based on my Presidential Address before the Linguistic Society of America at New York, 29 December 1951. See chap. i, n. 3, above.

human rights. It is possible to defend, with better logic, the thesis that man has no rights, but only complete freedom, and therefore complete responsibility. But we are not directly concerned with this question of man's right to knowledge, which, on the particular occasion, served merely as a peg on which to hang a searching criticism of the methods of literary scholarship. With much of what Professor Kroeber said I find myself in sympathy. In particular, as this entire course of lectures is intended to maintain, a new approach to the study, and a deeper understanding, of Greek and Latin literature is possible through the use of methods more in accord with modern thought than the traditional methods of criticism, both literary and textual. I cannot imagine that among the scientists I should be accepted as one of them; and the rumor reaches me occasionally that the "humanists" (a disdainful term, with its air of self-righteousness) regard me as something of a renegade. But I seek the best of both worlds, the scientific and the humanist, and I believe that there is a unison and concord between them that needs to be made clear. If, therefore, I speak still as *grammaticus*, even, if you will, as a grammarian, it is with the purpose of trying to set forth the nature of that unison and concord, a profound conviction of which is my *religio*. I never read the comment of Byron with which this lecture began, without being reminded of an experience of my own. From time to time, for one reason or another, I still lecture on a Classical text, notwithstanding the divergent character of my primary interests for more than thirty years. The last time was at Radcliffe, just before the practice of separate instruction at that College was abandoned, with the result that I read through the entire *Aeneid* for the first time since I was an undergraduate. My first conclusion was (and remains) that Vergil is an author for mature minds, and that the understanding of him by students whose knowledge of Latin, not to mention the other things that Byron declares to be required, is inadequate, could not be other than deficient, and their whole experience of Vergil frustrating. To me the unity between the message of Vergil's epic and all the other things engaging my attention in those years, and since, was then clear for the first time; the poem "meant" for me something that had been completely unrevealed by the literary and critical studies in the midst of which I had been set to write that undergraduate essay (p. 12) on Vergil's philosophy of life and death.

Scholars among scholars and scientists among scientists, as well as scholars and scientists severally, clearly have, most of them, many quite different as well as conflicting standpoints, and yet may agree in regarding the unity of knowledge as a common ideal towards which their efforts are directed. Such agreement, however, is possible only if it is first agreed that unwarranted (i.e., nonscientific) speculation be excluded, the principles of logical analysis observed, and historical development recognized. It is evident that intellectual contradiction between scientist and scholar must imply error. The unitary doctrine of knowledge, for which I plead, is to be regarded as a methodological postulate which asserts the existence of a single principle to which all subordinate variants may be referred—for example, principles of symmetry, structure, stability, self-regulation, equilibrium, and especially order (and its opposite), of which more will be said (in lecture vii) with reference to Classical form in language and in literature. The essential presupposition of science is that there is and will be order in nature. Man's general experience confirms this faith in order and intelligibility; and therefore he is entitled to form a picture of himself and his situation as more or less unified. Increasing awareness in recent years that, after many decades of specialization, quite different disciplines have independently developed quite similar general concepts (regardless of their subject matter, which may be inanimate things, living organisms, social phenomena, behavior and activity, which includes language and literature), is leading in our own day to what is called "General System Theory,"[1] which contends that the convergence is not a mere string of coincidences, a chapter of accidents, but indicates a fundamen-

---

[1] See L. von Bertalanffy, in the *British Journal for the Philosophy of Science* 1, 1950, 134–165.

tal unity, a doctrine unrelated to the philosophical doctrines of monism, whether logical or "neutral." Thus, it has been noticed that formally identical or isomorphic laws apply in totally different fields, for example, the exponential law (with a negative or positive exponent, as the case may be) to such diverse entities as atoms, molecules, bacteria, animals, human beings,—and books; the mathematical law is the same, different as the functional mechanisms are; or again, the principle of least effort, which appears in mechanics, economics, physical chemistry, electrodynamics—and linguistics. Nor is it always necessary that a particular law should be mathematical: *Gestalt* perception in psychology is said to follow principles strikingly similar to those of the formation of a whole animal out of a divided sea urchin.

But there is one important reservation, namely, that generalities of the kind we have mentioned apply to classes of complexes, that is to say, to *systems*. A system is defined as a complex of interacting units, that is, of units which stand in varying relationships to one another with corresponding variations in their behavior—exactly the case of linguistic units in articulate literary form. Certain systems, for instance, approach a steady state. Hence it is possible to derive certain "general system laws" which apply to all systems of that type, without reference to the distinctive properties of the units or system concerned. Like probability theory, which may be applied both to thermodynamics and communication, to genetics and life insurance, "General System Theory" is intended to apply to all fields of knowledge which have to do with systems, some of which are well enough adapted to mechanism as a principle, others not; systems of symbolism, on the other hand, which includes all varieties of discourse, raise problems of orderliness, of organization, and of regulation, which in their turn are dependent upon the mutual relationships of their constituent units. In particular, "General System Theory" allows the application of statistical laws such as Boltzmann's (the Second Law of Thermodynamics), wherever (as in language) these yield "results consistent with experience," and within a previously constructed "theoretical system" (here, linguistic theory, in which the statistical law "describes the average result of the behavior of a great many individual" units). The important point is that "General System Theory" not only sanctions the transfer of principles from one field of investigation to another, but obviates the necessity of separate discovery of the same principle in isolated fields, and at the same time excludes merely superficial analogies; above all, it substitutes a scientific theory for a vague metaphysical dogma of "wholeness," is much more, even, than a metaphysical interpretation of science.

Progressive segregation, in which a state of "wholeness" (according to "General System Theory") passes into a state of independence of units, may be observed at work in all kinds of discourse, but not to the extent that there is an increase of mechanization or a loss of self-regulation in the system—there are simply independent chains, in varieties of discourse, as exemplified by different works or authors. Their individual behavior may be summed; however, a change in a given unit is "amplified" in the entire system, leading to progressive individualization. But at the same time, at least in linguistic systems, the system aims at equilibrium, without which there could be no intelligibility (witness the fragments of Hipponax, in which the entry of new, in part non-Greek, materials seriously disturbs the equilibrium), and to that extent the system is self-regulating, largely by means of "feedback"; that is, part of the "output" is returned as "information" back to the "input," so as to regulate it and thus stabilize and direct the action of the system. This implies purposiveness or foresight of a goal which directs present action. "True purposiveness is characteristic of human behavior, and it is connected with the . . . symbolism of language,"[2] and (we may add) of literature. The upshot is that in the investigation of many forms of behavior which have been considered inaccessible to exact formulation, it becomes practicable to seek and perhaps to reach such a formulation in terms

---

[2] L. von Bertalanffy (as cited in note 1 above), p. 160.

of the concepts of "wholeness," summation, hierarchy of order, steady states, and structural uniformity, thus narrowing, if not closing, the gap between the sciences and the "humanities." Neither of these, notwithstanding the claims made sometimes for the one, sometimes for the other, closes the cycle of knowledge; neither by itself realizes the unity of knowledge.

Not that there will ever be an end: doubt always arises to dispel certainty. But it is now generally agreed that literature is primarily a product of cerebral activity, being, in short, a form of communication, and thus capable of measurement as "information" (in the sense of communication theory). If a poet is to do those things which enable him to achieve his purpose of writing poetry, he must receive "information" (again in this technical sense). By this is meant that the system (the poet himself) is capable of reacting in such a way (among others, by the writing of poetry) as to maintain its own stability. A simple model of such a system would be a modern servo-mechanism, a construction which not only receives information (input) and acts upon it, but also exerts control (output) in such a way as to ensure that its own activity continues in a steady manner.[3] Biologists assure us that living things behave in a comparable way, are self-regulating, maintain a steady state and tend to correct deviations from it, a form of behavior that has come to be known as "feedback" (that is, the return of part of the output so as continually to correct reactions to the input). A poet's writing may, by a not very remote analogy, be regarded as part of his self-regulatory behavior, keeping him in a "steady state" as a poet, even to the degree that if "feedback" is excessive there is a swing in the opposite direction, to restore that maintenance of order, against the forces of disorder, which is characteristic of vocabulary and of other literary features, and to which we shall come in the next lecture. Meanwhile let us merely observe, what is incontrovertible, that one of the chief means by which human beings maintain stability is communication. What we learn from engineers, biologists, and neurologists about human communica-

---

[3] See N. Wiener, *Cybernetics*, New York 1948.

tion has thrown new light on the nature of language, spoken and written, as part of the human system of control; and, within this system, poetic discourse is of at least as great moment as scientific. The poet's great contribution to communication is his poetry, without which we should be very much the poorer; it is hardly an exaggeration to say that without it our own stability or self-regulating systems would be greatly impaired, and modern methods of communication, the so-called "mass media," are failing in their duty by making so little and so poor use as they now do of poetic discourse, essentially a way of talking to ourselves about ourselves and therefore about human organization.

Now just as statistical methods have succeeded in describing more accurately than before not only human behavior in general (as in biology), but also communication behavior, such methods may illuminate also that special form of communication and organization which we call literature. For a literature is always part of the status of a language, to the description and understanding of which the statistical method, we now know, is peculiarly appropriate. The selection of any particular response is statistically controlled: this is what gives the response meaning (as we saw in chapter iv), enables us to interpret our environment and our age. But here we are not acting as it were altogether "naturally," but rather as the result of long years of "learning" or experience, that begins in earnest only with learning to talk. The rules are built up as a system from infancy, whatever individual extensions of them (analogy) or departure from them (anomaly) are made later in life. But the rules are first learnt by the combination of sensory input with the motor acts of output (talking or writing) which satisfy each individual, poet, philosopher, historian, or the plain "man in the street" who is none of these, in the sense of preserving for him his own status as a living human being. To be sure, a poem may "mean nothing" to others or to many others, just as some painting or musical composition "means nothing" to anyone but the poet, painter, or composer, or only to a few others. But this is beside the point. It is the way, however, in which the poet or painter fits himself to the world and the world to him: the matching is both a cerebral and a statistical process. Each brain forms its own rules (within limits) and develops its own way of modifying them; the essential thing is the preservation of balance, of a state of equilibrium.

The necessary factors in the system appear to be: (*a*) that it operates with a number of units that ranges from a very small limit (phonemes), gradually increasing (morphomes, words, constructs), to an extremely large number (vocabulary and meanings) which though not infinite is apparently always capable of temporary enlargement and certainly is subject to permanent loss; (*b*) that the "information" carried by each unit is simple, restricted, and well defined; (*c*) that this "information" is "matched" (just how is not well understood) with cerebral "patterns" and thus acquires its symbolic value in the system, a process helped, it would seem, by convergence and mixing of different kinds of "input";[4] and (*d*) that at each of these steps there is "feedback" to the preceding one. The remarkable habit, on the part of the gifted among us, of writing poetry (or painting pictures, composing symphonies, or the like) is hardly to be explained otherwise—like science itself, it is in essence a high order of the formation of symbols as links in the many chains of human communication. Every sentence of poetry is, as it were, a means of sustaining communication among all those who read or hear it. By means of it we see relations between elements of environment of which we were previously unaware or only dimly aware. The effort that goes into its production is comparable to, and worth as much as, the effort that goes into other activities that bind a human society together, not disrupt and destroy it, from the simplest or most menial to the most elaborate and most admired—say, great feats of engineering like road building, bridge building, or architecture.

The unifying media vary from age to age: both drama and architecture in Periclean Athens; religion in the Middle Ages; science, and its special forms of discourse, in modern times. But

---

[4] See my *Language*, London and New York 1956, chap. xi.

each of these is a special form of "communication," and is far more unifying—not necessarily unitary—in character and effect in the form of the spoken and written symbol than any other. We are entitled to welcome every spread of literacy as evidence of the increased use and impact of this remarkably efficient, systematic, and orderly form of cerebral activity. Since the most serious deficiency of the systems of the natural sciences has been their tendency to overlook man, and of the "humanist" systems to neglect everything else, the urgent need of using both, and if possible uniting them, has now become paramount. My thesis is that both scientists and humanists will be the better understood if their work is regarded as the "output" of an organized cerebral activity than by any amount of discourse about such vaguely perceived qualities as "imagination" or "invention." The peculiar achievement of a poet seems to lie in his special ability, greater than that of the rest of us, to select among the excessively complex features of input ("noise" notwithstanding) and to vary the features of output. It is even suggested that both the theory and the practice of education may well profit from a study of current knowledge of cerebral processes, to the end of healing the present cleavage between "scientific" and "humanist" specialization, a cleavage that is largely artificial and without justification in "real" life.

Now precisely as a scientific theory is comprehended as a whole or not at all, so a work of literature should be taken in whole, not anatomically dissected or interpreted piecemeal. This latter is a method which the sciences are now recognizing as telling much less than the whole story; that the "humanities" should ever have borrowed it from the natural sciences is amazing enough. It would be even more ironical if it should be preserved longer in a field alien to that in which it originated. More and more minute critical dissection of works of literature is not likely to add to their understanding. Their basic character is, in fact, organization—not even the summation of the entities called sentences, still less words or morphomes, phonemes and their features. It is possible, indeed, that "General System

Theory" may in due course lead to new methods of learning and comprehension that will revolutionize education much as Aristotelianism revolutionized it in antiquity and again in the Middle Ages.

Students of language in all its manifestations are now faced with the necessity of making careful study of the theory of chance, of statistics and probability.[5] As a general principle, it appears true to say that the more highly organized literary form becomes, the less random its system, the more likely it is to propresent new relationships not previously incorporated into the system, either because they had not been noticed, or, if noticed, then considered not relevant. It is far easier to detect such linguistic formulations in scientific discourse—compare, for example, the language of Einstein with that of Copernicus; but the language of poetry obeys the same rules—compare Dante with Lucretius. An epic of the modern world might be written by a poet able to comprehend the significance of scientific achievement; his grasp of science would form his language. Again, a growing body of knowledge about the way in which the brain functions may be expected to illuminate our understanding of literary discourse: its model is likely to be mathematical and statistical, but not critical. Like the organization of a single human brain, so the organization of its total literary product is such that it may be compared with that of any large "population" (in the statistical sense of the term). If we are to obtain an accurate account of the "behavior" of the components of this "population," we shall need a suitable statistical terminology, which will supplant the critical and grammatical terminology that goes back to the days of Aristotle's *Poetics* and *Rhetoric*. Such a development will in itself tend to diminish the gap between the sciences and the humanities as fields of study, and to lead to a unity of knowledge that will further communication, where now the separation of knowledge into natural sciences, social sciences, and humanities only hinders it. My observation of the working of general education leads me to conclude that

[5] An easy introduction is H. C. Levinson, *The Science of Chance: From Probability to Statistics*, New York 1950.

attempts to instill (or is "distill" the correct word?) the essence
of each of these three divisions separately into the brains of the
young, though doubtless general, has not hitherto been unitary.
New ways of presenting subjects so wide apart, in present-day
discourse, as physics, politics, and poetry, hammered out in
strict logic, will, I believe (as part of my *religio*), give a truer
picture of mankind as a whole, in its features both of organization and of randomness.

It is impossible, I believe further, to go all the way with the
positivists, in demanding only what they call "clear, not symbolic" presentations, for language is by its nature symbolic. But
systematic presentation is both a desirable and a necessary goal,
and the trisection which splits one world into three, as known to
natural science, social science, and the humanities, must be rejected. Especially the sentences of the discourse which literary
criticism produces are at fault because characteristically their
form is not communicable, but partial—they are not connectible
with the rules of any language that would logically admit or
confirm them. Elucidation comes only by rigorous method, and
the only such method so far devised by which literary structure
may be elucidated is the statistical.[6] The development of a
scientific "General System Theory" of mutually connectible
fields of knowledge throughout the domain of human interest
would, if successful, be even more effective. As I have urged
throughout these lectures, in poetic discourse the units of everyday language are used in what is often an original, but still an
orderly, way, not in accordance with fixed rules of a theoretical
poetics, but rather by individual modifications of linguistic organization, form, and system, such as epic, lyric, and all the
rest, which will not be understood until scientific study of them
from this standpoint has progressed far beyond its present initial

---

[6] Compare the valuable work of Josephine Miles, *The Continuity of Poetic Language:
Studies in English Poetry from the 1540's to the 1940's*, University of California Press,
1951. I had hoped to find some discussion of Byron in this book (he gets only passing
mention on p. 368) in comparison with Donne. His misfortune is not, I suspect, to fall
between 1740 and 1840, so much as the want of a concordance. This is a great desider-
atum (cf. p. 171 n. 3).

stages. Talk about free play of imagination, value, the music of poetry, poetry of color, even about symbolism (in the jargon of literary critics), and the like, has amounted to little more than a collection of slogans which tell us nothing about poetic discourse, the characteristics of which, in all its functions, will be established only by careful analysis based on accurate quantitative data.[7] Such an analysis will show clearly that a work of literature is what it is and nothing more, namely, a manner of speaking; how its constituent linguistic units have been used, even created, as the work progressed; that it is worthless to read literary critics as compared with reading the original works in the original language; that a work of literature is comprehended by a single act of understanding not to be had by assigning and adding up "points" after the manner of judges in an agricultural show, a method in which the fact that the work of literature is a structure, an articulation of linguistic elements, an orderly organization, is entirely concealed.

In the October 1950 issue of the *American Journal of Philology* founded and for many years edited by the pungent Gildersleeve, there is a contribution in which Professor Combellack of the University of Oregon remarks that "like all successful [*sic*!] religions, [Homeric] Unitarianism can boast of a number of distinguished converts." Now, in itself the entire dispute about the authorship of the two Homeric epics is of no moment; what matters, and the only thing that matters, is the truth, in the terms of symbolic logic, according to which all meaningful (i.e., connectible and communicable) statements fall into one of two groups, either (*a*) those expressing a statement of fact which can be tested by experience—such statements are data, namely, sentences expressing and indicating experienced, that is, experimental facts;—or (*b*) those statements which, independently of all experience, are true or false by virtue of their wording. Such true statements are called "tautological"; the false are called "contradictory." Tautological sentences form the content of all axiomatically formulated theories.

---

[7] See Rudolf Carnap, *Logical Foundations of Probability*, Chicago 1950.

There are now several impressive applications of the method of symbolic logic. This method involves first the systematization of factual data, then the framing of generalizations, and finally the most rigorous proof of theorems, i.e., the consequences of hypotheses, as "tautological" (in the sense explained); or dis-proof as "contradictory." As C. I. Lewis observed: "The logistic method is applicable wherever a body of fact or of theory ap-proaches that completeness and systematic character which be-longs to mathematical systems. And by the use of it, the same assurance of correctness which belongs to the mathematical por-tions of scientific subjects may be secured for those portions which are not stateable in terms of ordinary mathematics. . . . What seems certain is that for the presentation of a systematic body of theory, for the comparison of alternative hypotheses and theories, and for testing the applicability of theory to ob-served facts, logistic is an instrument of such power as to make its eventual use almost certain."[8]

A beginning was made in doing this for biology nearly twenty years ago by J. H. Woodger. Biology has in the past notoriously given the impression of being a tissue of *ad hoc* hypotheses, in which systematization of factual data and generalization lagged far behind. Of philology the same impression is even more ob-vious, for philology has lent itself all too readily, even when it has professed (but only professed) to deal with such a manifestly comparative and historical problem as the Homeric question, to appeals to anecdotes, truisms, and slogans. Substitute now for this subjective argument, though argument is not the name to call it by, the rigor of mathematical system and of axiomatic and logistic method, and the only correct answer to such ques-tions is to hand. The axiomatic method, particularly that part of it which deals with descriptive as well as historical data, re-veals elements that are so disparate in time and place as to make unity of authorship an absurdity, especially when it is remem-bered that the poem was not written down until quite late in its

---

[8] *Survey of Symbolic Logic*, 1918 (Univ. of California Press), p. 371.

transmission. As for statistical method, it is a necessary preliminary to analysis, since it furnishes precise data.

The factual data are subject to "information" (better, "conformation") theory, which refers to repetitive pattern; the
formula for it is quite general. Next, the statement that the
Iliad was composed by a single speaker simply cannot be de-
duced logically from the data; that is, it is contradictory, or
false. The religious fervor of the Homeric "unitarians," which
amounts to a conspiracy of falsehood, is inexplicable except by
their obsession (to use Nilsson's words, quoted by Combellack)
with the magic formula of "the creative genius of Homer," itself
a meaningless statement of literary criticism since it cannot be
verified either by experience (i.e., data) or logic. That such a
statement is widely accepted is symptomatic of the negativism
of large tracts of humanistic interpretation, which is essentially
a revolt against reason that accounts for the decline of humanistic studies.

In the three-and-thirty years that have passed since my career
as a teacher began, the same years toward the end of which
Vergil appeared in a new light (p. 184), the study of language
has emerged from a crisis the severity of which is lightly or not
at all apprehended by some of the younger generation of students, and apt to be grossly exaggerated by the rest of them. The
elder are less prone to the error of exaggeration since they are
more aware of the emergence of new doctrine from old, of an
essential continuity; but the need to abandon or revise much of
the theory and method of linguistics with which they were in-
doctrinated by their own elders, to the extent of reorganizing
and even destroying great wads of lecture notes, certainly has
demanded awareness of the revolution on the part of my generation, whatever the caution with which we may have greeted it.
The interlude has been chaotic.

When I speak of linguistics as scientific, scientific is what I
mean; and when I speak of crisis, that also is what I mean. It
might be supposed that the terms could not possibly be misunderstood by any academic audience. That would be to speak

in haste; all things are possible. By scientific I understand an evolving and fruitful conceptual scheme the quantitative methods of which are expressed in objective, communicable, and verifiable theorems. By crisis I understand a time not of danger, but of decision, a decisive turning point. Now it is from such a moment of decision that we have recently emerged; earlier claims to the other term were an abuse.

The very etymology of *religio* is an interesting and disputed question. Its meaning is not, of course, "religion," any more than *uilis*, for example, is "vile," granted that many things that are "vile" are both "cheap" and nasty. Two etymologies were current in ancient times. This is far from being a unique case, for "the ancients," it has been well said, "took leave of their usual sanity whenever they dabbled in etymology." Nor, on reflexion, do I find it very astonishing that the moderns also are divided, for whoever has spent much time with etymological dictionaries must have wondered, at times, about the sanity also of some of their authors. What is striking is that the etymologies that are proposed and disputed today are the same two as in the last century of the pre-Christian era; except in the pages of the immoderately cautious, who are so afraid of being wrong that they refuse to make any decision at all. Thus, Ernout and Meillet state the alternatives: first, *religio* related to Latin *relegĕre* (like *legio* to *legĕre*) and to Greek ἀλέγω "to pay attention to, heed, care for," though *relegĕre* means "to go over again, traverse," or "to repeat, relate," save in contexts in which the meaning of *religio* itself is being discussed (e.g. Cic. *N.D.* 2.72), where it is paraphrased *retractare* and thus comes close to something like "reconsider, meditate, contemplate"; and, second, *religio* related to Latin *religāre* "to fasten, bind, fetter," so that *religio* would refer primarily to the restraints imposed by faith and conviction, and even by superstition. But having stated evidence and opinion, and having referred to modern discussion, which is prolix on the part of students of religion, Ernout and Meillet content themselves by declaring that no one can be sure: "pas de certitude." I am not so sure about that. Ernout and

Meillet may, if they wish, record their own despair, but I know no right whereby they pronounce this finality of judgment, and I certainly refuse to have their etymological distrust pinned upon me.

Hofmann favors the relation of *religio*, which is as old as Plautus, with *relegĕre*, itself a later compound, probably first in Vergil. That is not really any better. But there is a further question to be asked now. *Religāre*, everyone will admit, is a compound of *ligāre* "to bind." But is *relegĕre* connected with *legere* "to read," and with Greek λέγω "to say"? And is Greek ἀλέγω "to heed" connected with Greek λέγω "to say"? This is one of the situations in which the sanity of the moderns too is called in question. No, says Hofmann, in what amounts to little more than an *ipse dixit*. The same position is taken by Pokorny, who indeed sets up three "Indo-European roots":

1. *leg-* "to collect, gather, assemble";
2. *leg-* "to drip, leak";
3. *leg-* "to heed, pay attention to."

Of these the second is indeed irrelevant and may be set aside. But the other two are properly regarded as identical by Buck; or at least he sees *legere* "to read" in *religio*, and I concur. The older meaning of *legere* was "assemble, collect, select," and also of λέγω "to say"; for "to speak" and "to read" (or for that matter also "to write") is "to choose" i.e. "to select" the appropriate sequence of phonemes and morphomes, of graphemes and of orders, of constructs and of lexical items, which make up the pattern of a language. It is now a well-recognized fact that discourse is at bottom a code, consisting of a sequence of discrete symbols, phonematic or graphematic as the case may be; and also that the symbols constitute a finite set in the case of each particular language.

Now the problem of homonymous so-called "roots" is one commonly faced by etymologists who occupy themselves with Indo-European, or with any linguistic history that, by using the method of comparing recorded languages, seeks to recover and to probe unrecorded utterances—an undertaking which has an air of improbability, if not impossibility, about it. Indeed, strict honesty, I think, requires us to admit that when comparison leads back to Indo-European homonyms, then, unless the semantic criterion is trenchant, we must be content with a solution that is, at most, plausible but not probable (i.e., not susceptible of proof). Since Indo-European writings are not yet among the things to be hoped for, at least not in this world, the rigor of analysis in phonological and morphological method must be matched by a similar rigor in semantic technique, something which remains to be developed, though there are encouraging signs (see chapter iii) of attempts to face this difficult and extremely complicated task.

For when we can avail ourselves of recorded forms, whether contemporary or not, a problem of this kind is not so hopeless, provided that a technique suited to the task is used. This I judge to be an extension of a technique that has been markedly successful in linguistic analysis, namely, the technique of oppositions or contrasts within the environment of a context. But in the realm of meaning it will take a far greater measure of learning and of judgment than in phonematics or even in morphomatics, in both of which some who call themselves linguists produce work that indicates only that they are mechanics. Now a semantic analysis of *religio, religāre*, and *relegĕre* conducted on the lines I have mentioned leads, I think, to one and only one conclusion. So far as phonology and morphology go, either etymology of *religio* is beyond reproach. A semantic analysis of *religio* in contextual oppositions shows that we have to do with two distinctive semata, if not two distinctive epilegmata. In Lucretius it is *religio* "restraint," but in Cicero it is *religio* "choice, consideration, awe." The older terminology would speak of conflation; so the correct conclusion is not, as Ernout puts it, a matter of indecision, but an acceptance of both sources.[9] Tested by a device of communication theory, the result

---

[9] There is of course no possibility of a relationship between *religare* (as old as Livius Andronicus) and *relegere* (note *religens* Trag. inc. 148 ap. Nigid. Gell. 4.9.1) comparable

is the same: in a certain context, is it *religio* "restraint"? Yes or No? If No, is it *religio* "awe"? Yes or No? And so in each other context. As Weaver puts it, "the powerful body of theory concerning Markoff processes [i.e., processes in which the probabilities depend on the previous choices] seems particularly promising for semantic studies, since this theory is specifically adapted to handle one of the most difficult aspects of meaning, namely, the influence of context."[10] Meaning is always involved in a complex of contextual relations. Thus, in the end, *religio*, like any other significans, is concerned with the attitude taken by members of the speech community, to whose usage the word belonged, toward certain elements in the sum total of conditions under which they lived. *Religio* was for example Cicero's, or for example Lucretius', attitude in the face of what were taken to be supernatural powers manifesting themselves in the universe and the human means taken to achieve harmony with them.

It is in some such sense as this that I speak to the theme *religio grammatici*, my attitude or conviction vis-à-vis certain elements in my environment, among other things chiefly my present subject matter, the understanding of Greek and Latin literature. These obviously are included, and obviously they occupy a large place in my environment; moreover they inevitably affect, and are affected by, my attitude toward a substantial part of the raw material of literature, namely, language. Conviction, it need hardly be pointed out, is requisite to forming an attitude.

In the first place, then, the study of language has emerged from the crisis which was produced by conflict between historical and structural methods, foolishly contemptuous as some structuralists have been and still are of the older discipline; for the conflict itself has now been resolved by a convergence that supplants it. This follows from the final proof that continuous dis-

---

to that between *sonare* : *sonere*, *lauare* : *lauere*, *dicare* : *dicere*, *fodare* : *fodere*, *parare* : *parere*, and many other pairs, notably in compounds (e.g. *aspernari* : *spernere*, *elegans* : *legere*, *compellare* : *pellere*).

[10] See C. E. Shannon, *Mathematical Theory of Communication*, Urbana 1949, p. 117.

course is readily rendered discrete by a quantizing process. For myself, I declined to admit the claim of linguistics to the title scientific until this final step was taken a few years ago. It is significant that the step was not taken by linguists, manifestly because the mathematics even of the most scientifically minded of them is far from being equal to the task. But the mathematical formulation applies convincingly to any linguistic status, historic or contemporary. Hence it reconciles convincingly the discord, that has lasted some twenty-five years, between the diachronic and the synchronic approach to language; and in future the practitioners of either one will do well to pay more attention to the other, for they are complementary. Accordingly there is no longer any need of reservations of the kind expressed even by Sturtevant so recently as 1947 when he wrote that "linguistic science must . . . be grouped with the humanities." For there is now a prospect of a real union of the ways. This also was the view of von Mises (*Positivism*, p. 217), that humanistic interpretation may become scientific in method, and in the same sense and degree as the natural sciences. But the present failure of the humanities to work to this end is too glaring to be glossed over, and the area of disagreement among the humanists themselves too large.

To repeat, then, a linguist has the conviction not only of the correctness, both presumptive and inferential, of scientific method, but also that his subject matter is amenable to scientific method. But I do not admit that I have crossed a dividing line between the sciences and the humanities, or that I must abandon any notion of combining both fields. What I do decline is to occupy myself for one moment with such trivialities as the place of Vergil's birth, a paltry and meaningless problem over which humanists so prominent as Rand and Conway between them spent nearly four whole years; with the contradictory, i.e., false, assertion of single authorship of the *Iliad*; with quibbles such as that about the authorship of the *Satyricon* of Petronius, or about the authenticity of the epistles attributed to Plato— both of which have been debated, without finality, for centuries.

This flogging of dead horses, this threshing of old straw, and all of it in the name of humanism, is a betrayal of the cause of humanism, or, at best, indifference to it. If this seems like intolerance, the reason is precisely that I am not indifferent to the frittering away of intellectual endeavor upon these idle and vapid problems.

For a man who has convictions finds that there are some things of which he will not be tolerant. But *religio* demands more than the courage of conviction; it demands also faith in conviction. And it always leaves open the door to heresy, which means choice, and which is something not to be evaded; as the existentialists among others remind us, to refuse to choose is to make the choice not to choose.

Faith is the certitude, I do not say certainty, that the consequences of what one has done in the past will be what one intended. Without it, one's own actions are distrusted. It is a prime requirement of scholarly as well as scientific endeavor. Notwithstanding von Mises' special pleading, there is today no contrast more marked than that between science and the form of scholarship which is vaguely called interpretation or criticism or evaluation of a pre-modern writer—epic, lyric, dramatic, historic, or philosophic. At best there is a strict verbal exegesis; at worst, a subjective "explication" (to use the fashionable term) which attempts to say (for example) what Plato "meant" that amounts to no more than an assertion of what Plato *might* have said, an assertion made, moreover, by some one reader now separated from Plato by more than two thousand years and four thousand miles, with all that that implies of the differences between a modern twentieth-century technological environment and the fifth-century Athenian city-state shortly after the death of Pericles; it being of course *never* admitted that Plato *might* have said these things, if only it had occurred to him to say them, which demonstrably it did not. There can be no argument here, since all the work of Plato has been preserved intact. Presumably Plato said what he meant, and meant what he said. The case is the same with a historian, say Thucydides, despite

the common implication—or explicit assertion—that certain
situations in the Peloponnesian War are amenable to prophetic
generalization of history still to come. General propositions contained in, or drawn from, the recording of events by historians
are not comparable to scientific prediction; they are, moreover,
apt to be falsified by the course of events. As for a writer whose
work is imperfectly preserved, e.g. Aeschylus or Sophocles, the
case is worse. There is at least an even chance that in the unlikely event that their works were suddenly revealed to us complete and entire from the sands of Egypt, the literary critics
would at the same time be revealed as totally misleading. The
clarity of vision attributed to Sophocles has become somewhat
dulled, the penetrating insight of Thucydides has lost its edge,
and the brilliant intuition of Plato is unenlightening, under the
sheer weight of explanation and interpretation.

The only thing is to stick to the text. Nowadays this is heresy
in philological circles. But *religio* or conviction, as I said, always
leaves the door wide open to heresy, to choice and decision, to a
departure from orthodoxy, to reformation. No scientific principles, it has been repeatedly observed, are sacrosanct; no scientific theory is ever held with religious conviction (except the
theory that no theory is so held); . . . all the "truths" of science
are provisional. This atmosphere of provisional hypothesis and
verifiability constitutes what has been called the "homely air"
of science, and is part of its strength. Science has adopted the
pragmatic criterion of truth, and hence science has been successful. In fact, its success is not possible on other terms. There is a
disinterested passion for logical truth such as is rarely found in
any other human activity; the truth is an end in itself. The
scientist who distorts observations or falsifies argument is very
soon exposed and loses his standing; the experiments are repeated by others and observation corrected; the reasoning must
be verified or rejected. Unless a doctrine affirmatively satisfies
the question, "Is it true?" the mere prestige of its proponent is
without weight, and the fact that much of the subject matter of
scientific investigation is usually not such as to arouse emotional

opposition detracts not an iota from the moral integrity of the scientific process. But there is an unsuspected element of self-deception in the arguments used by literary critics to defend their preoccupation with problems of authenticity, of textual emendation, and the like, even of interpretation, which a disinterested observer finds repellent. On page 2 of a work of some importance to them, which yet seems to have escaped their notice almost altogether, I read:

The controversy on the authorship of the book [*de Imitatione Christi*] seemed to me mostly quite foolish, a matter of historical and pathological rather than actual interest, but I had read some few of the works relating thereto and in these ... the vocabulary and diction of Thomas à Kempis are discussed as evidence. These discussions left in my mind a sense of inadequacy. They did not tell me what *I* wanted to know. They dealt with such details as his use of words and idioms taken literally from the Dutch—like the well-known *exterius* in the sense of *by heart* in Lib. I cap. 1 of the *Imitatio;* of words used in unusual, non-classical senses; of italianate words, and so forth. All these are mere details, ... *they give no faintest notion as to what his vocabulary is like as a whole.* To tell me that there is a small mole on Miranda's cheek may help me to identify the lady, and may in conceivable circumstances be quite useful information to the police, but it hardly amounts to a description of her alluring features.

These words are quoted from G. Udny Yule's work, published in 1944 by the Cambridge University Press, *The Statistical Study of Literary Vocabulary*. The author, a Fellow of the Royal Society and of St John's College, was Reader in Statistics to the University of Cambridge from 1912 until he reached the age of retirement. I mention these facts as vouching for his academic and professional standing; his training was, of course, that of a mathematician. He himself insists (p. 281) that the methods which he developed are not important solely, or even mainly, for endeavors to solve controverted questions of authorship or chronological order (questions which he regards as quite insipid and jejune): "They are methods," he writes, "for studying language-in-use, ... and ought to find their due position in the study of the living tongue, past and present . . . [whereas] we cannot, at present, . . . give definite answers to even the most obvious questions [of characteristics of vocabulary]."

I have succeeded in finding only one review of Yule's work in American periodicals, and that in the *Journal of the American Statistical Association* (New Series 39, 1944, 527), though there is a reference to Yule's treatise of 1922 on the theory of statistics in the interesting and important article on "Quantitative Linguistic Analysis" by Mr David W. Reed of the University of California, in *Word* 5, 1949, 235–247, and J. W. Greenberg (*Word* 6, 1950, 168) has used statistical methods in his study of the patterning of root morphomes in Semitic. Of the other five reviews of Yule known to me, two are in statistical publications: one, by Leon Isserlis, in the *Journal of the Royal Statistical Society* (107, 1944, 129–131); the other, by M.-L. Dufrénoy, in the *Journal de la Société de Statistique de Paris* (87, 1946, 208–219). Three are in English reviews of language and literature, viz., the *Modern Language Review* (39, 1944, 291–293), the *Review of English Studies* (21, 1945, 77–78), and *Medium Aevum* (14, 1945, 51–56), by Greg, Grebenik, and McIntosh respectively. It is astonishing, even all allowance being made for the momentous events of the year 1944, that no attention whatever was paid by students of language to a work of great importance in the statistical analysis of language. As for the three reviewers last named, they are faintly contemptuous, which is not astonishing from Grebenik and McIntosh; but one might have expected more interest on the part of Sir W. W. Greg, who himself is the author of an essay in textual criticism called *The Calculus of Variants* (published at Oxford in 1927).

A review, to be worth recording, should possess the distinction of adding something to the subject. Accordingly, those by Grebenik and McIntosh may be dismissed as worthless. Greg's is somewhat better, for he admits that questions of disputed authorship may be settled by purely statistical tests. But it is only the statisticians themselves, Isserlis, Rider, and above all Dufrénoy, who saw the true significance of Yule's work. It would almost appear that contemporary "literary scholarship" treats literature as no more connected with language than with music or the fine arts. This is not Yule's fault, since he pointed out, at least incidentally, that his methods are concerned with the repetitive process of language in use. Not that he came to grips with the problem of applying the calculus of semantic choices to the sequence of discrete symbols generated by a stochastic process from a finite set, which is what language is, or at least a mathematical model of language. There are other shortcomings, too: a failure to take into account the time element; limitation of Yule's study to nouns only; the curious idea that, if not so limited, still it would be correct to ignore such items as words of high frequency of occurrence (usually short words, with low semantic content, such as the article or the verb *to be*).

It is, therefore, not astonishing either that Yule reached no broad generalizations. However, he set out to study a different problem, and a narrower. And he showed up the weakness of merely subjective, impressionistic judgment; he established also the validity and comparative ease of sampling in order to secure typical, representative, unbiased specimens from the mass (what the statisticians have in mind when they speak of a "population"). It is here that we part company with the scholar who is not a statistician, who depends on memory or vague impressions to do the work of a statistical computation, and so picks out a number of items, not usually very large, which are, in his judgment, typical. His judgment of typicality may indeed be correct, but it cannot be accurate or precise. The method is obviously bad, even untrustworthy, because of its personal (i.e., subjective) character, when the issue can be decided only by a method that is quite impersonal, namely, that of simple random sampling.

This is what Yule did with the *Imitatio Christi*, and also with selected works of Bunyan and Macaulay, in order to discover the distribution of vocabulary. His results are quite important. He demolishes, for example, the delusion, to which literary critics commonly resort, that the field in which an author is working may be held to affect the *total* vocabulary at risk. Yule "begins with the frequency distributions of nouns in samples of an author's work. The mode occurs at nouns used once only. There is a long tail of nouns used many times in extracts that have a total number of only a few thousand occurrences. The following is an illustration. A sample of the Latin theological works of the fourteenth-century writer Gerson shows 8,196 occurrences of nouns. The number of different nouns is 1,754. One noun (*Deus*) occurs 256 times, and 804 nouns occur once only. An extract from Macaulay's essay on Bacon long enough to contain about the same number, viz., 8,045 occurrences of a noun, includes 2,048 different nouns. One noun, this time *man*, not God, occurs 255 times, and 990 nouns occur once only."[11]

The fact that *man* is Macaulay's most frequent noun, *Deus* that of Gerson, might at first sight seem not to need comment. But statistical studies of vocabulary show that words of high frequency of occurrence are also words of low semantic content. Here again there would, I suppose, be agreement about *man*. It is so colorless that often another word displaces it, so that the other word may then be said to have changed its own meaning (meaning being a complex of contextual relations). For example, *dog* (which we may define closely enough for the present as a hairy quadruped), in the statement not "He's a bad man" but "He's a sad dog," where a certain association, perhaps in moral laxity, between the hairy quadruped and the not so hairy biped, leads to the use of the word of low frequency in place of the one of high frequency (the proportion is 1 : 8.5)—provided always that there is a point of association in the complex of contextual relations. So a young man will say, "She's a peach," not "She's a fine girl" (the proportion is 1 : 22)—the association of sweetness, if not ripeness, being the semantic link; or, "She's a lemon" (the proportion is 1 : 11 this time, the implication of which may be left to the imagination). But what about *Deus*? The answer is that in Gerson's Latinity a statement containing this expres-

---

[11] Here, and a little further on, I quote from an article of my own in the Festschrift für Albert Debrunner (1954), pp. 441–446.

sion is a sentence only in the sense that it satisfies the routine rules of grammar; it may indeed form part of a system of moral norms that, rightly or not, enjoyed a certain popularity. But the claim to be apodeictically certain or à priori true renders the expression indefinite; and, therefore, the semantic content of Gerson's *Deus* at least no higher than that of Macaulay's *man*.

"Yule considers that an author has W nouns at his disposal. In any of his writings each noun is exposed to the risk of being not used, used once, twice, or any other number of times. The risk is different for different nouns. There is an immediate analogy with the liabilities of factory workers to meet with accidents. The practical application of the Poisson series is, however, necessarily different. In accident distributions we deal with the numbers of workers who in a given period of time meet with 0, 1, 2, 3, · · · accidents. In the study of a piece of writing we observe the number of nouns used 1, 2, 3, · · · times in a 'sample' containing a certain total number of noun occurrences. So long as the meaning to be attached to the words 'size of sample' is clearly understood, this difference causes no difficulties. But there is a difficulty in the fact that we do not know how many nouns the author has not used at all. On the basis of the Poisson exponential distribution a characteristic constant is K proportional to

$$\frac{S_2 - S_1}{S_1{}^2}$$

where S_1, S_2 are the first two moments of the frequency distribution about zero of occurrences of nouns.

"Thus Yule was able to determine one rather complicated quantity indicative of the form of the frequency distribution, and independent of the size of the sample within reasonable limits. This quantity he terms the Characteristic and denotes by K: it may roughly be said to measure the 'concentration' of the vocabulary, the degree to which the author relies upon the commoner words. In the foregoing illustrations, if, in order to avoid small fractions, K is

$$\frac{10^4(S_2 - S_1)}{S_1{}^2}$$

Yule finds $K = 35.9$ for Gerson and 27.2 for Macaulay (i.e., Macaulay depends less on a commonplace vocabulary). The square of the coefficient of variation of the liabilities of nouns to occur is

$$10^{-4} \cdot W(K - 1)$$

where W is the number of nouns in the author's vocabulary.

"This leads Yule to an interesting section on the probable value of W. He distinguishes between the number of words an author has actually used in the finite field of his writings and the total number of words in what he calls the author's 'treasure chest.' This last, which clearly is de Saussure's *la langue*, is, he thinks, much larger than the estimates usually given of an author's vocabulary. Rough sampling counts show that there are nearly 60,000 nouns in the *Concise Oxford Dictionary* and that 32,000 of these (or 23,500 on a stricter basis of rejection of words probably not known to him) were somewhere in Macaulay's treasure chest, liable to use if the need was felt and the word came obediently to his mind.

"The starting point of Yule's research, we remember, was a desire to obtain some objective criterion for use in the problem of the disputed authorship of the *Imitatio Christi*. Having introduced the characteristic K, he examines how far it is consistent for different samples of the same size (in the sense used above) for the same author, and how it differs from author to author. Samples from Macaulay's essays on Milton (written when Macaulay was a very young man), Hampden, Frederick the Great, and Bacon, give K (as a mean of six samples for the essay on Bacon), 27.33. The variations are considerable when compared with the values of K for other authors—Gerson 35.9; Thomas à Kempis all works 59.7, *Imitatio* 84.2; St John's Gospel in Basic English 141.5, in the Authorised Version 161.5," this last a striking measure of the redundancy both of Biblical English in general, and of Basic English in particular.

Yule was concerned with a limited problem. The statistical investigation of linguistic data covers the entire field; and its justification calls for no special pleading. I have no wish to belittle the achievements of descriptive analysis. But it should be obvious that mere description is not enough—this is generally admitted in the case even of the much-admired Pāṇini, to whose work modern analyses show some striking likenesses, notably that economy of statement which is apt to be confounded with accuracy but which renders both Pāṇini and his modern counterparts somewhat impractical as well as unreadable. It must also be conceded that the presuppositions upon which modern descriptive technique rests now at last begin to demand a general theory that will systematize the analyses that result from structural investigations. There is, in fact, a good deal of resistance, passive and now and then even active, to the introduction of mathematical and quantitative methods. The course of development in other fields of study concerned with human relations and activities has been quite similar, as for example in law, sociology, and economics: at first, for many years, if not open opposition, at least an admission of the usefulness of statistical procedures that was at best merely tacit. On the other hand, some of the adherents of such procedures carried their enthusiasm for figures so far as to refuse to allow any place for mere descriptions at all. Sooner or later the two schools converge, each admitting the importance of the other's point of view. There is still a hostility, especially among scholars, toward statistical inquiries into the nature of human behavior.

The matter is neatly put by Mr Reed in the article already referred to: "If one wishes to analyze the data, a purely qualitative analysis is incomplete. A qualitative study discloses the nature and variety of form, but in no way indicates its frequency or magnitude. In theory, at least, any and every form which occurs but once is entitled to the same descriptive emphasis. Thus the description presents a picture entirely in terms of the nature and variety of its contents; it is like a recipe which describes qualitatively the ingredients of a pudding without indicating the proportions in which they are combined."[12] Similarly, in 1948 at the Sixth International Congress of Linguists it was emphasized that results based on numerical investigations "must take the place" of vague estimations and appreciations. The kind of information needed: totals of words current, calculation of the quantitative relations between types of word order, and of context.

As for the discussion at the Congress itself, one or two matters are worth noting: (1) It is of prime importance that the units in any enumeration be derived from the *qualitative* language system. Yule's work at least made clear this necessity. On the other hand, deviations supposed to be inherent in style or subject matter may be eliminated, as Yule showed, if the count is based on a large number of brief texts. (2) An objection raised by some speakers, namely, that the calculus of probability should be invoked, may now, I think, be discounted, since the formulae of communication engineers satisfy that requirement. (3) In dealing with literature, we must keep in mind the distinction between "la langue" and "la parole." Actually it is the facts of both that we wish to obtain; but, so far, hardly any attempt has been made to cope with the extremely difficult problem of obtaining statistical information from "la langue."

Since I have discussed the mathematical theory of communication several times in recent years, it is unnecessary to dwell on the importance of the application of probability calculus to the statistical data except to point out that Shannon himself has now refined his formula, so as to provide for an upper (i.e., maximum possible) and a lower bound of entropy, and that Leon Brillouin, until recently Gordon MacKay Professor of Applied Mathematics at Harvard, has confirmed Shannon's results in a series of three articles in the *Journal of Applied Physics*, March and August 1951. Brillouin shows that efficiency in the use of "la langue" is concerned with probability distribution and that the Shannon formula is absolutely general in its applica-

---

[12] "Quantitative Linguistic Analysis," *Word* 5, 1949, 247. I somewhat compress the quoted passage.

tion. Moreover, the discussions of the relation between written and spoken forms begun by Uldall and Vachek in *Acta Linguistica* (Vols. 4, 1944, and 5, 1949) and continued by Pulgram (*Word* 7, 1951) indicate the validity of written sequences for statistical computation, notwithstanding certain internal inconsistencies. Modern research into statistical regularity in language, as carried on by the engineers of the Bell Telephone Laboratories, is fundamentally an investigation of the degree of determinacy in linguistic sequences.

More attractive to students of literature is the prospect of applying statistical and probability theory to meaning. The structure of all human utterance is such that sequences of more than a very few phonemes may also be described in terms of higher-order units. These can be defined by the same two methods that are applicable to phonemes, viz., the formal and the functional. The formal definition of a higher-order unit may consist merely of a statement of its composition in terms of units of a lower order; for example, morphomes are usually described in terms of phonemes. The functional definition involves the "meaning" of the form, but does not differ qualitatively from the familiar functional definition of phonemes; that is, it consists of a statement of the environments in which the unit in question is found. For example, contexts such as *The X barked and wagged its tail* or *Xs like to chase cats* almost certainly determine the occurrence of the English morphome-word *dog*, and hence constitute a minimum definition of *dog*; i.e., they establish its identity by contrast with any number of other morphomes or words in the language, the occurrence of which in the same contexts is highly unlikely, e.g. *bog, cog, fog, frog, hog, jog,* or *log*. Such a functional definition is essentially different from definition by reference, and offers greater possibility of exactitude; indeed, the difficulties of defining words by correlation with features of practical situations are manifold. It would seem that descriptive technique will be obliged to include quantitative criteria at this level.

Now the application of quantitative criteria tends to demon-

strate what was said in an earlier lecture (chap. i), by now
something more than a conviction, namely, first, that equivalent reproduction of a text in a foreign language (i.e., translation) is impossible; and, second, that comment upon and criticism of a text do not amplify, but distort and subtract from the
original message. These simple basic facts have serious consequences for accepted procedures in the study of literature.

Exposure to Homer, or Vergil, to Dante, or Grillparzer, even
to T. S. Eliot, may, or may not, be a major experience; that
depends. But if and when it is, its majesty is diminished or destroyed both by translator and by critic. If this be heresy, make
the most of it. Letters, like music and the fine arts, contribute
to human understanding, in a measure at least not inferior to
the sciences, *at the creative level*—this perhaps is what von Mises
means. But once they fall into the hands of the translator or
professional critic their message is reduced or impaired.

I conclude with an appeal for mutual understanding on the
ground that disharmony tends toward negation. By this I mean
the trend opposed to scientific method which has always had
considerable support and seems once more to be marshaling its
forces in a new anti-intellectual movement.

Whitehead, in the preface to a volume of essays in honor of
H. M. Sheffer, *Structure, Method, and Meaning* (New York
1951), is quoted as agreeing with Sheffer's derivation of negativism from inconsistency. This suggests that interpretative
scholarship fosters the very alienation against which it protests
so vociferously. Continuity in language, like continuity in life
itself, if I read Schroedinger aright, is, to borrow Brioullin's
coinage, a matter of negentropy, that is, it is behavior which
maintains itself at a fairly high level of orderliness. Not an or-
ganism, language, in all its manifestations, is nevertheless an
activity of organisms, and obeys the same laws. The convergence of historical and comparative, of structural, and now of
statistical methods, upon this conclusion is convincing; it is the
conviction that language partakes of a law (entropy) that (in
Eddington's words) "holds the supreme position among the laws

of Nature"; a faith that the study of literature will continue, in harmony with other sciences, to deepen understanding so long as life itself continues. This is the very foundation of the *religio* of at least this *grammaticus*.

In a word, it is my contention that a poem, or any work of literature, like a scientific theory, both itself is, and also pro-presents, a fraction of τὰ φυσικά, that the birth of a poem is like the birth of a child; whereas literary criticism partakes of all the fatal flaws of metaphysics that call for the elimination once and for all of both criticism and metaphysics in favor of more logical and positivistic views. Positivism is redeemed from solipsism or privacy by linguistic usage, in which the first person is objecti-fied by the other persons, any one of which becomes any of the others alternately. Poetry, like all literature, is a form of know-ing, a *scientia*—that is, a "grasping, comprehension," which is what *scientia* means. There are no "laws" of poetry, however, just as there are no "laws" of nature; but we make a model of a fraction of the universe of knowing, whether in poetic or in scientific discourse, as for example Shakespeare did in his de-scription of a hurricane in *The Tempest* (Act I, scene 2, lines 1–5, 201–205) and as meteorologists do on their maps or in their articulate reports of the conditions that betoken a hurricane—temperature, barometric pressure, velocity and direction of the wind, and all the rest. From these models we derive our prop-ositions, which are no more than constructs, yet valid within the limits of the case. Other accounts of literature tend to de-generate to mere exchanges of opinion, and even, in extreme cases, to what can be counted no more than a guessing compe-tition.

VII

Order and Disorder

Classical Form

THE FRENCH symbolists—Baudelaire, Rimbaud, Mallarmé, Apollinaire, Claudel, Valéry—stressed poetic form,[1] the true nature of which has only recently been discovered, at least with respect to distribution of vocabulary.[2] This and other attempts to state more precisely wherein consist order in literary form, and its opposite, disorder, are based upon the hypothesis that the most important and most significant feature to be considered is the relative frequency of occurrence of the several constituent elements in the underlying linguistic pattern. It is already known that the length of words is strictly related to their rank, their rank to their frequency of occurrence, frequency of occurrence to semantic variation. Hence, if a particular verse, the French alexandrine, for example, excludes long words, which are not well adapted to the flow of that verse, the immediate consequence is that the semantic, morphological, and phonematic structure of poetic discourse (as it appears in works composed in that particular verse) is correspondingly modified. There is always some deviation of frequency distribution from the arithmetic mean of the total observations made; and the sum of the deviations may be corrected by reducing it to the median on the assumption that the observations are evenly distributed. Depending on the particular text studied, the deviations indicate precisely that feature known to critics as "style," the formulation of which for a given author or genre has so far remained subjective and therefore vague.

---

[1] See C. M. Bowra, *The Heritage of Symbolism*, London 1943, p. 99, cf. p. 23.

[2] P. Guiraud, *Les Caractères statistiques du vocabulaire*, Paris 1954, pp. 75–107.

The evidence may be regarded from a very different point of view, namely, that of the theory of communication.[3] From study of the mathematics of telegraphic transmission, the conclusion has been reached that the entropy, or distribution of signs, in such a system corresponds to the distribution of linguistic units in discourse; and hence that there is a human apparatus for the transmission of spoken and written messages, those parts, that is, of the nervous system that produce and control speaking (which includes listening) and writing (which includes reading); and that the structure and operation of this system of signs (language) obeys the same laws as electrical transmission.

The symbolists are now being charged with having been escapists who used symbolism as a means of getting away from reality. One answer, at least, to this charge is to show that their works have significance in virtue of their inherent structure, and some of the new critics have seen this. Thus a reviewer of R. P. Blackmur's essays *Language as Gesture*, writing in *Thought* (28, 1953, 615–619), naïvely speaks of the creation of order as a new adventure in language. But it has always been there, and it is as real as cosmic order. Every complete work shows an internal coherent "economy" or (to coin a word) "glossonomy" that is the basic determinant of its particular style, to the same degree that its style can be shown to evince a latent deviation from the theoretical norm of usage. But this is by no means either an "adventure" or "new."

A first step in the determination of the structure of vocabulary is to ascertain the distribution of frequency of occurrence in the total number of words used by an author or in a given body of text, distinguishing between words of low semantic value (the definite and indefinite article, prepositions, and suchlike) and then words of increasing semantic value (auxiliary verbs), and finally those of genuine semantic content—all in descending order of frequency, for example *homo, poeta, lasciuus*, in Vergil 51 : 9 : 3 times respectively; or, to quote Guiraud's example,

---

[3] B. Mandelbrot, in *Publications de l'Institut de Statistique de l'Université de Paris 2*, fasc. 1–2, 1953, pp. 2–121. A simpler account may be found in *Word* 10, 1954, 1–27.

animal : *dog* : *Pekingese* : *my Pekingese*. The words of highest frequency ("empty" words) may be disregarded in the search for individual characteristics, which cannot dwell there. Instead, there must be computed the values:

N: total number of occurrences of "content" words;
V: total number of different "content" words in the text;
V_1: number of such words that occur once only.

For example, Donne has 3,944 words used once only, the alphabetical initials of which conform to the probabilities of the corresponding phonemes, words which also run in about the same proportion as "once"-words in the French symbolists. From these values it is possible to calculate the extent of an author's lexicon, and the degree of dispersion and concentration of his vocabulary; but it is necessary also to know the incidence of features of poetic discourse, such as rhyme; the relative frequency of different parts of speech (noun, adjective, verb, adverb); and the corrected deviation in the frequency distribution of an agreed number of the most frequent "content" words— say, fifty. Comparisons between one author and another, or between any of them and the "entire" language, are significant even within the range of these first fifty words. In a list taken to be representative of normal usage in the French language,[4] as compared with a computation of the frequency statistics of Mallarmé's *Poésies* compiled by Guiraud, for a copy of which I am indebted to its author (Groningen 1953, mimeographed), we find the following order of classification (by frequency):

	Vander Beke	Mallarmé
pas (ad.)	1	3
faire	2	25
plus	3	14
dire	4	16
y	7	20
aller	8	6

[4] *Bibliographie* 5B.84 (G. E. Vander Beke, *French Word Book*, New York 1929: based on a count of 1,147,748 running words in French prose 1850–1920).

	Vander Beke	*Mallarmé*
voir	9	12
comme (ad.)	11	1
vouloir	14	9
si (ad.)	15	46
savoir	17	8
enfant	23	19
où	24	2
non	25	27
beau	28	36
ainsi	29	37
très	31	38
seul	37	4
toujours	43	33

Striking divergences here are *faire*, *plus*, *dire*, *y*, *si*, commonplace words which Mallarmé uses more sparingly than the language as a whole; *comme*, *où*, *seul*, which are more frequent in Mallarmé than in normal French usage. But, to take single examples, *homme* (rank 6 in Vander Beke) does not occur in the first fifty items of Mallarmé, and *azur* (rank 5 in Mallarmé) does not occur in the first fifty of Vander Beke. As a result of his statistical studies, Guiraud (p. 80) describes Mallarmé's *Poésies* as having "lexique étendu, normalement dispersé" and "vocabulaire riche," adding (and this is the important point) that richness of vocabulary depends not only on its lexical extent, but also upon the exploitation of its range, i.e., upon structure.

But such descriptions of style, in articulate qualitative terms, lose in precision what they gain in easy intelligibility, and fail to measure accurately the qualities that distinguish an individual from his fellows as much as they fail to indicate the overall feature of any form of human activity, literature among them, into which choice, conscious or unconscious, enters. This can be done only by means of statistical analysis, by enumerating and classifying all observable facts; for such analysis gives the most efficient known method of observing, measuring, and interpreting both the common features of a "population" and the deviations of any particular members of the ensemble. So much has been recognized for many years in the investigation of other kinds of human behavior, e.g. in psychological studies. Linguistically, statistical analysis is concerned with "la parole," the individual rendering or act of speech, as well as with "la langue," the totality that is the "norm," and not merely with its minimum units.

The question of form and structure, therefore, may be related, if I mistake not, still more closely to information theory. An accepted model of communication goes like this:

$$\text{information} + \text{transmitter} \rightarrow \boxed{}^{\text{signal}} \rightarrow \text{receiver} + \text{destination}$$
$$(\text{message}) \qquad\qquad\qquad\qquad\qquad (\text{message})$$

The signal may be disturbed by interference ("noise") from any external source. A variation of the model stresses a "literary" rather than an engineering approach, but does not differ essentially:

$$\left.\begin{array}{l}\text{"intentive"} \\ \text{behavior of} \\ \text{the writer}\end{array}\right\} \rightarrow \begin{array}{c}\text{encoding} \\ (\text{writer})\end{array} \rightarrow \text{message} \rightarrow \begin{array}{c}\text{decoding} \\ (\text{reader})\end{array} \rightarrow \left\{\begin{array}{l}\text{interpretative} \\ \text{behavior of} \\ \text{the reader}\end{array}\right.$$

Linguistics is concerned with the code and the message; literature, with the "intentive" and interpretative behavior, less with the coding processes. Encoding involves the sequence of partly automatic "choices" permitted by a given linguistic pattern and their emergence as signals (in the human being performed by his motor system in speech or some other gesture, e.g. writing). The "choices" and their sequence manifest, at any particular occurrence, a high degree of determinacy, which is given in part by the nature of the "information," but more by "feedback" from previous utterances, heard and spoken, or written and read, all reinforced by previous experience. Encoding need not be overt— the vocal or gestural behavior may be suppressed, but can always be produced at call.

The *message* is both overt and, apart from random variations comprehensively labeled "noise" (i.e., disturbance or distortion), systematic. The systematic recurrent features are words and arrangements of words or sounds (phonemes) and their arrangements within the types and patterns of a language, and occasionally outside them. Decoding involves the hearer (but observe that we all are by turns indifferently speaker and hearer), that is to say, perception of the message and discrimination between different messages, all the way from phonemes to literary form—lyric, dramatic, and the rest. The immediate context of one or more elements, and the total environment furnished by a completed text, contribute to the process. And inconsistencies of any kind between sender and receiver of the message, and especially in the command of or use of the language concerned, give rise to "misunderstanding," especially if the language is one in which either of them is completely at home and the other not (cf. chap. i). The hearer, finally, may (or may not) respond either in further verbal behavior or in nonverbal action. This is his interpretation.

Defects of various sorts in verbal behavior, such as stuttering, seem to be, in part, the consequence of faulty coding at the phonematic or higher levels of speech. But speech disorders, which sometimes culminate in complete aphasia, are far from being well understood, and are by no means solely linguistic. On the other hand, many behavioral manifestations that ostensibly have nothing to do with language are clearly, on closer inspection, accompanied by linguistic correlations. Consciousness itself takes verbal forms more commonly than any other; and such features as repression, to take one simple example, are often detected by a distortion of verbal activity. However that may be, the kind of disorder that we shall have to consider in a work of literature, although personal, is very different. It is concerned, for example, with departures from established poetic features such as length of verse, metrical or grammatical anomaly, rhyme, stanzaic pattern, types and agreement of strophe and antistrophe, and similar arrangements of order.

There are certain obvious analogies between mechanical communication systems, such as the telegraph, and human speech, which is not to be wondered at, since they are founded upon speech. The sender encodes a message by turning it into signal units; the message is carried over a channel, is received, decoded, and reaches its destination. This, in the most general terms, is what has happened when, after a time lag of variable length, since the author was at work, a reader has occupied himself with a work of literature. It is no objection to say that communication theory merely quantifies the telephone company's commodity. As a poem is read, that is, as the message reaches its destination, entities are being received the original utterance of which depends upon the choice of those particular entities by the author. This is not a conscious, or fully conscious, choice—to put any such meaning into this cardinal principle of communication theory is a naïve misinterpretation. The choice (*la parole*) is determined, step by step, by structure inherent in the system (*la langue*) and in the particular genre and literary form; whence the structure of the poem, or whatever it may be, emerges; at the same time, it is an emergent form characterized by the individual author—his "style." If there is no option, no choice, that is, if the only answer to the question whether this or that entity is to be accepted, is "Yes," no structural contribution has been conveyed by that answer—it was known already. If the answer is either "Yes" or "No," then whichever answer is given does make such a contribution; if it is "Yes" or "No" or "Perhaps," then a greater contribution is made. The more possibilities there are, the more "formation" or structure emerges; the measure of its amount depends upon the number of possible answers. There is a close relation at this point between the technique of communication theory and word (or morphome) boundaries: as a sequence progresses, the amount of "structure" decreases, being more and more conditioned or predetermined by the pattern (the norm, *la langue*), but at intermediate stages (morphome boundaries) it suddenly increases with the onset of each new morphome. By using this technique it is possible to observe the degree of "structure" in Catullus (or any other author) in, for example, his use of words such as *castus, lasciuus, pudicus* (or any other such feature) as compared both with any part of his work in which the observed feature does not occur and with the usage of other Latin authors of his own age, or before him and after him.

In other words, structure and form correspond to the orderliness of language; within limits, disorder may be introduced— then an entity is *not* predetermined by the structural probabilities built into the language. Structure and form result from making adequate choices; if each unit in the system is adequate to represent x alternative choices, then the number of units in that system to give one out of N possibilities (cf. pp. 15–16, 136 above) is $\log_x N$. In a system of electrical relays $x = 2$; that is, the system is binary. Now the remarkable thing is that this situation corresponds exactly to language in use in all its manifestations, literary composition included. Everything proceeds by binary choices—since that is the way the human nervous system operates, by a "Yes"-or-"No" mechanism.

Linguistic symbolism, with its derivations, is the most effective attempt to apprehend and control the world of experience. By using verbal formulations as surrogates, we are better able to cope with infinitely numerous and complex memories of experience, to record insight and intuition, even to venture prediction. As the recorded resources increase in range and volume, we modify our formulations of them in the interests of consistency, or of uncovering verbal magic which, at bottom, rests on mistake, incoherence, inconsistency, and imprecision. The fact that the signaling units of speech are not equiprobable is accommodated by the well-developed theory of Markoff chains, a method of calculating conditional probabilities. Redundancy, as defined in communication theory, has as its correlate in literary form contextual clues to what is going to occur next in the sequence; for the form is continuous in the channel although it is composed of discrete units which, as encoded or decoded, trigger a response in the receiver of the message that corresponds closely to the "choice" of the sender.

In other words, all psychological considerations may be eliminated; the message is the consequence of physical and physiological laws of communication. But (cf. chap. vi) it does not
follow that teleological considerations must be abandoned; the
structure is purposive, structure and purpose also are correlates;
and even qualitative values emerge from the over-all structure
such as is revealed most clearly in literary and especially in
poetic Classical form, e.g. in a play of Sophocles. But choice is
still not haphazard—it was there in the first place, before the
rhapsode began to sing, Sappho to compose her lyrics, before
Catullus put pen to paper. Hexameters are a failure in English,
the saturnian failed in Latin, Olympian odes do best in Greek,
the *triṣṭubh* in Vedic Sanskrit. The "choice" of this or that unit
is dictated not only by the need for its use, but even more by
order: so that "information" is not what you learn, but the
element of surprise.

   In the graph inserted at page 202 in my book *Language* I have
given not only Zipf's harmonic law, the formula $p_r = P/r$ (here
r is rank, p_r its corresponding frequency, P constant), but also
Mandelbrot's canonical law, expressed in his formula $p_r =
P(r + \rho)^{-B}$, in which ρ and B also are constants, and only in the
special case where $B = 1$ and $\rho = 0$ is the harmonic law valid.
But B and ρ must always have a particular value, since the
number of words and the number of meanings at the disposal of
an author is metastable (p. 231). Variety comes in the use which
the author makes of the available vocabulary, different combinations of words (within the same structure) being infinitely
large. One may ask, therefore, what the critic means when he
speaks of "well-chosen" words. The answer would seem to be
that, since each unit has a predetermined frequency of occurrence, the intrinsic quality that distinguishes one sequence from
another is variety. A good text is that which shows the maximum
variety compatible with a minimum duration or cost or effort of
decoding. It is perhaps unfair to condemn Hipponax on this
ground as a "poor" text, for we have only a fragmentary text.
But this text would not have survived at all had there not been

considerable delay (that is, abnormally prolonged duration or cost) in its reception (or decoding), which even for readers in the direct line of the Greek tradition seems to have far exceeded the minimum permissible length; his "variety" came far too high, it cost too much, even though it must have satisfied Mandelbrot's canonical law, which is good for the dialect of Ephesus (or Clazomenae) as much as for standard English. This statement sounds paradoxical, if not impossible; that is because the canonical law involves parameters, which are defined as "variable constants," also a seeming contradiction. But consider a number of concentric circles of different lengths of radius; the ratio of the length of the circumference of any circle to the diameter (twice the radius) is of course constant ($2\pi r$, $\pi = 3.14159 \cdots$), and the radius itself is of constant length if confined to any given circle, but a radius drawn from a common center varies in length from one concentric circle to the others if conceived as belonging to the whole system of concentric circles—this radius is a parameter. A more homely illustration is a suit of clothes, which while remaining a constant, qua a suit of clothes, must be cut to fit the wearer. An individual writer wears, so to speak, a linguistic suit of clothes cut by himself to his own fit. But the variations are selective, just as a suit of clothes is selected, out of many cuts, for "fit"; only the selection, which is sequential, is made by the writer himself,[5] and his suit will not fit everybody, perhaps not anybody else at all. Here also the purposive quality of a text appears; Catullus is a well-made text, and its selective variations are almost all decoded (see chap. ii) at low cost. Every text, then, has its own parameters which nevertheless are such as to satisfy the canonical law. Exceptions are the outpourings of schizophrenics; and, at the other extreme, Esperanto and Basic English (Mandelbrot, p. 21), and, it must be added, Homeric "usage." If the parameter B is high, then the resources of

---

[5] On selective variation in the history and origin of language see *Newsweek* 30 July 1951, p. 62; and my papers in the *Scientific American* April 1952, pp. 82–86, and the *American Mercury* June 1953, 120–124. I was expounding the theory in my lecture room in 1941, as appears from Harvard Examination Papers of that year. Parameters are variables of the linguistic status, not of historic change.

the lexicon have been put to good use, and even "rare" words appear with appreciable frequency, and the text may be described as "closed" in the sense that the potential number of different words may be accurately predicted (e.g. in the works of markedly purist poets); if B is low, then the text is "open," the potential number of different words used is indifferent, words are not put to good use, and rare items remain at very low frequencies, or occur but once or even not at all (e.g. the language of children, especially those of poor general, and especially of poor linguistic, ability).

Classical Greek and Latin authors, so far as some preliminary calculations may be trusted, show a mean "informational" variety. But the *Iliad* is one exception, and has a very large deviation; another is Hipponax (although the bulk of text is perhaps too small),[6] and a third is the *Satyricon* of Petronius (the authorship of which is disputed). But Vergil (in the *Aeneid*) stays close to the mean, and Catullus departs very little from it. These judgments are based on samples of a particular stated size (except in the Hipponax sample, which was arbitrarily raised) in order to avoid possible error of incompatible ratios, which would make the figures almost as meaningless as any impressionistic judgment. Of the possible ratios between the four quantities special vocabulary, special occurrences, total vocabulary, and total occurrences, one (namely, the ratio special vocabulary / total vocabulary) is fallacious, a second (special occurrences / total vocabulary) is meaningless, a third (special vocabulary / total occurrences) is open to misuse, leaving the fourth (special occurrences / total occurrences) as most useful. But this is precisely the ratio that is most difficult to assess from subjective impressions: take, for example, Catullus 77.8 [Scaliger] *sauia comminxit spurca saliua tua*, and 99.10 *tamquam conmictae spurca saliua lupae*, which surely need no comment. Their tremendous impact on the reader is not at all confirmed statistically.

Any class of patterns may show a certain amount of disorder

---

[6] I have no figures for Pindar. If the text is trustworthy at *Ol.* 6.54 (βατείᾳ ἀπειράτῳ), it is remarkable to have two *hapax legomena* together. L.Sc. explain ἀπειράτῳ as -ῃτο- (cf. πειραίνω).

(entropy), as well as varying measures of "information" or order. Literary forms, like language in general, are more strictly associated with negentropy, i.e., with good order, which increases relatively with the increase of probability in the type of pattern. Thus literary form, even from the mathematical point of view, does show greater orderliness than nonliterary, verse than prose. This, as we shall see, may be the reason why poetry is found to be more quickening than prose, "good" literature than none at all, since life itself is normally negentropic. Here I am poles apart from Wiener's curious and crude notion that "what has been said before may not be worth saying again; and the informative value of . . . a piece of literature cannot be judged without knowing what it contains that is not easily available . . . in contemporary or earlier works" (!); the effect we are concerned with follows from the greater degree of orderliness, quite apart from content. After all, the content of the Classics is well known, it has been absorbed into the cultural life of the West, so much so that to some the Classics appear to be chiefly source material for compilers of a handbook of familiar quotations. Their true import is revealed only by an intimate familiarity in which each work is seen as a well-ordered unity; and this can be done only in the same measure as their readers' (or, if a single reader, his) receptor organs are adjusted to the author, the effector organs (a modern servo-mechanism being a reasonably appropriate model of human communication), namely, by knowing his language. However anomalous it may seem, it is nevertheless true that this improved insight into the nature of literary form and appreciation should have been given so vividly by communication engineers, not by literary critics, who persist in pursuing the wrong objectives and, far worse, in reading mere selections, and in offering translations.

But it is time to return to the question of linguistic symbolism with which this chapter began. Language has been called a systematic symbolism and an ergodic process. It is both of these; and both are implied in an expanded definition which says that language is a communicating system consisting of a finite num-

ber of regulated vocal (or graphic) symbols with several levels
of restricted syntactic relationships and unrestricted designatory capacity, a definition well suited for accommodating literature and its forms. At least this definition attempts to account
both for form and for function, and for the relation between the
two; the definition "systematic symbolism" is perhaps more
philosophical, and is based implicitly on a functional interpretation of the procedures of language; the other definition, "ergodic process" (a specialization of Markoff process), is based
upon a purely formal observation of the behavior of certain elements which the mathematician recognizes as linguistic (e.g.
phonemes and morphomes, the sequence of which in any utterance exhibits certain statistical regularities that may be described by the mathematical techniques of combinatorial analysis). The expanded definition is more meaningful than the two
brief attributive phrases. But it also begs the questions that we
say that it answers; for it implies the knowledge of what is a
"communication system," and what is the place occupied in
such a system by "symbols."

A communication system implies the existence of two variables, a sender and a receiver, with a fixed function and a fixed
relation to the system. The finite number of regulated vocal (or
graphic) symbols constitutes collectively the code; and the unrestricted designatory capacity is the frame of reference, which
may be coterminous with the universe itself. As for the several
levels of syntactical relationships, this factor is a peculiar complication of language, that is, of this particular communication
system, and not a fundamental constituent of any communication system whatever. In fact it is really a further specification
of the nature of the code. But it may also lead to considerable
modifications in the usage of any individual speaker or writer.

A communication system is a system designed to transmit
messages from one point to another, both points being part of
the system, both the "source" and the "terminus" or destination. In language, but by no means in all communication systems, source and terminus may be identical, or at least the same

person may serve indifferently as either, now the one, now the other. Now the messages thus transmitted may contain "information"; thus, if a certain message is *selected* from a repertory at the source, and this message is such as to permit the terminus to make the same *selection*, then "information" has been transmitted. Fundamentally, "information" is the ratio of the probability of making the right choice from a repertory after the transmission of the message to the probability of making the right choice without any such message. What I get from Homer or Catullus is what I cannot get from myself.

The working of a communication system is a process of encoding the message at the source, transmitting the coded message to the terminus, and of decoding it there. This is fundamentally the same as the situation of literary forms, where one has the writer (source) and the reader (the terminus, this time *not* reversible); and, as for the symbol and referend, a genetic (encoding) and expressive (decoding) process, respectively. A significant feature that is usually ignored is that of feedback, which enables the writer to correct his own message, to counteract interference or distortion (technically called "noise"), in situations in which the transmission is impaired. At least, that was originally true; the author's function unhappily is now usurped by scholars, who call it emendation; and by critics, who call it interpretation. The process is a highly refined one in literary as compared with nonliterary discourse; but it is not really different, biologically speaking, from the "feedback" process that occurs in childhood, when as infants we learn to talk and the problem of correction is acute. In later life it becomes firmly integrated into the linguistic system, so much so that when deprived of its "guidance" we find it difficult, in different degrees which may rise as high as temporary aphasia, to talk at all. So with the poet: if feedback fails, peculiarities of order enter, as in the mystic Hopkins; or "inspiration" fails, because in examining the roots of his work ("feedback"), the poet finds that some of it, so far from being clairvoyant (cf. pp. 203, 263), is almost nonsense, and then he ceases to believe in the importance of what

he himself is doing—all through the failure of a particular factor
of form, namely, the code; that is to say, the loss of order.

This matter of code, therefore, into which the message is
shaped, is all-important, and in short absolutely indispensable
in any communication system, literary discourse being no exception. Literature, I conclude, is a special variety of communication system, and form is an integral part of the code, especially
in verse. Neither linguists nor communication engineers have
yet recognized literary *form* as part of the code: at this level the
problem is that of striking an efficient equilibrium between the
capacity of the channel (the binary units of "information") and
conflicting factors ("noise") which now take the shape of inhibitions imposed upon the writer by the demands of form. Nowhere has this problem been posed with greater complexity, or
resolved with greater ingenuity, genius in fact, than in Pindar's
odes; but Pindar is the hardest Greek there is for a modern
reader to comprehend at all, if ever he *can* read Pindar as Pindar's own contemporaries read him.

The code is also influenced by the nature of the frame of reference; what limits, if any, are imposed upon the range of symbolization? Theoretically, none: the frame of reference in language is the entire universe. Even in practice a writer is free to
treat anything within his experience, primary or not. Conse-
quently the code must be relatively intricate; this intricacy is
achieved as follows. First there is a phonematic code of conven-
tionalized vocal symbols which, within the particular system
to which they belong, are easily and as a rule almost perfectly
differentiated. This code may vary in the number of units
(generally averaging around thirty to thirty-five, and telegraphy
—Morse code—may go no further), taking everything else
ready-made from language which has the necessary complexity
of its symbolization, thanks to the device (a "universal" of
language) of combining and recombining these primary elements
into series of relatively higher and higher units—the syllable,
morphome, word, the phrase, the sentence, the stanza or paragraph, the poem or chapter, the "book," the entire work, the

collected works of one author, the collected works of all the writers of a century or country, and so at last all the works of all authors of all ages and places. In any one of these, there obtain significant rules of ordering the elements: contrast Japanese and English or Greek poetry.

One of the most important types of ordering is of words, that which we call syntax. This is formally a modification of the code in terms of general communication theory, but in fact it is the most striking feature of language as a whole. The factor of "several levels of restricted syntactic relationships" is so potent that it is fair to speak of composition, as well as of language itself, as a form of order.

Throughout this chapter the term *form* has been used, perhaps ambiguously, not in the sense of linguistic form (a recurring vocal feature merely), but with reference to a feature far above the syntactic level, to that disposition or arrangement of its parts that gives a work of literature its particular *diathesis*—or, to coin a word, the *morphopoiesis* itself—as distinguished from a mere ensemble of units of which a given piece is made up; gives it, in the finest pieces, its *beauty* (a term which even in common usage often has *form* almost as a synonym), its grace and elegance. So much has been written about the restraint by which this result is attained in Greek and Latin authors that there is nothing which I could profitably add.

Yet there is still more. There remains what may be called extralinguistic context that plays an overwhelmingly large part in poetry, not crude meaning, for which I cannot find a better word than the threadbare *symbolism* and *symbolic*. But these *are* threadbare, and therefore I shall not adhere to them. The function appears to be to expound, even to enhance, that which a word or phrase says, beyond what, in strict lexical or ostensive or other definition, it might convey, by raising it to some power not defined, perhaps not definable, an allegorical, not algebraic, x: possibly *exponent, exponential* will serve my need, meaning as it were symbolic powers, or orders of reverbalization. The word as a linguistic unit is closed; the word as a symbol is open-ended.

It is not at all "information" in the technical sense that is transmitted, nor is literature "communication" as such, but a specialized variety of a particular system of communication that
might be called "supercommunicable" as well as extralinguistic:
les sons ne sont jamais expressifs qu'en puissance.

Language *is* a self-sufficient totality, but it is more than that.
It is precisely because language is more than what is said that
we seek a constant which underlies all languages, and all their
processes and fluctuations, in a word the system beneath the
external form, a constant anchored in the reality of which linguistic units are only the exponents, and which different authors
present from their several selective points of view, combining
formal characteristics with critical contexts in figurative language. It is sometimes urged that the universal language is the
"language of symbolism." But this seems to me a misappro-
priation of the word "language," much as in the expressions
"animal language" or "language of flowers," that amounts to
nothing more than mere punning and is a source of confusion.
The arts, or music, are *not* languages, nor have they in any
proper sense of the word their own languages; but language is,
or may be, for all human beings, a universal exponential symbolism, the others (art, music, and the rest) nothing remotely of
the same kind for most of us. If a successful "universal language," that is, a means of interlingual communication (commonly called an "international language"), is ever to be devised,
it will be through electronic, not linguistic, symbolization.

Literature, then, is concerned with understanding, not with
criticism. The critic dissects, indicates, paraphrases, interprets;
but he does not, and cannot, restate the content which literature pro-presents abstractly (as displaced speech). Its order is
metastable, that is, stable compared with all states differing only
infinitesimally from the given state. But language has its own
therapeutic measures and restores its own equilibrium. Just as
biological "links" are rare (being short-lived), and "new" stars
of temporary and usually short duration, so symbolism has its
startling deviations, also usually short-lived, from the system;

it presents problems which (fortunately) are inherent in the nature of linguistic expression, and liable to constant renewal. Notwithstanding the temporary, if brilliant, bursts of energy that accompany it from time to time, giving rise to a kind of disorder, symbolism, like literature at large, is orderly, since it is part and parcel of the dynamic, purposive activity of language itself. Language, like life, seems to have been in its origin a supreme form of symbolism, and both appear to be maintained in good order by obedience to the law of "information" or "communication" theory,[7] the principle of negentropy which averts both death and disorder. In this, language and literature alike partake of the cosmos and furnish an exit from the anarchy and disorder of human societies.

What was said above about the Classics as a mass of familiar quotations has a reverse application. Familiarity with these storehouses of symbols means, in the language of the day, that their content acts—or used to act—so as to "trigger" responses common to Western civilization. Obviously form plays no part, or but a little, in this function; yet the formal characteristics were often involved, if not realized, in the particular contexts, especially when figurative expressions were absorbed, and thus influenced personal or multipersonal practices. This is an aspect of Classical form that greatly needs investigation. But it is not literature, or literary form, that needs exegesis. It is the "exact" forms of discourse that call most loudly for recognition. Complete stability is not attainable in normal linguistic situations, nor even desirable. If symbolic logic aims at it, or scientific discourse, like law and religion, professes to attain it, this is a delusion. In symbolic logic, stability is achieved only at the cost of inhibiting change, which sooner or later will burst the bonds of any system of logic; in the natural sciences, the law, and religion, the use of normal language, whether a vernacular or a

---

[7] See Homer Jacobson, "Information Theory and Life," in *American Scientist* 43, 1955, 119–127, Schrödinger, *What Is Life?* (Cambridge 1946); my papers cited in note 5 above; and L. von Bertalanffy in the *British Journal for the Philosophy of Science* 1, 1950, pp. 141–162.

petrified legal or religious language (e.g. Sanskrit, Coptic, Old Church Slavonic, Latin), will constantly demand new definition and exegesis, and logical syntax is founded upon, and individually learnt from, "ordinary" language. In strongest contrast to this, literary discourse is its own best commentary: even sense and sound go together and supplement each other, but not in the interpretation that certain phonemes or groups of phonemes carry, and carry universally, inherent meaning. What *is* true is that meaning may be acquired by, and so come to inhere, as it were by abstraction, in a particular speech sound or group of such sounds, in some given language, from a very few words—two or three will do—and then be extended to others. Thus English initial *sl-* is said to be depreciatory; but historical considerations show that English words beginning with *sl-* are of quite diverse origins, and that the *sl-* itself varies correspondingly in respect of source. No Latin word begins with *sl-*, no Greek word except the foreign and uncertain σλιφομάχος. In what sense, then, do "we react to the sound of the words, rather than merely to their meaning"? Is not the "sound," even of a word of unique occurrence, part of the meaning? The phonemes and their sequences give conventionally, almost arbitrarily, the meaning—English *table* has meaning, *letab* or *eltab* has not. Why? The phonetic entities are the same, or nearly enough the same; the phonematic patterns are widely different. But even at the phonematic level, form plays a greater role than sound, and the same sequence of sounds may totally differ in meaning, not only when reversed (*God : dog*), but in words differing only by a single phoneme. Thus may we seriously maintain that *-ame* [eịm] is filled with a content of meaning for its "pleasing" sound? Surely not: we all remember *South Pacific*—"There's nothing like a *dame . . . same . . . name . . . frame.*" Rhyme would be impossible if it had to depend on meaning inherent in sound and nothing else. Now the same is true at every level. *Table* is a *verbal* symbol. So, in like manner, *and* or *beer* or *have* or *embryo* or *drunk* or *man*. Now when we have occasion to use such a verbal symbol, we do so in a systematic way. Thus the verbal symbols "table and embryo have drunk beer," placed in that sequence, are so unsystematic in arrangement as to symbolize nothing, unless possibly dementia on the speaker's part; but "the man has drunk beer," by adhering to the system, retains the symbolic integrity of each symbol, and the arrangement enhances their symbolic values.

One other way of putting what has just been said about the systematic character of linguistic symbolism is to say that, at any given status of its history, a language is found to show a statistical regularity which may be put in terms of formulae that are concerned with classical probability of frequency of occurrence of the constituent elements, and of permitted combinations of them within the pattern of a particular language. Objectively, therefore, a language may be described as a body of physically discrete events in which relations of similarity occur in a statistically definable pattern.

If a permissible sequence of symbols that makes a word, for example the series *furious*, is followed by anything at all, then those following symbols are already prescribed and limited; in this case they must be *l y* or *n e s s* (not normally *e r* or *e s t*) and nothing else. In other words, the symbols *ly* or *ness*, in this particular sequence, are determined by what went before, and therefore may be said to add nothing to the information conveyed. Determinacy is in such an instance close to 100 per cent.

The argument that language gives reality carries no conviction whatever; and it is just as difficult to answer the question, What (if not reality) gives language? It seems likely that each author selects certain features of his nonlinguistic environment for linguistic expression, and that some linguistic devices are more fitted to the making of distinctions than others. Wherever the inflexional method is, or has been, well developed, there seems to be considerable aptitude for abstracting a great variety of features from the physical environment for linguistic designation.

Now since order and form are paramount at each stage from

phoneme to sentence, and are in part latent in certain of these stages, it would seem reasonable to suppose a corresponding relationship of equilibrium between form and function in outward form all the way from an epigram consisting of a two-line couplet, through melic poetry, to drama. It is commonly said that melic poetry consists of three elements—words, melody, and rhythm. To these form or structure should be added as an obvious fourth: triadic structure (strophe, antistrophe, and epode) manifestly guarantees equilibrium. What could be structurally more defined than a Greek tragedy (prologue, parodos; first episode; first stasimon + anapaests; second episode; second stasimon + anapaests; third episode; third stasimon + anapaests; fourth episode; fourth stasimon; fifth episode; fifth stasimon or hyporcheme; exodos), creating a pattern comparable to those to the breach of which we are so sensitive in musical composition; or a comedy of Aristophanes (prologue; parodos; parabasis with ode, epirrheme, antode, and antepirrheme; first and second syzygy; agon; second parabasis; episode; second agon; exodos)? Much as editors differ about detail, strophic correspondence in the *Peruigilium Veneris* is generally admitted—not irregular groups of lines followed by a refrain. Restoration of order, disturbed in the manuscript tradition, carries its own proof. Here is rich and abundant material for statistical investigation. But the important feature is manifest and patent order. The disorder exhibited by some modern writers of verse—Ogden Nash or e. e. cummings for example—is best matched by the disorder of advertising copy writers (*Ibath, Eye-gene, Eye-cues*), which depend upon appeal to the eye, not to the ear (*blimpwich, traxcavators, exercycles*), and is likely to vanish for the same reasons—that it violates the law $r \cdot f = K$ by overloading in the "input-output" channels, that it is totally irreversible and therefore lacks the correction of "feedback." Everyday discourse may not dispense with these requirements; the safeguard of poetic discourse, which makes them unnecessary to it, is precisely its good order (cf. pp. 223–227 above).

All the recorded data of literary composition belong to history, whether a phonographic recording of a new poem made by Macleish yesterday afternoon, or the oldest parts of the Vedas. But in practice we are obliged to take into consideration data that belong to a relatively brief segment of time, during which it is assumed that there are no changes in the subject matter under study. This is a fiction. If we had sufficiently detailed observations of Attic Greek in Athens during the span within which Sophocles composed the *Antigone*, even the span within which a single performance of the *Antigone* could be gone through, we should be compelled to observe divergences within even such brief periods of time as these—the shortest possible sufficient for the accumulation of the data. Distortion may be excessive, as witness James Joyce; or nearly at a minimum, Sophocles. But to specify form at all implies (*a*) that it has been observed, and (*b*) that it will continue to survive for some time longer. In their turn these implications lead to the assumption of a certain degree of determinacy. If we had no tradition at all of Classical form, or of the works which embrace it, and then by some fortunate accident came upon a supply of recordings—papyri or manuscript, or, better still, tape recordings of an actual performance—an intelligent observer, curious to know the nature of these documents, would quickly notice the recurrence of specific features that could not be regarded as random, rhythmic movements so complex they could not entirely be overlooked, and yet not a merely oscillatory pattern, but correlations in sequence. But the longer the sequence, the more likely it would be that the identity of any given component would be determined by that of other components; or, in other words, the minimum definition of any such element is given in terms of the sequences which determine its occurrence; and as a sequence is extended, the determinacy of successive enlargements at first increases and then drops off abruptly, giving wavelike fluctuations. This is clearly a contextual situation which is better approached by measurement than by literary consciousness, in which subjective error becomes cumulative. Moreover, events taken out of context notoriously are ambiguous, their true meaning being inaccessible until related facts are known; in the case under consideration, by means of distributions in quite large contexts.

So far as items of vocabulary go—now we are coming back, as promised, to *castus*, *lasciuus*, and *pudicus*, and surely there is no ambiguity of natural language in any of these three items—one might take contexts with one preceding item (p 1), or one item following (f 1), two preceding (p 2), or two following (f 2), both of these four complexes (b 1, b 2, i.e., one or two units both preceding and following), or the entire context (c). No context at all infers ambiguity of varying dimensions in most cases; context reduces the ambiguity by more than 45 per cent for p 1 and f 1, by just less than 50 per cent for b 1 and p 2, more than 50 per cent for f 2, nearly 60 per cent for b 2, 75 per cent for c—whether context of vocabulary, of meter, or grammatical form. The reduction is contributed by units not more than two items away; the context acts quite specifically, and markedly in a b 2 context which is almost as efficient as c, for example both "it smells" and ". . . the guinea stamp" (see p. 120) reduce the ambiguity of *rank* by their substantive and not merely syntactic function;[8] or both $- \cup \cup \mid - \cup \cup$ and $\cup - \mid \cup -$ remove any ambiguity in $\mid -- \mid$ taken by itself; or κρατῆσαι not κρατήσειν (at Thucydides 2.3.2) is guaranteed by both ἐπιθέμενοι and ἐνόμισαν (the subject of both verbs being the same).

The principle may be illustrated by graphs; a probability 1 (certainty) means that no other unit is possible, a probability 0 (impossibility) means that anything at all will do (and this *is* impossible). All the curves show a pronounced but irregular (not oscillatory) pattern, with a higher degree of determinacy for "learned" words (*noris nos : docti sumus*), especially if they are also "long" words.

The relation between actual sequences of restricted length and potential sequences of any length is instructive. The numbers cannot be determined by counting for the latter, and only

---

[8] Cf. A. Kaplan, *An Experimental Study of Ambiguity and Context* (P-187, Rand Corporation, Santa Monica, Calif., 1950). As for word length and letter frequency, see also A. G. Oettinger, "Design for an Automatic Dictionary" (Harvard doctoral thesis, Applied Mathematics, 1954), Appendix C. On English *rank* compare *Language* p. 74.

for the briefest sequences (two or three units) for the former,
but must be obtained by extrapolation—indeed they rise astro-
nomically (potentially 10^{24} for 13/14 units; actually 100,000+,
potentially 10^7, even for 4 units) for any but the shortest sequences, and the ratio between the two series increases geo-

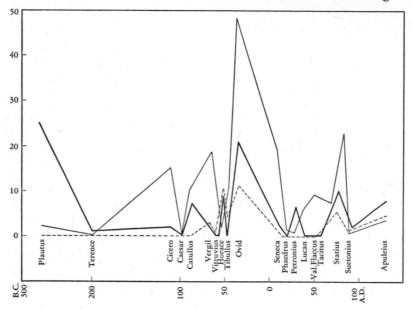

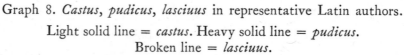

Graph 8. *Castus*, *pudicus*, *lasciuus* in representative Latin authors.
Light solid line = *castus*. Heavy solid line = *pudicus*.
Broken line = *lasciuus*.

metrically by a constant factor. Applied to concrete limited
samplings, this technique seems to lead to the conclusion that
the functional saturation of any special variety of vocabulary
(learned, poetic, obscene) is decidedly below that of ordinary
discourse, in which only the function of reference checks entropic degeneration to the prolonged *a-a-a-ah* of a new-born
babe. The opposite extreme is supplied by such compounds as
appear conspicuously in Sanskrit, for example in Navya Nyāya
philosophy, in which a tautology of contraposition, in most con-
texts best expressed symbolically $(\bar{p} \sim \bar{q}) \equiv (\bar{q} \sim \bar{p})$, may easily

both be made articulate and exemplified at the same time by this very means (compounding).

In the graph given above (chap. i, p. 16), I have reproduced the formulae of Zipf and Mandelbrot which are representative, in their respective applications, of the normal situation with

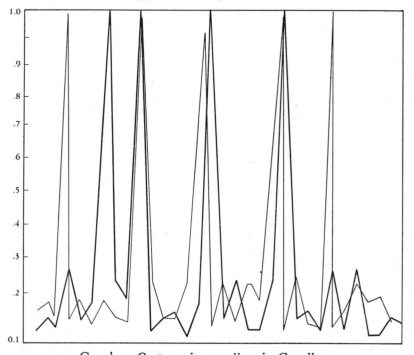

Graph 9. *Castus, pius, pudicus* in Catullus.

Light line = nam castum esse decet pium poetam (16.5).
Heavy line = pudica et proba, redde codicillos (42.24).

respect to frequency of occurrence, length, and perspicuity (or conspicuousness). For example, a *hapax legomenon*, which is rarest in recorded occurrence (once only) is long, shows high determinacy, high "information," low functional saturation. The appended diagrams[9] present (graph 13) certain functional

---

[9] For the graphs of *castus, pudicus, lasciuus* I am indebted to my student Harvey Sobelman; for the charts of functional saturation to a former student, Robert Abernathy.

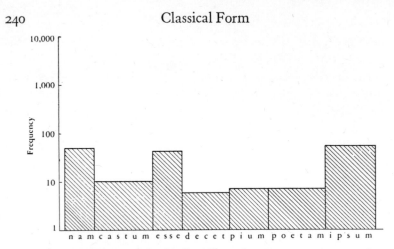

Graph 10, A. *Castus, pius* in Catullus 16.5: nam castum esse decet
pium poetam / ipsum, . . .

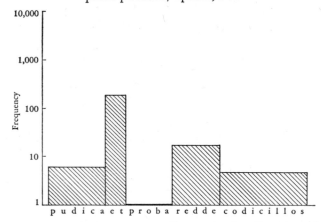

Graph 10, B. *Pudicus* in Catullus 42.24: 'pudica et proba,
redde codicillos.'

variants and (graph 14) functional saturation. Pro-presentation
is a third dimension of language; it is that displacement of
speech that liberates from the here and now, the goal of which
is not solely, or at least not chiefly, informative. A proposition
may be true or false; a unit of significance (within a contextual
complex) neither true nor false, but a variable. Thus poetic discourse is not primarily informative, but dynamic and emotive.

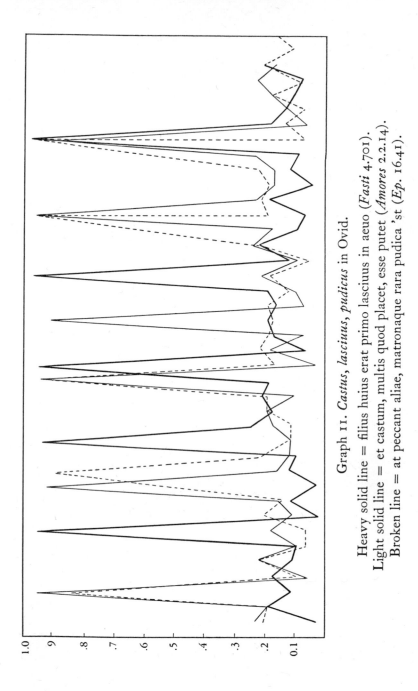

Graph 11. *Castus, lasciuus, pudicus* in Ovid.

Heavy solid line = filius huius erat primo lasciuus in aeuo (*Fasti* 4.701).
Light solid line = et castum, multis quod placet, esse putet (*Amores* 2.2.14).
Broken line = at peccant aliae, matronaque rara pudica 'st (*Ep.* 16.41).

We now come back to the problem (chap. ii), How does a given author stand in relation to other authors; specifically, how does Catullus stand to other Latin writers? We may remind our-

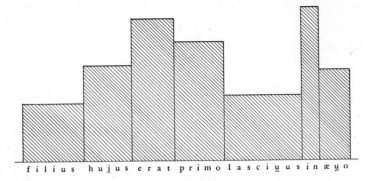

Graph 12, A. *Lasciuus* in Ovid *Fasti* 4.701: filius huius erat primo lasciuus in aeuo.

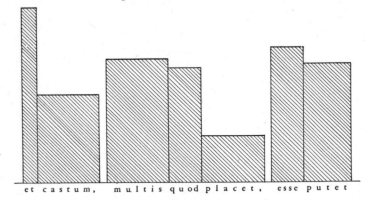

Graph 12, B. *Castus* in Ovid *Amores* 2.2.14: et castum, multis quod placet, esse putet.

selves at once that "information" (in the engineering sense) is high: the discourse of Catullus is by no means commonplace (*odi et amo; salaputium, ploxenum,* and the like). Here is negentropy clearly in evidence, the maintenance of equilibrium notwithstanding synonyms, homonyms, identity, total differentiation, ἅπαξ λεγόμενα, redundancy, and all the rest. Graph 13 pre-

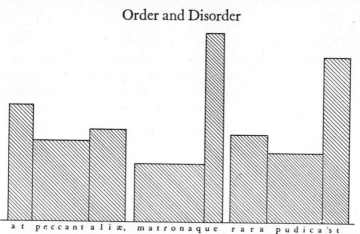

Graph 12, c. *Pudicus* in Ovid *Ep. ex Pont.* 16.41: at peccant aliae, matronaque rara pudica 'st.

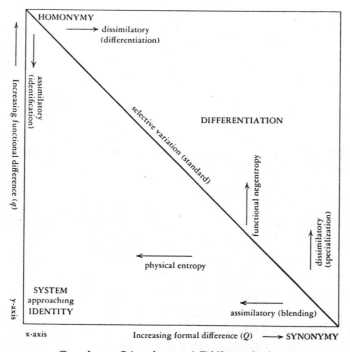

Graph 13. Identity and Differentiation.

sents functional and formal relationships as dimensions of a finite two-dimensional continuum. Resemblances among members of a system decrease proportionally along the two axes (x functionally, called q; y formally, called Q). Qualitative appreciations are added for purposes of interpretation, but the dia-

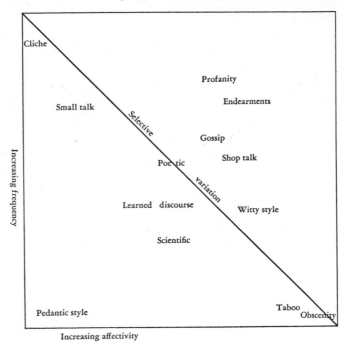

Graph 14. Functional saturation.

gram is not based upon them; and they are only approximations. There is in language neither complete identity nor complete synonymy. A recent, not very good, collection of Latin synonyms (by Gustav Humpf, 1954), intended for young composers in Latin, lists only 297 items; only 7 have more than six synonyms (no. 3 *old*, 37 *image*, 39 *ask*, 111 *think*, 173 *sacrifice*, 236 *kill*, 263 *property*), and of these 7, 4 only have seven synonyms: no. 39 has nine, 11 and 236 have eight each; there are, of course, many with four to six. Further, when units come one

after another without premeditation, which seems to have been
Ovid's case (*Tr.* 4.10.26, *quod temptabam dicere uersus erat*) as
well as Pope's and Byron's (and Isaac Watts's), there is an increase in determinacy at very low cost, or expenditure of energy,
in the working of the system, tending ideally toward a state in
which the probability of any form in any context is unity—decidedly not the case of Catullus.

The problem is that of stating affective values quantitatively,
not under special conditions of emotional stress, but the conventional affectivity of form. In such a formulation we have a statement of the literary syndrome of affective value: low frequency
and low determinacy. The difference between a cliché and an
epigram is that the cliché is frequent, the epigram rare; between
a pedestrian literary style and an "inspired" style, that the
former employs consistently the most probable units and sequences of the system in any context. Modern writers, aware of
this fact, have drawn the false conclusion that to use the most
improbable units will produce a brilliant style. This vicious
"originality" quickly produces unintelligible writing instead.
Still, many figurative forms are essentially variants called up by
the selection of the less probable in place of the more probable;
this also is negentropy, especially when what began as figurative
becomes the convention. But we should add that there is an
emotional upsurge, and that the drive which accompanies this
increase in affectivity, a little recognized type of selective variation, is what keeps structure "alive"; it is a force that counter-
acts entropic degeneration. Contrariwise, the progressive loss of
distinctive structure and function is commonly accompanied by
a loss of affective force, as is clear enough in the literature of the
centuries immediately following the disappearance of Classical
forms. It was that very scholastic preoccupation with theology
and philosophy, the final intellectual product of the Middle
Ages, that fed fuel to the flame of "humanism," once acquaintance with the old literatures was renewed. What I am stressing
now is the correlation between different degrees of frequency
and determinacy on the one hand, and affectivity on the other,

which once more gather around a line (roughly) −1 (or 45° slope). As to Catullus and obscenity in particular, observe that the low frequency is accompanied by high affectivity—the tendency to increased frequency would (and does, in some writers, Aristophanes for example, perhaps Hipponax) lessen affectivity; again a matter of negentropy, in which the vitality of the form (invective and satire in the ἴαμβος and Old Comedy; and, so far as metrical form is concerned, the scazon in Hipponax and Catullus) is not squandered, but sparingly used. Certain utterances have a peculiar potency of their own. Polite letters are likely to see their center of gravity shift toward inanity; their polished elegance refines their potential out of existence—witness Matthew Arnold.

What is commonly called "sound symbolism" appears to be an illusion. The writing of Catullus or Hipponax is not characterized by any such phenomenon, and items like *pius, castus, pudicus, lasciuus* certainly do not show it. So-called "symbolic forms," for example onomatopoetic words and interjections (the latter being strictly extralinguistic), owe a certain deceptive appearance of force, not to any real affective value, but to their association with responses that hardly rise above mere reflex actions. More valid is the view that structural tension decreases as specific meaning (the referend) increases in scope; that is, an obscene term is taken not literally, but symbolically, in its context (there is no reference here to *sound* symbolism): contrast *meio, mingo,* ὀμείχειν with what is used as an equivalent in French or English; wherever vulgar Latin *pišare* came from, it was not from Greek πίσσα, πίττα (š is the phonetic value of σσ, ττ), or from any of its derivatives borrowed into Latin. Whether the contrasts *m : p* and ʒ : š are relevant, only statistical investigation would show.

If the theory of these lectures is sound, I shall (no doubt) be challenged to predict the course of literature, or at least of poetic discourse. I do not think the challenge fair, since we have not yet arrived at explanations of the facts exact enough to give rise to predictions. It would be worth while to discover, if possible, the causes which make human activity seem unpredictable, if only in order to eliminate or at least reduce them. It may be that the scope of chance has been too severely narrowed, and the assumption of laws of chance too readily accepted. If so, there is indeed enormous scope for prediction—but a conditioned and restricted prediction.

We can predict how large populations will act, but not what they will do as individuals. If a machine is ever made that will compose sonnets—not an impossibility,—it will be because knowledge of the problem (in probabilities) is in fact a part of the very statement of the problem, in which the machine will be "instructed." The possibility of solution to such a problem is always bound to reflect the accuracy and clearness with which it was stated in the first place. The great number and complexity of the factors involved, the risk of independent modification of them before prediction can be made, the autonomy of some of the phenomena, the difficulty of experiment when phenomena are not repeated exactly, possibly even the changes of trend evoked by a technical civilization—all these may honestly be pleaded. But over and above them all is the urgent necessity of growth in "humanism" to match that of "science": the restoration, that is, of the concept of an equilibrium between these two forms of activity, perhaps the best element in all our ideas of man, society, and nature, to be inherited from the Mediterranean tradition.

VIII
Confessio Fidei
Classical Humanism

THOSE WHO have heard or read these lectures so far must have had enough of linguistics, philology, science, and autobiography. I too shall retire willingly enough from this invasion of territory now somewhat distant from my proper field. In fact, I begin this last lecture with a certain sense of inadequacy which would not have beset the confidence with which I might have approached its topic when I was thirty years younger. But the treatment would have been very different, and, I dare say, more acceptable to humanists. *Humanism*, so far as I can make out, is a term applied to a phase of the Renaissance, not of Classical antiquity. It did indeed find its ideal in a return to the study of Classical literature; but can there be said to be a Classical humanism? And if so, in what sense?

Fascist has the same formation as *humanist*, and *Nazism* as *humanism*, being one of those "foreign *-isms*" against which, as being also recent, we are warned; older ones, though alien, being acclimatized are usually considered no longer dangerous (e.g. *Romanism*). There are usually also verbs in *-ize*, parallel to the nouns, as *nationalize : nationalist : nationalism*, some of them quite innocent, like *pulverize* or *macadamize*. One original model seems to have been a mere handful of denominative verbs like Attic ἐλπίζω (Homeric ἔλπομαι), older *ἐλπίδίω from ἐλπίς (-ίδος), which, out of the small class of nouns in -δ-, gives us a pretty example of the analogical extension of a whole series of productive suffixes. The association with a manner of speech (ἑλληνίζειν, σολοικισμός,[1] βαρβαρισμός) or with politics (φιλιππίζειν) is already

---

[1] Cf. E. Bickel in *Annuaire de l'Institut de Philologie et d'histoire orientales et slaves* 5 (Brussels 1937), 69–76.

ancient but rare; with a school of thought (πλατωνίζειν, Origen ca. 185 to ca. 254 A.D.) or religion (*christianizare*, Tertullian ca. 160–240 A.D.) it is later. Now these are all areas of usage in which prejudice is present, or into which it readily enters, together with the derogatory flavor that attends many "-isms" as named by those who wish to depreciate the practice or opinions of others. The "practical" man speaks scornfully of *philosophism* or *psychologism*, the humanist of *scientism*, all secondary formations based upon existing nouns in *-ia* or of that type (*philosophy, psychology, science*), which may have something to do with the escape of *humanism* from a pejorative connotation, being formed, as it is, directly from the adjective *human(us)*. But that is not the sole reason; scientists, whose training and habit excludes prejudice from their inferences and judgment, do not, so far as I have observed, even those few of them who disapprove of *humanism* in education, use the word as a term of reprobation in the way in which, and this I *have* observed, certain humanists have taken up, if they did not invent, the recent formation *scientism*, a neologism designed chiefly, it would seem, in order to express distrust of science in education.

There is no such opposition between the human (or humane) and the scientific in Classical authors, whose view appears to me to be the correct one. It has been pointed out that *humanism* is itself a comparatively recent coinage, "having been created as late as 1808 by a Bavarian schoolteacher,"[2] and he used it in opposition to "Philanthropismus," not to *science*. The first occurrence of *humanist* is 1538 (the Italian *umanista*). Compilers of dictionaries of synonyms (for example, Webster's, 1942) catalogue the humanities with literature, letters, or belles-lettres as if science were not also concerned with the "activities, interests, and progress of man" (p. 514). The restriction to Greek and Latin specifically has not, in the long run, done either the term or what it stands for (in this narrow sense) any good. The use of

---

[2] B. Snell, *Geistige Welt* 2, 1947, pp. 1–9 (and now in his *Discovery of the Mind*, Cambridge Mass. 1953, see pp. 246, 320), after W. Rüegg, *Cicero und der Humanismus*, Zürich 1946, pp. 3, 129.

"humanist" in the meaning "Classical scholar" is an exaggerated claim, explicable only historically. It arose simply in opposition to "philosopher" or "theologian" at that time, during the Renaissance, when the rediscovery of Greek and Latin literature brought about a revolution in education which had become concentrated on the production of divines, priests, and monks. The antonym of *humanus* is surely *inhumanus*, a binary "yes-no" choice. But the disjunction is usually evaded by an appeal to words like *natural(ism)*, *supernatural(ism)*. There is an element of illusion about *humanism* as currently used by Classical scholars that they would be quick to detect in the terminology of other fields and that arose from the transfer of the word from its historical setting, so that it has now become a concept out of context. The anxieties of the times in which we live seem to give it a certain justification, which, strangely enough, has communicated itself to some natural scientists and to many sociologists. This, despite the recognition, by both of these, that the evolutionary process implies not only change but also stability. During historic times there has been no fundamental change in human physiological or psychological capacities, or in human aptitudes produced by biological evolution. What man has done in the twentieth century of our present era was inherent in man in the fifth century of the preceding era. What *has* changed has been the extension of his memory through the means of making and preserving human records, all the way from simple pictographic devices to the most recent and elaborate of machinery for recording, coding, and retrieving information. This is the problem of modern man: his brain remains what it has been all along, but the amount of information which he is feeding into it, with its limited input channels, has become vastly larger, causing what is essentially a breakdown of the system, freely recognized as such in individuals. Hitherto this modern problem has been met, not solved, by the device of specialization, since so few possess the necessary faculty of synthesis, the power, that is, of acquiring a comprehensive yet valid view of the world as an ordered whole, a cosmos not a chaos: which is something very

different from what Matthew Arnold meant. In such a view the
humanities and the sciences are equal partners, each contribut-
ing its own message, at times even adding new messages (cf. pp.
185, 213). Such a partnership was implied in the ancient theory
of man's place in the universe, which made no sharp separation
between language and literature, as one thing, and science, as
another.

A familiar formulation is the first stasimon of the *Antigone*.
What effect do you suppose these lines of Sophocles had upon
his contemporaries? Nothing like that which they now have
upon any modern reader either of the Greek original or of a
translation, both of which read like antiquarian jargon. I expect
to be adversely criticized for what I am about to say: that the
speculations of the chorus, there at Athens in the mid-fifth century of the pre-Christian era, an Athens which drew upon the
whole of her world both for material goods and for intellectual
stimulus, speculations about Promethean human invention and
discovery, and the peril as well as gain that these confer, are
comparable here in Berkeley, California, or in Cambridge, Massachusetts, in the mid-twentieth century of our era, to the speculations of a philosophically minded biologist or physicist (those
doubtful specialists), recruited possibly from abroad, along with
foreign "-isms" and foreign goods. To produce the same sort of
effect, what he might say would go something like this:

The species *homo sapiens* is biologically unique. He has an enor-
mously exaggerated brain, to which he owes his remarkable power of
intellect. He has, in consequence, become superior to all other animals,
and has succeeded in dominating the world through his readiness to
try experiments. Feats of engineering enable him to reach and to
communicate with any part of the earth, to increase the production
of food, to control the conditions of life, and to protect himself against,
or even modify, extremes of climate—all this despite the fact that
physically he is the poorest equipped for defense and survival among
all species. His expectancy of life has been greatly prolonged. His intelligence is adaptable to many varieties of purpose; the human species, in fact, is likely to become cleverer. But man's superior scientific

knowledge, applied to the conduct of his affairs, is productive of evil as well as of good—

σοφόν τι τὸ μηχανόεν
τέχνας ὑπὲρ ἐλπίδ᾽ ἔχων τότε μὲν κακόν,
ἄλλοτ᾽ ἐπ᾽ ἐσθλὸν ἔρπει.

I do not think that I have exaggerated, or not much, the "modern" ring in this modernization of the thought of Sophocles; note especially such items of vocabulary as μηχαναί, φύσις, παντοπόρος, μηχανόεις, τέχναι. Lucretius went much further; he built his poem, his entire view of existence, on a scientific theory. Humanistic theory, man as the subject of man's own study, as it appears in Greek and Latin literature, is something quite different from what is now understood by *humanism* in any of the recognized meanings of the word, and stands as close to what we should consider the sciences as to literature. But the science of the ancients has no longer any but historical value. Scientific theory is impermanent; humanistic, even when it takes a diabolic turn (Southey called Byron's poetry "satanic"), more lasting; but what it gains by endurance it loses in dynamic quality.

In Greek and Latin authors the opposite of "human" is not usually "inhuman," which is the modern contrast or antonym, but either "divine" or "brutish, beastly." Yet, concerning the most striking distinction in which man differs from the animals, the ancients and moderns are agreed—the power of speech; even the barbarian Triballoi talk, only not Greek. In evolutionary terminology this power is now called a "biologically unique capacity," the latest step in evolution. The orators, both Greek and Latin, encouraged the deliberate cultivation of this power, in the shape of eloquence and persuasiveness, as part of the necessary education of the citizen who was to take part in public affairs. Your modern evolutionist, if he is very daring, may venture the opinion that man's peculiar capacity of talking is itself capable of further refinement and sharpening; to me it seems more likely that the future may bring the development of some nonlinguistic form of symbolism and the substitution of this for linguistic symbolism, at least in world-wide interlingual communication, something more fitted to modern methods of transmitting messages than age-old speaking and writing. The sophists, too, had urged the importance of rhetoric; but Plato, in the *Gorgias*, warns against it. He contrasts a genuine and a pretentious education of the human ψυχή, and places sophistic and rhetoric together as pretentious, much as a modern critic might protest against the misuse of words in moronic broadcasting. Plato would have been skeptical of one of the chief tenets of modern humanism, that is, its uncompromising opposition to specialization. It was Plato's view, in the *Republic*, that there is no more fertile source of misery and crime than the pursuit of that for which a man is unfitted by nature; his ideal of civic justice is τὰ αὑτοῦ πράττειν, that everyone should do his special professional work, and not meddle outside his proper competence.

It is not astonishing, the uncertainties of translation considered, that the relation of *humanitas* to φιλανθρωπία and ἀνθρωπισμός (yet another *-ism*) is in doubt. On the whole the Latin word appears to overlap the content of both Greek terms and to convey something of both. In Snell's words, "from Cicero onward *humanitas* combines the humane with the humanistic; a special blend of unself-conscious ease and gracious affability is paired with a study of the classical authors who teach the art of speech,"[3] a lame conclusion that has little in it to command the attention of modern man.

The other contrast in which man may be set is with the divine, which is hardly distinguishable from everything that is external to man. Here also there were two interpretations: the first, which again has a peculiarly modern ring, stresses the insignificance of man either "in the sight of God" or as compared with the universe; the second springs from the rise of scientific thought. The modern equivalent of the injunction set in letters of gold at one side of the porch of the temple of Apollo at Delphi, the

[3] Snell, *Discovery of the Mind*, p. 254.

maxim γνῶθι σεαυτόν, is not the translation "know thyself" (I
have never met anyone, student in college or outsider, who could
give any clear account of this English rendering), but, as J. T.
Sheppard used to teach us, "bear in mind that you are not Al-
mighty God, but merely human"; and then the other injunction
at Delphi comes into play, μηδὲν ἄγαν "remembering this, do not
go to extremes," a play on the Greek virtue of σωφροσύνη, that
sense of the middle which characterizes the man of sound mind,
the observation of due moderation in all things, the recognition of number, of order, and of the mean. This implies that to
the Greeks the universe is a cosmos, that everything is controlled
by good order, in itself a tautology since the very word κόσμος
(in Latin mundus, a semantic borrowing) has both meanings—
"good-order" = "world-order." This -sm- formation has nothing
to do with the -isms; it is a simple -mo- derivative from the same
base as Latin censere, thus inferring a view of the world not unlike that implied by the word of God, either the "God said" of
the Old Testament or the λόγος, the divine "plan" of the Fourth
Gospel, the "choice" or "selection" of an appropriate order of
arrangement of utterance that appears in λέγειν "to say" and
legere "to read" and, in part, in religio, of which confessio is the
public proclamation. This belief in order and stability is by no
means exhausted or obsolete. In particular a linguist cannot but
regret that mankind betrays the cosmos of his speech by nearly
all the rest of his behavior. Nonlinguistic human activity in
general is disorderly compared with linguistic behavior.

In the earliest Greek literature, in Homer, we find the physical man, with all his physical parts and qualities, and a characteristically extensive Homeric vocabulary with which to designate them. There are words for the breath of life, the vital force,
for the departed spirit, which was thought of as a ghost or
specter dwelling "in the house of Hades," and some dubious
hints of words corresponding to what we call "understanding"
and "emotion," as well as the names of specific emotions, but
the concept of "mind" is lacking. Even intelligence and emotion
in Homer are physical attributes more than mental. There is in

fact more attention paid to the external world, the forces out-side of man, and to the way in which they affect him, than to anything that could be called ἀνθρωπισμός or "humanism" in the modern sense.

In due course this interest in the world external to man gave rise on the one hand to an interest in nature, which led directly to the origin of scientific thought, on the other to an attempt to deal with certain aspects of human existence that could not be explained as natural but came to be considered as supernatural or divine. Both of these developments, it must be noticed, were, at least in their origin, part of Greek ἀνθρωπισμός—they were directly related to an exploration of the nature of man and his environment, of the mutual relations of man and the world out-side him, of what man can do to or with his world and of what it does to him. Hence it is altogether justifiable to regard early Classical thought about what we should call scientific problems (I omit at this point any consideration of the gods or of God) as inherently part of Classical "humanism" itself, of the ancient view of man and his nature. There is a unity of thought on this question, divergent as the theories of particular philosophers or schools of thought became, which modern humanism does not even seek. Indeed our dictionary of synonyms (p. 249) explicitly excludes from humanism "the supernatural or natural (i.e., the world external to man)," and its definition of modern usage is, if I mistake not, also altogether justifiable. Less partial accounts are to be had in modern times, not from humanists, but from writers such as Sir Charles Sherrington in his Gifford Lectures of 1937–38 (*Man on His Nature*, Cambridge 1940); or from Ernst Mach's *Analysis of Sensations and the Relation of the Phys-ical to the Psychical* (Chicago 1914), which laid down theoretical principles that have been frutiful, however much outmoded the details of von Mach's treatment may have become.

What Latin writers have to say about science or scientific subjects is rarely original, but based directly on their Greek predecessors. This, I think, is largely true even of what is now called "applied" (as distinguished from "pure") science, although the Romans had greater opportunities for putting their scientific knowledge to the test of practical application and actual performance. Apart from this, scientific terminology remains still more Greek than Latin.

It is maintained by Snell[4] that the development of the Indo-European demonstrative pronoun into a definite article played a decisive role in adapting the Greek language to the expression of abstract scientific concepts. In a measure this is true; but the assertion that "if the definite article had not permitted the forming of these 'abstractions' as we call them" (that is, abstractions such as τὸ ὕδωρ, τὸ ψυχρόν, τὸ νοεῖν), then "it would have been impossible to develop an abstract concept from an adjective or a verb, or to formulate the universal as a particular"—this assertion goes too far. I know no instance of linguistic structure or pattern preventing the speakers of a language from saying anything that they have need to say. As for the infinitive with the article (τὸ νοεῖν), the reason for this is partly formal; I have suggested elsewhere that the determinacy of the simple infinitive, as a decayed case form, was such as to require the article (often with a preposition) in order to fulfill the required function. Whether this conjecture is well founded could be ascertained only by a careful statistical study of the infinitive with or without the article. So far as the Septuagint is concerned, the influence of Hebrew is generally acknowledged.

Statements about the relation between language and philosophy, or language and science, are apt to be, and in the same

---

[4] *Discovery of the Mind*, pp. 227–228. Snell speaks of the article as promoting "an adjective to the status of a noun, as in the case of the superlative: τὸν ἄριστον ᾿Αχαιῶν." But Latin has *optimum* as a noun, and expressions such as *summum bonum*, *pessimo publico*, in which of course *bonum*, *publico* are substantival, without risk of misunderstanding. Is there any Greek or Latin adjective, no matter what its degree of comparison may be, that may not be so used?

The need of distinguishing between the attributive and predicative use of the adjective had much to do with turning the demonstrative into a definite article both in Greek (ἀγαθὸς ὁ ἀνήρ) and in Germanic, which took the further step of using *n*-stem nouns with the article as adjectives (*hairdeis sa goda* ὁ ποιμὴν ὁ καλός as well as *hairdeis gods*, but this latter also means "the shepherd is good"; *þata managizo* τὸ περισσόν). The fact is that a formal distinction between adjectives and nouns that designate qualities is altogether foreign to Indo-European languages.

proportion, as misleading as they are facile. The reasons for the
development of Greek science, or for that matter of modern
Western science, and the entire failure of some peoples to par-
ticipate in it except as it is served to them ready-made, lie far
deeper than the definite article, deeper than grammar: a definite
article may be useful, it is not indispensable. We are told, for
example, that linguistic habits control nonlinguistic acts. This
also is a dogma which contains a measure of truth, but can and
does mislead the thoughtless, especially when it is pushed to the
extreme implication that "human beings are very much at the
mercy of the particular language which has become the medium
of expression for their society" (Sapir; cf. *Language* 27, 1951,
111). Whorf is the protagonist here, for I do not propose to take
Korzybski seriously. Nor do I propose to rush to the other extreme and ask the inane question, whether we say that things
are so because they are so, or whether things are so because we
say so, when the fact seems rather to be that a language is the
expression of the attitude of a certain speech community toward
its culture, that is to say, toward the sum total of conditions in
which it lives, both natural and as transformed by the activity
and hand of man—a combination of external phenomena and
of human responses to them, i.e., of human and nonhuman, together with the unceasing interaction of the one upon the other
and all its products, including man's sensations. That is an
awkward and cumbrous way of putting it, but it is a difficult
matter to put clearly and succinctly. It is what is meant by saying that language mirrors the psyche, and it the culture, of a
language community. There are no metaphysical assumptions
here. Indeed the gist of Whorf's argument is that each language
community has, as part of its own culture, its own physics—its
expression of its own attitude toward the whole of nature, human and nonhuman, and the entire complex of the interrelation
and interactivity of the two, with all their products. If I understand Whorf aright, he says that modern scientific doctrine does
not present to us a rationale of the universe, but is merely a
reflexion of the grammar of the languages which the scientists

speak, chiefly what he calls "Standard Average European," i.e., in the main the modern Indo-European languages of Western Europe and their expansions overseas. Specifically: "Newtonian space, time, and matter are no intuitions. They are recepts from culture and language. That is where Newton got them." (*Four Articles*, p. 33.) Presumably the same statement must be extended to non-Euclidean geometry, quantum mechanics, nuclear physics, the theory of relativity, electronics, communication theory, cybernetics, and all the rest; for while Whorf stresses the difficulties of modern philosophers and scientists in talking about their monistic, holistic, and relativistic views, precisely because these can only be talked about "in what amounts to a new language" (ib.), he overlooks the fact that Einstein, Riemann, Niels Bohr, Shannon, Wiener, and the rest are not the last word, any more than were Euclid, Copernicus, or Newton. Besides, it is unfortunately true that the results brought about by nuclear physics are the same for the speakers of an Indo-European language and of an American Indian one, alike— English or German, and Hopi or Shawnee. There is an empiric test; the faintest atomic explosion knocks the whole theory into a cocked hat. Even Whorf admitted (ib., p. 3) that every boat that sails is in the lap of planetary forces, and that includes, I suppose, as much the kayak of the Eskimo or canoe of the American Indian as the yacht of the New Englander or the German rotor on the North Sea. A less alarming example than an atomic explosion is any modern servo-mechanism—an up-to-date thermostatic control of an oil burner, or the elaborate controls of an elevator that will receive and obey a succession of orders from several floors, or antiaircraft firing-control mechanisms.

There is even a serious linguistic objection. Whorf dwells, with abundant illustration, upon certain features of Hopi and Shawnee, apparently under the impression that these features are unknown to Indo-European languages. He simply did not know, and someone should have told him, that they are not. I doubt very much whether there is a single instance that Whorf

cites as significant for his theory from American Indian languages to which a parallel may not be adduced from the Indo-
European languages at some stage or other of their history.
Thus (30) the Hopi for "to prepare," we are told, is "to try-for,
to practise-upon"; but this is exactly *prae-paro* (: *experior*);
again (13) Shawnee *l' θawa* is a "forked outline," both "toe" and
"branch (of a tree)"; but English *branch* is literally "*paw*"(*DAG*
220)—an etymology, like the Shawnee, which is suggestive in
regard to an early making of tools, and the date at which
speakers of Indo-European and of Shawnee respectively reached
and passed that stage in their cultures; and finally, most interesting of all, beside the Hopi (17) *rehpi* "flash there," i.e. "it
lightens," consider the so-called meteorological impersonals,
which are not properly verbs at all, but, as Brugmann showed
(*Syntax des einfachen Satzes im Indogermanischen*, 1925, 17–24),
e.g. Lat. *fulget*, are simply old *ti*-stems "lightning there," *pluit*
"rain there," *tonat* "thunder there"; and Whorf was quite
wrong when he said (17) that *tonat* (he used that very word)
is structurally and logically unparalleled in Hopi. It and
the Hopi forms are altogether parallel. But so long as Indo-
European stayed in the Hopi stage of development there was no
Indo-European physics. It will not do to say that if physics had
been invented by speakers of Hopi it would have had no concepts such as time, space, velocity, and mass; or that, if it had,
they would have been very different from those of modern
science.

On the contrary, speakers of Hopi would have had, and still
in fact have, no physics at all. They are not interested in that
kind of attitude toward natural phenomena. But that fact does
not falsify the correspondence theory of truth, or the expression
of physical concepts such as the Indo-European languages use.
The expression of time, for example, can be traced to an anterior
expression of the experience of motion or velocity; the expression
of abstract space, to the concept of solid objects (known by
visual and tactile impressions), and then of the intervals of
space which such bodies occupy. No, modern physics will not

be refuted by Hopi grammar, but—if at all—only by nature herself. The bridge over the Golden Gate still stands; the asepsis and anaesthetics of modern medicine are still your choice on the operating table, not the songs and rituals of the Navaho, or the squawbush twigs and feathers of the Paiute instead of the technique of modern obstetrics for your wife; the practice of the law is much more backward, precisely, I suspect, because by the very nature of its subject matter it is not amenable to the methods of the natural sciences—in fact the social sciences at large labor under this very handicap.

But why did not the American Indian develop scientific methods? And why did Western Europeans and their American descendants? And why just at the time they did? Is scientific discovery and its application destined to go on without end, granted that the new language, which Whorf (33) correctly says it must have, is successfully devised—as it easily may be and can be by the normal processes of linguistic development, and especially by selective variation? The dogma of the Communist Manifesto, to the effect that the economic climate determines the intellectual climate—that is, that modern science and the tremendous feats of engineering and processing that have derived from it are dependent upon economic prosperity—is, on the historical evidence alone, the antithesis of the truth, poles apart from it. It was, on the contrary, the very atmosphere of intellectual freedom, freedom of speech and enquiry, which conceived and brought forth at once both the French and American revolutions and also—as a later offspring—modern science, and which has since thrived and multiplied exceedingly in the scientific if not in the political field, and has also led to the twentieth-century economic prosperity of the Western world. That is the real reason why it is dangerous to shut the mouths of university professors. If we may not freely experiment, think, and say what we think, our civilization will shrivel and die. We shall become even as the Hopi, the Navaho, and the Shawnee with their tribal taboos that frustrate the individual mind, kill its genius, and stifle its expression—you fail to conform at your peril, and then intelligence withers. For intelligence is abnormal, it always implies a departure from the petrified routine and beliefs of former ages. The individual *is* at whiles intelligent, the *herd* NEVER. And, in fact, language and extralinguistic factors act and react with mutual influence one upon the other. "Life," in any of its phases, social and all the rest, does not in itself "give" language, nor language "life"; those who take the view that language gives such things as scientific theory should ask themselves the question of what gives language. The peculiarities of Greek grammar, to return to Greek science as part of Greek ἀνθρωπισμός, have no more to do with Greek science than the peculiarities of Hopi have to do with the failure of Hopi "physics." It was rather the Greek discovery of freedom that prepared men's minds for speculation and the formation of theories about man and nature. The language itself supplied in its syntax the logical framework for these, just as, in our own day, linguists having rejected the notion that syntax is logic, philosophers of the school of Russell and Carnap are rediscovering logic in syntax. There is even a forecast of the modern view that, in Hilbert's words, anything that can be an object of scientific thought at all, so soon as it is ripe for the formation of a theory, falls into the lap of mathematics. Sensory impressions, things as perceived by man's five senses, the only means by which knowledge comes to him, of and from the outside world, were to be transferred, so far as thinkers like Democritus and Heracleitus could do it, into terms of space, size, form, and number. Finally, it is worth observing once more (cf. p. 187) that teleological concepts, until recently discounted or totally rejected by science, have returned at least to the biological scene, just as they had an honored place in the scientific ἀνθρωπισμός of Greek thought.

What of the supernatural? Notwithstanding all the divine paraphernalia of myth and art, the former exhibited in the literature from Homer to Apuleius, the latter in material remains of all kinds—coins, vases, plastic sculpture,—cultivated Greeks and philosophically minded Romans of Classical times were, in the main, disbelievers. To venerate had been originally either "to fear" (σέβειν), the best remedy for which, in the realm of the supernatural, is simply to discover that there is, after all, no supernatural, and this Greek philosophy did, thus liberating man from superstition; or else "to regard as current coin" (νομίζειν). If some of the primitive regard for gods and daemons lingered on in everyday talk and customs, as many of the characters in Aristophanes suggest, still at the same time, in the very next breath, both reverence and fear vanish like smoke before the gusts of laughter released by a pointed joke which shows how far from seriously the gods were taken. Thus even the "average" man's vision of himself in the world around him was made clearer and less perplexing. The modernity of the Greek attitude of mind is obvious even on the surface. The field of psychic research is one in which the rules of logical syntax seem not to be applicable; its statements are neither connectible nor communicable, whether they are intended to cover "super-normal" phenomena or (more frankly) supernatural, not because they operate in a field which is "unscientific" or even extrascientific, but because (in J. J. Thomson's words, quoted a year or two ago by Conant)[5] scientific theories are not beliefs concerned with the nature of reality, but policies, practices that must work empirically.

It is all the more noteworthy, therefore, though perhaps not so much to be wondered at after all, since all ages produce such paradoxes, that the very one Greek writer who has appealed most strongly to such modern readers, Greekless or not, as are interested in Classical authors, namely Sophocles, runs counter to the trend of Greek thought of his own day in this very matter. A recent sympathetic, perhaps too sympathetic, interpreter of

---

[5] J. B. Conant, *Modern Science and Modern Man*, New York 1952, p. 53; and especially p. 101 n. 4 (in the last chapter, on "Science and Spiritual Values": "I doubt if believers in astrology, bizarre interpretations of astronomy, or modern necromancy will find any comfort in these lectures. A basically skeptical outlook, even if it denies the ability of science to provide a map of the structure of the universe, can hardly provide a platform for the superstitious. The extension of commonsense ideas by domesticated scientific concepts provides the framework of the modern world. The burden of proof is heavy on one who claims to have found a new effect contradicting accumulated practical experience."

Sophocles puts it like this: Sophocles' "well-known piety, which appeared to be so eloquently reinforced in public by the tenor of his plays, recommended him as the last great guardian of the myths . . . and won him a title almost the equivalent of the defender of the faith."[6] We may let the comparison with Henry VIII pass. But the use made, in the dramas of Sophocles, of all sorts of supernatural machinery, epiphanies, oracles, curses, and suchlike, does not prove that Sophocles himself was full of superstitious convictions, for they are woven into his presentation of the old stories that he had read in Homer. Yet they cannot have been wholly uncongenial to him, and the "insight" ($\gamma\nu\acute{\omega}\mu\eta$) ascribed to Sophoclean heroes is closer almost to divination or clairvoyance than to intuition. The Sophoclean world order, even, is one thing for divinity, another for humanity, and both somewhat visionary.

The essential presupposition on which these lectures have been based is that of fundamental and pervasive good order, not only in nature—there, I suppose, most investigators would concur,— but also, if he will, in man. I was led to this view of mankind by the discovery that inherently language is orderly. But language is the one thing that marks man off from the rest of animate creation. His achievements as a toolmaker, which are sometimes said to be another distinguishing feature, are secondary to his capacity to talk, even if it is possible that man evolved simultaneously as both the talking and the manufacturing animal. Readers of the *Gorgias*, that work of Plato which, in my haphazard education, I read long before I read the beginners' staples of the *Apology* and *Crito*, will not need to be reminded that, according to the theory there set forth by Plato, who probably found it in Pythagorean teaching, excellence or virtue in anything the structure of which is fashioned, whether vitally ($\zeta\tilde{\omega}o\nu$) or only mechanically ($\sigma\kappa\epsilon\tilde{\upsilon}os$), from a multiplicity of parts, depends upon the order ($\kappa\acute{o}\sigma\mu os$) or arrangement ($\tau\acute{\alpha}\xi\iota s$) proper to the particular structure in question. Those things in

[6] C. H. Whitman, *Sophocles*, Cambridge Mass. 1951, p. 6; and see the whole of *his* final chapter ("The Metaphysic of Humanism," pp. 241–251).

the ancient literatures which humanists prize most may be regarded as manifestations of this rule or principle; all that conflicts with them, as due to its neglect or breach. Let us take a single example. Beauty (τὸ καλόν) in literature is dependent upon form—design, pattern, unity, order. The structure of a Greek tragedy, or of an ode of Catullus, their significant form, is an illustration of this principle unrivaled, or at least unsurpassed, in any literature.

Now, if I mistake not, this perfection, this excellence, is also directly related to certain concepts of morals and ethics. Falsehood, for instance, is a perversion of the pro-presentative function of language that, when not so perverted, gives language all its power.[7] Thus the Platonic ideal of "the true" depends entirely, even on the merely linguistic level, upon order and arrangement of the linguistic units in accordance with preëstablished pattern; but this linguistic order or structure reaches its highest level in literary form, where it has passed far beyond both morphomatic and syntactic structure.

If I should lay down my pen here, giving the impression that I have no interest in the content of the two great literatures of the Ancient Mediterranean, that would be to leave a false impression. The "humanism" of the last century, and as it was presented to me in the early decades of this, was for the most part a form of antiquarianism. There was also a rather absurd exclusiveness in the claims which it advanced and, if I mistake not, still advances in some quarters, as the "best" in education, in literature, and in many other things, which, had I been less naïve, would not have deceived me, which I see clearly now to have been the excessive defensiveness of a losing cause, and which had never had any real warrant, not even during the Renaissance itself.

Now we are in a very different, a technological, age, in which the value of the "humanities," and not in education only but in the entire civilization and tradition of the West, lies in their

---

[7] See my essay, "On an Underestimated Feature of Language," in *Studies in Honour of Gilbert Norwood*, Toronto 1952, pp. 248–254.

spiritual and moral worth. The educational fight has been fought, and lost or won, depending on your position. But there has never been any fight over the spiritual and moral values to be either lost or won; these are permanently lasting, they are imperishable. Some may choose to deny or to ignore them, to their own loss. But although a young American, or European for that matter, never masters Latin or Greek, still he gets something of what the Ancient Mediterranean has given to our civilization through the post-Renaissance Western European tradition, much of it in the form of the so-called modern "humanities"—he cannot, in fact, escape doing so. But, to be honest with ourselves, is there any more justification for asking our youth to devote much attention to these studies exclusively than there would be in asking young Italians or Greeks to obtain a masterly command of the languages and civilizations of the Near East, since the ultimate springs of Mediterranean civilization lie there? There must always be a few who are equipped to reinterpret the literatures to their own generation, and their command of Greek and Latin *should* be masterly. I shall be asked about translations, despite all that I have said already: the answer is that if Mr X must translate, say, the *Antigone* of Sophocles into English, the title page should read, "The Antigone of Mr X, with reminiscences of Sophocles," which is what in fact it would be.

"Poetry gives most pleasure," said Coleridge, "when only generally and not perfectly understood," to which Housman added that "perfect understanding will sometimes almost extinguish pleasure";[8] and Samuel Johnson observed of Shakespeare that "his works . . . are [perhaps 'should be'] read without any other reason than the desire of pleasure," that the subjects discussed [by critics] "are of very small importance," and that "now we tear what we cannot loose, and eject what we happen not to understand," instead of sitting "down quietly to disentangle Shakespeare's intricacies and clear his obscurities."[9] The

---

[8] *Name and Nature of Poetry*, Cambridge 1933, pp. 36, 39.

[9] Preface to the *Plays of William Shakespeare*, Vol. 1, London 1765, pp. vii, xlvi, lvi, etc. etc.

enjoyment of good literature has been restricted by the desire
to understand in the narrow and pedantic sense of the word to
which both Coleridge and Housman objected, the explainings
and textual hagglings of the laboriously learned commentary,
seeking meanings that are "unimportant or virtually nonexis-
tent," instead of leaving the reader to take in, as comprehensively and comprehendingly as he may, an entire structural
unity.[10]

My own conviction is that true humanism concerns man in
every part of his being—not letters merely, ancient or modern,
but, like the Greek ἀνθρωπισμός of Sophoclean Athens, all realms
of knowledge, even the sciences. "The proper study of mankind
is man"; yes, but only if it take all knowledge for its province.

Accordingly, ἀνθρωπισμός and *humanitas* are to be understood
as they were in the Classical world, that is to say, as a comprehensive theory or way of human life, not as a mere academic
discipline, and not at all as disciplines in conflict with others,
or with one another, but as embracing both the sciences and the
arts; a theory of life, that is, which implied a conviction of, and
a belief in, the unity of knowledge, what might be called a unified science of *anthroponomics*. It is true that after the time of
Aristotle there was a tendency to divorce what we should call
science from ἀνθρωπισμός; in fact, a hint of such a divorce is
visible already in Plato. But if we think of the very name *Museum*, the institution that was founded in Alexandria about 280
B.C. and lasted 600 years, the abode of the Muses, at once we
find that it is not only song, music, and the long tradition of
composers and executants, but the very concept of a *universitas*
of scientific knowledge and human experience, that shines like a
beacon light over the multitude of the separate parts, so that
their mutual relations are preserved and illuminated; the Sciences and the Arts walk hand in hand. Now contrast the totally
different concept by which *Humanitas* has chosen in recent cen-

---

[10] See, for example, an attempt to deal with the comparatively simple material of
fairy tales in this way, by Anna B. Rooth, *The Cinderella Cycle*, Lund 1951, known to
me only from (not altogether favorable) reviews.

turies to tread a divergent path by herself and all alone, a matter
on which A. J. Toynbee has delivered himself of some telling
comment in the ninth volume of his *Study of History* (Oxford
University Press, 1954, pp. 705–719; cf. Vol. X, pp. 24–35 and
145–154), which I commend heartily to my readers. It is not
simply the frittering away of brilliant gifts and of energy over
mere compilations, translations, critical editions, anthologies,
dictionaries, encyclopedias, that delusion of "coöperative" but
declining scholarship that damns the humanities; what is more
serious is the failure of too many of its practitioners ever to
bring their pigs to market at all. They read, but form no plan
of work; or, if they form a plan, they do not execute it or even
work steadily at it. The familiar apology of perfection, and the
even more familiar repudiation of usefulness, either are lame
excuses for idleness, or a tacit admission that the humanist's
occupation *is* useless. A "classic," it seems, is never to be in the
mother tongue, being like the foreign expert who is always the
best expert, far above the native product; pedantry takes command, all the way, to borrow Toynbee's excellent terminology,
from sheer and showy extravaganza to utter inanition: "The
difference between a Humanist and a lunatic is in fact one of
degree. . . . Judicious discrimination in the pursuit of their
follies saved the Humanists from the madhouse, but it also condemned them to be hustled off the stage of Modern Western History after a vogue which lasted no longer than two hundred years
in the Transalpine provinces of an Occidental pseudo-Hellas." It
is sad to reflect that the successors of the very humanists who
at the rebirth of learning had derided as a hotbed of Aristotelianism the Padua that was destined to play a leading role in the
growth of science are once more ready to obstruct a technological and scientific revolution, and at universities even such as
Harvard the revival of a pre-modern Aristotelianism makes itself heard in a community of learning which has been in the
forefront of modern scientific discovery for almost a century.
The simple and bare fact is that the Classical humanism of
antiquity was both scientific and humane, that there was in it

at first no separation between the pursuit of science and pursuit of the arts.

Students of the psychology of animals tell us that if, when an animal has learned to solve the puzzle set before it, the puzzle is then changed, the animal either will sulk in despair in a corner or will turn into an enraged fighting fury. Man's endless puzzle is to live his life upon this planet, and to solve its ever-changing problems intelligently, without fury and without despair: for despair and fury are unintelligent attempts to find a solution which breed inaction or, at their worst, armed conflict. If there is in our day increasing resort to fighting or to sulking, by turns or both together, it is because the puzzle has become insoluble to a generation in which humanism is enfeebled, futile, and outmoded, through its own refusal to learn from contemporary knowledge in its own time. A scientific humanism and a humane science in unison, however, have it in them to find solutions to most of the modern puzzles that are baffling us: yet the human mind cannot but be able, *ex hypothesi*, to understand and to cope with what the human mind has done, and now we must bend our hearts and minds to this task. No one knows yet but that new genetic mutations even may turn out to be not all of them bad or not entirely bad.

One of my predecessors in the Sather chair, Professor E. R. Dodds, has made it clearer than ever that Greek rationalism and intellectual discovery more than once, between the foundation of the Lyceum about 335 B.C. and the end of the third century of the present era, stood upon the brink of a tremendous triumph. Greek science had passed from the stage of mere guessing, conjecture, and superficial generality, a confused medley of speculation, to the development of abstract sciences, mathematics, and astronomy, and had advanced their study to a point that was not to be reached again until the sixteenth century. Geography, zoölogy, botany, even the history of language, literature, and human institutions, were not neglected in this comprehensive intellectual range. In fact, there was no specialized science; it was not an age of specialists. All the great names,

Theophrastus, Eratosthenes, Poseidonius, Galen, Ptolemy, even the elder Pliny, are the names of men of the widest interests. The breakdown of Greek rationalism was internal. There was no further experimentation, no technology, not because (as some argue) there was an abundance of slave labor that made technology superfluous; nor, as Professor Dodds holds, because the boredom and restlessness of intellectuals led to a paralysis of scientific thought.

Was it not rather the collapse of the political system of Greek city-states, and the substitution of Macedonian authoritarianism and totalitarianism that changed the tenor of Greek thought, its science and its philosophy? The economic argument as an explanation of Greek scientific stagnation is merely an upside-down, a back-to-front argument. Intellectual status is the parent, not the offspring, of economic prosperity: freedom of thought gives rise to discovery and invention, to scientific and technological achievement, and these bring abundance and material well-being in their train; mere economic advantage, on the other hand, is no sure guarantee of intellectual growth. What stifles advance in the realm of thought is an economic or political system that controls or seeks to control thought. Technology produces prosperity; and while prosperity, once it has been won, does not ensure technological progress (unless it also grants freedom of exploration and expression), it need by no means suppress or bring to an end the flow of magnificent and beneficent additions that science and technology make to every aspect of human life, provided always that thought is left unfettered. A mere abundance of servile labor is no more reason for the failure of Greek science than our contemporary abundance of mechanical labor need be, subject to the rule of freedom to experiment, to speak, to teach, and to publish, without restraints devised for political or economic purposes. The success of a polity or of an economy depends at bottom upon powers of intellect and insight; these are not evoked by the material status and do not depend upon it, at least once the material status has been raised above the level of want and poverty; but the administration of such a status can and often does kill the tender flower of the mind. In modern times a stagnant humanism may wreak serious mischief by its lack of interest in science and desertion of science; in ancient times it was a stagnant science that did the mischief by deserting the arts.

I deplore, therefore, such a title as that of *Machines or Mind?* (a pamphlet written, as an introduction to the Loeb Classical Library, by W. H. D. Rouse, London 1912), with its implication that the one excludes the other; far wiser is a title of a new book published in 1954, *Minds and Machines*, which, like Classical humanism, sees in man the master of his own destiny, inseparable from nature. I deplore equally the insistence by some educationists, for example the present president of Princeton, upon the stagnant concept of the so-called "liberal" (!) arts college; how much better is the move made last year by the Massachusetts Institute of Technology to establish a new degree of Bachelor of Science in the curriculum of which the Humanities will be joined with the Sciences! But observe that this forward step has been taken by scientists, not by humanists. Lucretius was thoroughly scientific in temper, even to the extent of using an adjective such as *manabile* (1.534 sc. *frigus*) in a quasi-instrumental (not "passive") meaning, although the verb *manare* is intransitive, a piece of scientific slang in his vocabulary (there are other such adjectives in *-bilis*), exactly like Greek πύραμις "pyramid" (for "wheaten cake"); but he was also a thoroughgoing humanist, and the poet and scientist in him support each the other. The terms used by Plato to distinguish long-range and short-range activity, ὁ θεωρητικὸς βίος and ὁ πρακτικὸς βίος, have been misconstrued to infer a false suggestion of an antithesis between theory and practice, between action and inactivity, between the poet and philosopher and the scientist; and to justify the plea on the part of the humanist for inaction, his "occupational disease," as Toynbee calls it (Vol. 10, pp. 35–36), a phobia against action, that is apt to end in mere inanition; and above all to hint that ὁ θεωρητικός is somehow superior to ὁ πρακτικός, a medieval notion which set back the advance-

ment of science for centuries. It will be calamitous if this episode
of human history is to be repeated now; fortunately the prospect of the consummation of such an anti-intellectual event
seems unlikely, the current revival of superstitious beliefs and
practices notwithstanding.

For to a Greek, say to a man like Pythagoras, or of his generation, science was intimately blended not only with politics, but
even with religion; it was a system of behavior, of an attitude
to the universe and to the forces that manifest themselves in it,
by which man might acquire mastery over his environment,
that is to say, it was his *religio*. Form and design were to be
found already embodied in nature herself; and number, according to Philolaus, was the first principle in the being of gods and
of men. What finer blend of science and *humanitas* can be found
than in Hippocrates? Indeed, speculation upon the divine, to
the neglect of the human, is rare in the older Greek philosophers
of nature; and the Ionians actually had a startlingly modern
outlook on the world, aimed at a control over nature to be exer-
cised by craftsmen, artisans, and technicians, as well as by
scientists and philosophers, in a free society.

It is of peculiar interest to record the observation of Democritus (fl. about 420 B.C.), perhaps original with him, though it
would have suited the mathematical world of Pythagoras (about
572–500 B.C.) equally well, that out of a tragedy a thoroughgoing
transposition of the sequences and arrangements of the letters
(as we should say, the phonemes) might produce a comedy. This
is more strikingly modern, though not less fundamental, than
later discoveries, recorded by Diodorus Siculus, but not original
with him, that the meanings of words are a matter of convention; and hence that we cannot hope to understand nature philo-
logically, a prominent but altogether vicious supposition made
in still later Greek thought, but that we must understand words
through their use in human history, which, broadly interpreted,
means science as well as the arts, the social as well as the natural
sciences, and understand them at that without any recourse
whatever to the device of supernatural invention. Even Plato

saw that those arts which make their contribution to life with
the help of nature—agriculture, architecture, spinning and
weaving, medicine—are of prime importance, a truism which
still holds: not the scholar or humanist, but the farmer, the
artisan and craftsman, the builder, all of them supported and
sustained by modern science and technique, still come, and must
come, first. And even Aristotle realized the intimate connexion
between nature and society. As for biography, in the modern
sense, that is a literary art barely known to the ancients. Thus
the view that the form and therefore the meaning of the world
lie embedded in matter, familiar enough to Greek science, was
lost to the world in the humanistic revival of the Renaissance;
and when, a few centuries later, it was recovered, it was not
humanism, but science, which recaptured this view, a view still
unhappily denied or ignored by many humanists. Astronomy,
like music, showed how man might learn through his senses the
fact of order in nature, and then apply it to his own institutions
and to his own life. Indeed, as we saw in an earlier lecture (IV),
cosmologies have more than once been used to justify a system
of politics as well as of poetics. Already science is becoming a
dominant and vital inspiration of some modern arts—architecture, for example. It should reach poetry, if the kind of aberra-
tion which appears already in the *Timaeus*, a departure from the
scientific point of view, is not perpetuated by humanist doctrine.
A poet-scientist (or, if you will, scientist-poet) has in this age as
great an opportunity as ever presented itself to Lucretius or
Dante, which would, if seized, powerfully revitalize humanism
itself.

Knowledge of human nature is now grotesquely out of step
with modern command of science. The remedy is not the liberal
arts college, preached in season and out by contemporary educa-
tors possessed of one and only one idea, but the scientific direction of humanism; an end, once and for all, of the fatal separation of science and the arts, as if either could possibly yield
its full meaning alone, apart from the other. Science is a human
undertaking, and other human undertakings such as the arts

need it. True Classical humanism had precisely this combination, this coherence, in its very roots and being. It was a latter-day Greek philosophy that divorced science, with deplorable results. Modern humanism bids fair to repeat the error by turning its back upon science, a wellspring that will, if allowed, fertilize it into a new life of abiding virtue.

The theory of ideas, despite its social aspects, took the wrong step of abandoning any attempt to develop the science of nature, and then itself became an obstacle to such a development. This error led directly to "thought about thought," which is as sterile as "language about language"; which always ends by becoming pure formalism, and so looses the all-important thread that guides us through the labyrinth of matter, the concept that natural order is rescued from chaos by the imposition of form upon matter. But for Aeschylus in the *Prometheus Vinctus* (436 ff.), as for Sophocles in the *Antigone* (p. 251 above), the mastery of techniques in the infancy of human evolution had evoked and accompanied, step by step, the growth of intelligence. The later loss of this outlook, the fatal arrest of Greek science, was accompanied by the decay of Greek society: are we to repeat the same mistake? At least some Greek thinkers saw that magic does not work, that its adherents accomplished nothing; but now we are being exhorted by some foolish linguists, forsooth, to form a theory of language on the basis of our knowledge that Hopi, Paiute, and Navaho have no physics, no science, and then govern ourselves by magico-superstitious linguistic formulations that inhibit all action! The Hopi too, who would satisfy well the modern political dogma of absolute conformity to the prevalent pattern of social or ethnic taboo, likewise do nothing. The real culprit is social or tribal compulsion; if we listen to these, then surviving subhuman emotions in the human ethos are not likely to be removed or abated by all the resources of humanism, not even with the help of that powerful weapon, language, a unique biological capacity, which, properly sharpened and wielded, might yet rid us of magic and superstition, falsehood and misrepresentation. For Greek thought also had passed its zenith when the arts and sciences were divorced. True understanding is far more than a mere verbal exploration; it is action deliberately and consciously directed to achieve a perceived and desired end: true meaning is, and has always been, of necessity, goal-directed activity.

It was a most unkind mischance that Plato, whose influence was destined to be so deep, so powerful, widespread, and long-lasting, despised the technical application of science to human life. The science of experiment and of the laboratory is at least not less significant in application than in theory, as witness the use to which isotopes are now being put in medicine. Problems not foreseen in theory arise in the world at large, and by their demands for solution stimulate new research and discovery, thus bringing illumination back again to the laboratory. It is the old question of the relation between the active and the theoretical life, a question misunderstood by Plato's successors and not again realized in its full import until the growth of modern science, which, profiting from the freedom of thought that the rationalists secured, has gone into action with the full force of highly coördinated teamwork, exactly as in sport, where a team of athletes realizes clearly the value of orderly and directed activity.

Those who doubt or question whether in fact nature imposes form and order on matter—in human and other living forms—should study Sir D'Arcy Wentworth Thompson's *Growth and Form* (new edition, Cambridge University Press, 1945). This factor of good order is characteristic also of that variety of human behavior which we call *language* or *literature:* it has been copied in scientific and athletic behavior, in music, in drama, in the dance (I am thinking of the ballet), to some degree in the management of men's private affairs, hardly at all in social, political, and international life. The self-stabilizing control inherent in language and in letters still waits to be extended to these other areas of human activity; even one-tenth of its orderly processes might well cure effectively the mass neuroses of our day.

Greek psychologists, from Alcmaeon to Aristotle, a span of two centuries, except when they fell under the influence of the theory of ideas, understood the need of correspondence between theory and action—the "correspondence theory of truth," as it has been called, the connectibility and communicability of the positivists. The Epicureans were self-confessed anthropologists, who believed in the evolution of man; the Peripatetic treatise on *Mechanics* actually reveals a brilliant endeavor to render even human activities amenable to mathematical treatment—something that is only now being tried once again, under the name of General System Theory.

Thus scientific knowledge unfurls its banner over the whole scope of human experience—music, song, poetry, composition, and performance, traditional or innovating, the humanities as well as mathematics, philosophy, and the natural and social "sciences"; each of these is at the same time an art, a τέχνη (to use the very Greek word that has given us *technique, technical,* and *technology*), as well as a science.

Thus also, Greek music led to the investigation of the dynamics of sound, and then it was discovered that musical composition is a *system* of sounds, that each sound alone is only distinctive, not significant: significance lies in the system and functions of the notes, their relations and intervals. In the same way it was seen that literary composition might be subjected to scientific analysis—the phoneme is like the musical note, insignificant in itself, significant in its function and relations to the other features of grammar, up through words, phrases, sentences, and finished works—a poem, or drama. The *Poetics* of Aristotle and the *Harmonics* of Aristoxenus follow parallel lines of exploration, and for Dionysius Thrax (fl. about 30 B.C.) grammar had become entirely functional—another modern way of looking at a subject matter. A little-read author, the Christian bishop Anatolius of Laodicea, who lived in the third century, is reported by a skillful and learned modern historian of ancient science[11] to

---

[11] On Greek Science see G. Sarton, *History of Science,* Cambridge Mass. 1952; Sir William Cecil Dampier, *A History of Science,* ed. 4, Cambridge Eng. 1949; Benjamin Farrington, *Greek Science,* London, two parts, 1944 and 1949.

have insisted upon the wisdom of using even pure mathematics in the cause of *humanitas*. What would Greek architecture have been without the principle of *entasis*? Perspective, optics, surveying, the use of the theodolite, harmonics, are by no means any further removed from the arts than is poetics.

The Romans found this spirit thoroughly congenial and exerted themselves to bring the literary and scientific culture of Greece—in a word, civilization—to the West, and usually for practical ends, the life of action in a bilingual world. The works of Cicero and Varro are conspicuous illustrations; so is the scientific poem of Lucretius, the main purpose of which, as of much—nearly one-half—of the best of ancient poetry, was first and foremost to instruct. To Lucretius, civilization rests upon the control by man of his nonhuman environment, and nature is not providential; history is the long recital of human trial and error; society needs technical as well as political improvements; human nature itself is to be made rational, and human progress is at once the history of science—that is, the story of the physical universe and of evolution—and the science of history. An acute observer has remarked that the writings of Varro and the century-later encyclopedist Celsus imply a program that reads like a university catalogue of courses of instruction. The same is true of the universal history of the elder Pliny, which ranges all the way from a description of the solar system, through geography and natural history, to the arts, agriculture, industry, medicine, architecture, painting, and sculpture, and technology.

Such were the gifts of Classical humanism to science, and through it to the life of men. Both the scientific and the humanistic spirit are threatened with defeat by any separation between them that brings in its train, as it must, the loss of all sense of history, human and nonhuman.

✧   ✧   ✧   ✧   ✧

Addendum (6 December 1955): I owe to Mr Harold A. Small, Editor of the University of California Press, a very interesting quotation from a letter of Chekhov's to A. S. Suvorin, dated

3 November 1888, in which Chekhov writes, among other things, that there are people who "want to find the physical laws of creation, discover the general law and formulae according to which the artist, feeling them instinctively, creates musical compositions, landscapes, novels, etc. We know that in nature there are a, b, c, d, do, re, mi, fa, sol; there are the curve, the straight line, the circle, the square, the color green, red, blue . . . we know that all this in certain combinations produces melody, poetry, or a painting, just as simple chemical bodies in certain combinations produce wood, or rock, or sea. We are only aware of the fact that this combination exists, but the order of this combination is hidden from us. . . . there is, in my opinion, only one way out—the philosophy of creation. All the best works created by artists throughout the ages may be gathered into one pile, and through use of the scientific method there may be discerned the common element that makes them similar to one another and determines their value. This common element will be the law . . . the *conditio sine qua non* of all works of art that lay claim to immortality."

[A. P. Čekhov, *Polnoe sobranie sočinenij i pisem*, T. XIV (Moscow 1949), pp. 215 ff.; translation by courtesy of Nina (Mrs B. C.) Shebeko, secretary to the Department of Slavic Languages and Literatures, University of California, Berkeley.]

POSTSCRIPT

THESE LECTURES were written between June and December 1954. The presentation of them in the lecture room at Berkeley in the Spring of 1955 was not at all a reading of the manuscript or of any part or parts of it, but was given from notes which added some things not in this book, and merely summarized, with suitable examples, such things as the discussion of the comic trimeter or the vocabulary of Hipponax, which, presented in full as written, would have wearied my audience. But lectures, which is what the several chapters are, and were written to be, often call for some repetition of argument, and I have let such repetitive passages stand as they were written, even (in one place) the same words, for that reason. Readers who read carefully enough to spot that passage are asked to accept this explanation.

Since 1954, however, I have gathered a large mass of new material about Linear B (and even more about Linear A); and I have enlarged, or otherwise modified, my views of some other things, notably of scientific discourse, but not of poetic, views which the publication of Housman's *Notebooks* (not to mention the outpourings of flocks of spring poets and autumnal "new" critics) only confirm. But the text is left as it was written, apart from minor corrections, and I shall incorporate the new matter and new views into my lectures to be delivered before the Lowell Institute in Boston in February 1957, *Language the Measure of Man*.

I must, nevertheless, mention here the following details: (1) Professor MacKay (*CP* 51, 1956, 88–89) suggests that *essentialist* and *existentialist* better describe the two schools of thought about "Homer" than Unitarian and separatist, which no longer correspond to their actual views. I agree. (2) Mr Ventris writes to me that his and Chadwick's achievement was less based on

279

statistical procedures than I have argued. We must, then, await his forthcoming book to tell us just how they did proceed. (3) The relation of *dropsy* to Greek ὑδρωπία was cleared up by Niedermann (see *CP* 51, 1956, 212). (4) Instead of negentropy or negative entropy I should now write *ectropy* everywhere. (5) In addition to Harris (p. 127) I should now mention also Hocket's *Manual of Phonology* (Bloomington Indiana 1955), which gives much more attention to symmetry in language (at least phonematic symmetry) than Harris, a topic to be developed in my Lowell lectures. And last, (6) the present lectures were written less than a month after I had finished my book *Language*. I was hardly able to escape quoting myself in a few places; for kind permission, therefore, to use some of the same matter and some illustrations again in this book I am indebted to the publishers of *Language*, Messrs Secker and Warburg of London, and the St Martin's Press of New York.

13 July 1956

Index

INDEX